Oxford Junior Illustrated Thesaurus

OXFORD
UNIVERSITY PRESS

Great Clarendon Street, Oxford, OX2 6DP, United Kingdom

Oxford University Press is a department of the University of Oxford. It furthers the University's objective of excellence in research, scholarship, and education by publishing worldwide. Oxford is a registered trade mark of Oxford University Press in the UK and in certain other countries

First published 2003
Second edition 2007
Third edition 2012
Fourth edition 2018

All artwork by Dynamo Design Ltd.
Photos: Pages 22, 24, 26, 92, 129, 190, 218-219 © Photos to Go: Pages 25, 144, 221 © iStockphoto/Thinkstock: Pages 27 and 67 © Goodshot/Thinkstock: Pages 34, 70, 113, 133 © Hemera/Thinkstock: Pages 36, 172 © Comstock/Thinkstock: Page 40 © photos.com/Thinkstock: Page 64 © Atlaspix/Shutterstock: Page 75 © Stockbyte/Thinkstock: Page 119 © Tatiana Popova/Shutterstock: Page 134 © REX/Shutterstock: Page 137 © Myotis/ Shutterstock: Page 141 © Ryan McVay/Lifesize/Thinkstock: Page 142 © John Snelling/REX/ Shutterstock: Page 170 © Makarova Viktoria/Shutterstock: Page 203 © Richard Whitcombe/ Shutterstock: Page 227 © George Doyle/Stockbyte/Thinkstock

British Library Cataloguing in Publication Data

Data available

ISBN: 978 0 19 276718 9 (hardback)
10 9 8 7 6

ISBN: 978 0 19 276719 6 (paperback)
10 9 8

Printed in China

Paper used in the production of this book is a natural, recyclable product made from wood grown in sustainable forests. The manufacturing process conforms to the environmental regulations of the country of origin.

The publisher would like to thank lexicographers Sheila Dignen, Morven Dooner and, for this new edition, Rosalind Combley and Jenny Watson for their contributions to this title.

Oxford Corpus

You can trust this book to be up to date, relevant and engaging because it is powered by the Oxford Corpus, a unique living database of children's and adults' language.

Contents

Introduction

Discover the power of words with this new edition of the **Oxford Junior Illustrated Thesaurus**. The pages are contemporary, bright and colourful which makes it easy to find the words you need. The text has been created using the Oxford Children's Corpus, and tested in the classroom with teachers and children. The headwords have been carefully chosen and are words that children are most likely to look up, and the synonyms and alternative words are a mixture of familiar and unfamiliar words that will stretch children's vocabulary. Example sentences, including some from well-known children's authors such as J. K. Rowling and Kenneth Grahame, show how the words are used in context. The supplement at the back of the book contains useful help and ideas for word building, planning and editing, and help with a range of types of writing for different purposes.

If you love learning about new words and language, and want to find synonyms for words that are not in this thesaurus, try a bigger thesaurus, for example, the *Oxford Primary Thesaurus*.

www.oxforddictionaries.com/schools

How to use this thesaurus

What is the difference between a thesaurus and a dictionary?

A **dictionary** tells you what a word means, so it gives you a **definition** of the word.

A **thesaurus** tells you what other words have the same meaning, so it gives you **synonyms** of a word.

You use a dictionary when you have read, or heard, a new word and want to know what it means. You use a thesaurus when you want to write or say something yourself and you want to choose the best word.

Here are some good reasons why you should use a thesaurus:

- **to find a more interesting word** Are there any alternative words to describe clothes that are very **dirty**? Look up **dirty** to find some other adjectives to describe dirty clothes.
- **to find the right word** What word might you use to describe **rain**? Look up **rain** to find the right word.
- **to make your writing more interesting** Instead of saying that someone ate a whole pizza, you might write: *He **wolfed** down a whole pizza!* or *He **polished** off a whole pizza!*

Synonyms are words that mean the same—or nearly the same—as each other. You can make your writing more interesting by using different synonyms, rather than using the same words all the time.

Imagine you are writing about what you did at the weekend. You might start like this:

I had a good weekend. The weather was not very nice so we went to the shops. I got a new top that is really nice. I met up with my friend and we went to see a film. I thought it was good but my friend didn't like it.

Can you see that the words **nice** and **good** are used over and over again? If you look up these words in this thesaurus, you will find a number of synonyms with a similar meaning.

*I had a **brilliant** weekend. The weather was not very **sunny** so we went to the shops. I got a new top and it is really **stylish**. I met up with my friend and we went to see a film. I thought it was **amusing** but my friend didn't like it.*

alphabet
the alphabet is given on every page with the letter you are in highlighted so you can find your way around the thesaurus easily

headword
is in alphabetical order, in blue and it shows you how to spell a word

word web panel
words that are related to the headword or are types of the headword

synonyms
words that mean the same, or nearly the same as the headword

writing tips panel
sentences and words to inspire you to write creatively

citations
from well-known children's authors show how the word is used

blew to boat

A Bb C D E F G H I J K L M N O P Q R S T U V W X Y Z

blew VERB (*past tense of* blow)

blob NOUN
*There was a **blob** of jam on the table.*
a lump
a dollop
a drop

block NOUN
*They covered the hole with a **block** of concrete.*
a piece
a lump
a slab

block VERB
*A huge lorry had **blocked** the road.*
to obstruct
to clog up

blow VERB blows, blowing, blew, blown
*He **blew** on his food to cool it down.*
to breathe
to puff

blue ADJECTIVE
navy blue
sky-blue
royal blue
turquoise
azure
bright blue

blush VERB
*She **blushed** a bright red whenever the teacher spoke to her.*
to go red
to redden
to flush

boast VERB
*She's always **boasting** about how good she is at netball.*
to brag
to show off
to gloat

boat NOUN
*We need a **boat** to get across the lake.*
a ship
a vessel
a craft

WORD WEB

Some types of **boat**:

an aircraft carrier
a barge
a battleship
a canoe
a dinghy
a ferry
a fishing boat
a kayak
a lifeboat
a motor boat
a raft
a rowing boat
a sailing boat
a speedboat
a tanker
a trawler
a warship
a yacht

WRITING TIPS

Here are some useful words for writing about **boats**:

- *The little fishing boat **bobbed up and down** in the water.*
- *The dinghy **drifted** slowly out to sea.*
- *We **floated** down the river on our raft.*
- *The barge **chugged** slowly along the canal.*
- *The speedboat **sped** quickly through the water.*
- *We **sailed** the yacht into the harbour and **moored** it to the jetty.*
- *We were worried our little rowing boat would **capsize** in the storm.*

He leant back in his seat and surveyed the cushions, the oars, the rowlocks, and all the fascinating fittings, and felt the boat sway lightly under him.—THE WIND IN THE WILLOWS, Kenneth Grahame

30

word class
shows what type of word it is, for example, noun, verb, adverb or adjective

catch words
show the first and last word on the page and guide you to the correct place to find the word you need

overused word panel
lots of alternatives for words that are used over and over again

example sentence
shows how the word is used—this helps you choose a synonym for the right meaning

opposite (antonym)
words that have an opposite meaning to the headword

numbered sense
if a word has more than one meaning, they are numbered

bob *VERB*
*The toy boat **bobbed** on the water.*
to float
to bounce

body *NOUN*

WORD WEB

Some parts of your **body**:

ankle
arm
armpit
calf
cheek
chest
chin
ear
elbow
eye
finger
foot
forehead
hand
head
heel
hip
knee
leg
lip
mouth
navel
neck
nose
shin
shoulder
skin
stomach
thigh
throat
thumb
toe
waist
wrist

bog *NOUN*
*He was sinking into the **bog**.*
a marsh
a swamp

boil *VERB*
*The water had started to **boil**.*
to bubble
to simmer

boiling *ADJECTIVE*
1 *Can we open a window? It's **boiling** in here.*
baking
scorching
sweltering
OPPOSITE **freezing**

2 *The soup was **boiling** hot and I couldn't eat it.*
scalding
piping hot
OPPOSITE **cold**

bolt *VERB*
1 *He **bolts** the door at night.*
to lock
to fasten

2 *The horse **bolted** from the stable.*
to run away
to flee

3 *She **bolted** her food as she was so hungry.*
to gobble down
to guzzle
to wolf

bone *NOUN*

WORD WEB

Some **bones** in your body:

a backbone or **a spine**
A collarbone is the bone from your shoulder to your neck.
A pelvis is the bone across your hips.
ribs
a shoulder blade
a skull

a b **Bb** c d e f g h i j k l m n o p q r s t u v w x y z

31

Writing tips

The panels in this thesaurus give you extra help choosing the best word to use. There are three kinds of panels. **Look for the icons!**

WRITING TIPS

OVERUSED WORDS

WORD WEB

You will find **WRITING TIPS** at these entries:

aircraft	**boat**	**dog**	**light**	**river**
bell	**car**	**horse**	**monster**	**water**
bird	**cat**	**insect**	**rain**	**wind**

The **WRITING TIPS** include words and sentences to show you ways of writing about the headword. For example, the **WRITING TIP** at **insect** shows how you can use words such as **buzz**, **crawl**, **scuttle** and **scurry** when you are writing about insects.

insect *NOUN*

WRITING TIPS

Here are some useful words for writing about **insects**:

an ant

- *The ladybird* ***flew*** *away.*
- *A wasp was* ***buzzing*** *around the kitchen.*
- *Bees come together and* ***swarm*** *when they are looking for a new hive.*
- *A fly* ***crawled*** *up my leg.*
- *The beetle* ***scuttled*** *away.*
- *Ants were* ***scurrying*** *around looking for food.*

Insects were swarming all over the earthen mound inside the container.—COLONY, J. A. Henderson

Overused words

You will find **OVERUSED WORDS** at these entries:

bad	eat	happy	look	old	say
beautiful	get	hard	lovely	put	small
big	give	like	move	run	strong
bit	go	little	nice	sad	walk
do	good				

When you are writing, look out for words that you use over and over again. Look them up in this thesaurus and you will find lots of more interesting synonyms.

For example, look at this postcard. The words **nice** and **good** are **OVERUSED WORDS** because they are used over and over again. We can make this postcard more interesting if we use a different adjective each time.

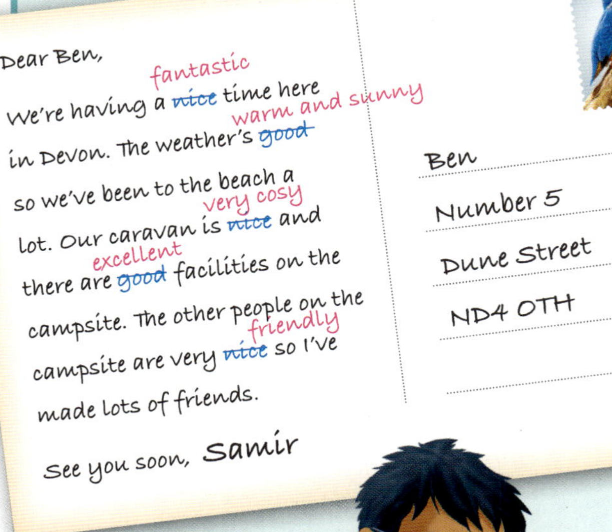

Dear Ben,

We're having a ~~nice~~ fantastic time here in Devon. The weather's ~~good~~ warm and sunny so we've been to the beach a lot. Our caravan is ~~nice~~ very cosy and there are ~~good~~ excellent facilities on the campsite. The other people on the campsite are very ~~nice~~ friendly so I've made lots of friends.

See you soon, Samir

Ben
Number 5
Dune Street
ND4 0TH

beautiful *ADJECTIVE*

OVERUSED WORD

Here are some more interesting words for **beautiful**:

1 *He married the **beautiful** princess.*
lovely
pretty
fair
attractive

Use **gorgeous**, **stunning** or **enchanting** if someone is very beautiful: *You look absolutely **stunning** in that dress!*

Use **glamorous** if someone looks beautiful and rich: *She looked like a **glamorous** actress.*

OPPOSITE **ugly**

2 *What a **beautiful** view!*
glorious
magnificent
spectacular
stunning

3 *The weather was **beautiful** for sports day.*
lovely
gorgeous
wonderful
fantastic

OPPOSITE **awful**

Word webs

You will find **WORD WEB** panels at these entries:

aircraft, amphibian, animal, athlete, athletics, bag, bat, bean, bed, berry, bicycle, bird, boat, body

bone, book, bridge, building, cage, car, cat, chair, clock, clothes, colourful, computer, cook, cup

dance, doctor, dog, farm, film, flower, fruit, hair, hat, horse, house, insect, jewel, job

light, material, meal, monster, music, paper, picture, plant, poem, religion, reptile, school, scientist, seat

shape, shoe, shop, snake, song, sound, space, sport, story, tool, travel, tree, vegetable, writer

Some words are not synonyms, but are related because they have similar meanings to your word.

For example, flower is a general word, which can mean any type of flower. The words **rose**, **daffodil** and **tulip** are related because they describe one specific type of flower. It can help your reader to 'see' what you are writing about if you use more specific words.

Instead of saying that a garden is full of **flowers**, you might write:

*The garden was full of brightly-coloured **lilies** and sweet-smelling **roses**.*

flower *NOUN*

WORD WEB

Some garden **flowers**:

anemones
bougainvillea
carnations
crocuses
daffodils
geraniums
hibiscus
jasmine
lavender
lilac
lilies
marigolds
pansies
petunia
roses
snowdrops
sunflowers
sweet peas
tulips
wallflowers

Some wild **flowers**:

bluebells
buttercups
daisies
dandelions
foxgloves
poppies
primroses

sunflowers

abandon *VERB*
*They **abandoned** the puppies by the road.*
to leave
to forsake
to dump
to leave behind *They **left** the puppies **behind**.*

ability *NOUN*
❶ *You are clever and have the **ability** to do well at school.*
capability
intelligence

❷ *He's a young footballer with a lot of **ability** for the game.*
talent
skill
flair
aptitude

about *ADVERB*
*There are **about** 30 children in our class.*
roughly
approximately
OPPOSITE **exactly**

accept *VERB*
*The children stepped forward to **accept** the prizes from the teachers.*
to take
to receive
OPPOSITE **reject**

accident *NOUN*
❶ *There was a nasty **accident** on the road.*
a crash
a smash
a collision

A **pile-up** is a bad accident with a lot of cars.

A **bump** or a **scrape** is an accident that is not very bad.

❷ *I'm sorry, it was an **accident**.*
a mistake
a mishap

ache *VERB*
*My legs were **aching** after the run.*
to hurt
to be sore
to be painful

Use **pound** or **throb** to describe a banging pain: *My head was **pounding** and I had to lie down.*

achieve *VERB*
*You have **achieved** a lot this term.*
to do
to accomplish

achievement *NOUN*
*Winning a gold medal is a great **achievement**.*
an accomplishment
a feat
a success

act *VERB*
❶ *We must **act** quickly if we want tickets for the concert.*
to do something
to take action

❷ *I would love to **act** on the stage.*
to perform
to appear

action *NOUN*
❶ *I like films that are full of **action** as they are exciting.*
excitement
suspense

❷ *His brave **action** saved his sister's life.*
an act
a deed

Aa

active ADJECTIVE
*Most children enjoy playing and being **active**.*
busy
lively
energetic
on the go *(informal)*
OPPOSITE **inactive**

activity NOUN
*What **activities** do you do outside school?*
a hobby
a pastime
an interest

actual ADJECTIVE
*This is the **actual** ship that Nelson sailed on.*
real
genuine
very

add VERB
*Mix the butter and sugar together, then **add** the eggs.*
to mix in

admire VERB
1 *Which sports stars do you **admire**?*
to respect
to look up to
to idolise
to hero-worship

2 *We stood and **admired** the lovely view of the mountains.*
to enjoy
to appreciate

admit VERB
*He **admitted** that he had broken the window.*
to confess
to own up
OPPOSITE **deny**

adult NOUN
*You must be accompanied by an **adult** at all times.*
a grown-up

adventure NOUN
*He told us about all his exciting **adventures**.*
an escapade
an exploit
a quest

advice NOUN
*He gave me some very useful **advice**.*
help
guidance
a suggestion *He made a useful **suggestion**.*

aeroplane NOUN
*The **aeroplane** flew over the mountains.*
a plane
an aircraft

afraid ADJECTIVE
1 *Are you **afraid** of spiders?*
frightened
scared

Use **terrified** or **petrified** if you are very afraid: *I'm absolutely **terrified** of snakes.*

Use **panic-stricken** if you are so afraid you do not know what to do: *We were **panic-stricken** when the fire broke out.*

2 *I was **afraid** the boat might capsize.*
worried
nervous
anxious

agree VERB
1 *Laura says chocolate is the best flavour and I **agree** with her.*
to think the same
to concur
OPPOSITE **disagree**

2 *I asked Dad to come and he **agreed**.*
to say yes
to accept
OPPOSITE **refuse**

agreement NOUN
*We made an **agreement** to help each other.*
a deal
a bargain

aim *VERB*

*He **aimed** his water pistol at his aunt.*

to point

aircraft *NOUN*

WORD WEB

Some types of **aircraft**:

an airliner
a biplane
a fighter plane
a glider
a helicopter
a jet
a jumbo jet

WRITING TIPS

Here are some useful words for writing about **aircraft**:

- *The aeroplane was **flying** high above the clouds.*
- *The jumbo jet **soared** up into the sky.*
- *Our plane **took off** at six o'clock and **landed** at ten o'clock.*

The aircraft stayed very low, following the coastline.—SHARK ISLAND, David Miller

alarm *NOUN*

*The fire **alarm** went off noisily.*

a signal
an alert
a siren

alert *ADJECTIVE*

*The sentries on duty must remain **alert**.*

ready
attentive
awake
on the lookout

alive *ADJECTIVE*

*The bird was injured but still **alive**.*

living
breathing
OPPOSITE **dead**

allow *VERB*

*They **allowed** us to use their swimming pool.*

to let *They **let** us use their swimming pool.*
to permit *They **permitted** us to use the swimming pool.*
to give someone permission *They **gave us permission** to use the swimming pool.*
OPPOSITE **forbid**

all right *ADJECTIVE*

1 *Were you **all right** after the accident?*

well
safe
unhurt
healthy

2 *The food in the restaurant was **all right**, but not brilliant.*

OK *(informal)*
acceptable
satisfactory

almost *ADVERB*

*I've **almost** finished making dinner, so we can eat soon.*

nearly
virtually
practically

amaze *VERB*

*He **amazed** us with his magic tricks.*

to astonish
to astound

amazed *ADJECTIVE*

*I was **amazed** when I saw his new bike.*

astonished
staggered
flabbergasted *(informal)*
stunned

amazement *NOUN*

*They stared in **amazement** at the huge ship.*

astonishment
surprise
wonder

Use **shock** when you feel amazement at something bad: *I felt **shock** at this terrible news.*

amazing *ADJECTIVE*

*What an **amazing** car!*

wonderful
fantastic
incredible

amount *NOUN*

*They ate a huge **amount** of food!*

a quantity

amphibian *NOUN*

WORD WEB

Some **amphibians**:

a bullfrog
a frog
a newt
a salamander
a toad

a frog

amuse *VERB*

*His jokes **amused** us all.*

to entertain
to make someone laugh

amusing *ADJECTIVE*

*He told us a very **amusing** story.*

funny
humorous
comical
entertaining

angel *NOUN*

*A beautiful **angel** appeared with a white robe and wings.*

a spirit
a guardian angel

anger *NOUN*

*She couldn't hide her **anger**.*

annoyance

Use **irritation** for slight anger: *He waved the flies away in **irritation**.*

Use **fury** or **rage** for very great anger: *Mr Evans turned crimson with **rage**.*

Use **outrage** for great shock and anger: *She felt **outrage** at the rude way he spoke to her.*

angry *ADJECTIVE*

*Mum looked very **angry**.*

cross
annoyed
mad

Use **irritated** if someone is slightly angry: *My mum gets a bit **irritated** if I keep asking her questions.*

Use **furious**, **livid** or **enraged** if someone is very angry: *My dad was absolutely **livid** when he saw what we'd done.*

Use **infuriated** if someone is frustrated and angry: *I got so **infuriated** when my computer wouldn't work.*

Aa b c d e f g h i j k l m n o p q r s t u v w x y z

animal *NOUN*
*My cat is a very loving **animal**.*
a creature

Use **a beast** for a large four-footed animal.

WORD WEB

a reptile

a bird

Some types of **animal**:

an amphibian
a bird
a fish
an insect
a mammal
a reptile

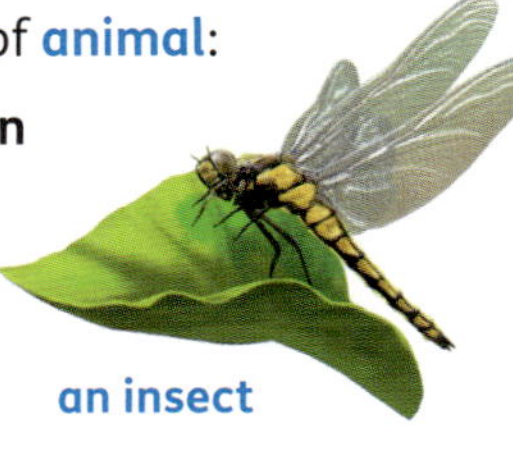

an insect

a fish

Some farm **animals**:

chicken
cow
duck
goat
goose
horse
pig
sheep

Some **animals** that are popular as pets:

cat
dog
gerbil
guinea pig
hamster
pony
rabbit
tropical fish

Some **animals** that you can find near water:

frog
newt
toad
water vole
penguin

Some wild **animals** you might see in Britain:

badger
deer
fox
hare
hedgehog
mole
mouse
pinemartin
rabbit
rat
shrew
squirrel

Some wild **animals** from hot countries:

alligator
baboon
camel
cheetah
chimpanzee
crocodile
elephant
gazelle
giraffe
gorilla
hippopotamus
leopard
lion
monkey
panther
rhinoceros
tiger
zebra

a rhinoceros

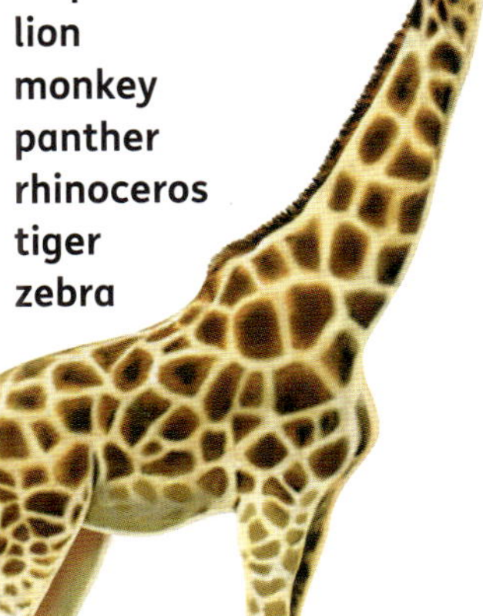

a giraffe

WORD WEB

Collective nouns for some groups of **animals**:

a flock of birds
a flock of sheep
a gaggle of geese
a nest of snakes
a herd of cattle
a litter of puppies
a pack of wolves
a pride of lions
a school of whales
a shoal of fish
a swarm of bees

a lion

a lioness

a snake

annoy *VERB*

❶ *The loud music was* ***annoying*** *me.*

to irritate
to get on someone's nerves

❷ *My little brother keeps* ***annoying*** *me!*

to pester
to bother
to tease
to bug *(informal)*
to hassle

OPPOSITE **please**

annoyed *ADJECTIVE*

My mum was quite ***annoyed*** *with me.*

cross
angry
irritated
exasperated

OPPOSITE **pleased**

annoying *ADJECTIVE*

Sometimes my sister can be very ***annoying****.*

irritating
tiresome
exasperating

answer *NOUN*

I called his name, but there was no ***answer****.*

a reply
a response

answer *VERB*

I shouted to her, but she didn't ***answer****.*

to reply
to respond

anxious *ADJECTIVE*

I felt ***anxious*** *about starting my new school.*

worried
nervous
apprehensive
uneasy
stressed

OPPOSITE **calm**

apologise *(also* apologize*)* *VERB*

I ***apologised*** *to my gran for being so rude.*

to say sorry

appear *VERB*

The ship ***appeared*** *on the horizon.*

to arrive
to come into view

to become visible

Use **emerge** when someone or something appears from inside or behind somewhere: *A man **emerged** from the house.*

OPPOSITE **disappear**

applause *NOUN*

*There was a lot of **applause** for our dance.*

clapping
cheering

Use **an ovation** or **a standing ovation** when the audience stands up to clap: *Our dance got a **standing ovation**.*

OPPOSITE **booing**

approach *VERB*

*I started to feel nervous as we **approached** the theatre.*

to come near to
to come towards

approximately *ADVERB*

*There are **approximately** 500 children in my school.*

about
around
roughly

OPPOSITE **exactly**

area *NOUN*

1 *There is a special **area** where you can play.*

a place
a space
a patch
a zone

2 *This is a very nice **area** of the city.*

a part
a district
a neighbourhood

argue *VERB*

*The children were **arguing** over the toys.*

to quarrel
to squabble
to fight
to fall out

To **bicker** means to argue about small things that are not important: *The two girls were **bickering** about whose pencil it was.*

OPPOSITE **agree**

argument *NOUN*

*They had a big **argument** over whose house they would go to.*

a quarrel
a squabble
a disagreement
a row
a fight

arrange *VERB*

1 *She **arranged** the books carefully on the shelf.*

to place
to set out

2 *We have **arranged** to meet at ten o'clock.*

to plan
to agree
to fix up

3 *My mother has **arranged** everything for my party.*

to organise
to plan
to sort out

arrive *VERB*

1 *We finally **arrived** in London.*

to reach
to get to

2 *Jessica **arrived** at the party two hours late.*

to come
to turn up

3 *When does the plane **arrive** in New York?*

to land
to touch down
to get in

4 *The boat should **arrive** at ten o'clock.*

to dock
to get in

OPPOSITE **depart**

Aa B C D E F G H I J K L M N O P Q R S T U V W X Y Z

art NOUN

WORD WEB

Some types of **art**:

drawing
painting
sketching
modelling
pottery
sculpture
graphics

painting

ask VERB

*He **asked** me how many brothers and sisters I had.*

to enquire *He **enquired** how many brothers and sisters I had.*

to question *He **questioned** me about my brothers and sisters.*

➤ **ask for**

*I've **asked for** a new bike for my birthday.*

to request

To **demand** something means to say that you must have it: *He held out his hand and **demanded** the money.*

To **beg** for something means to ask someone very strongly for it: *'Please, please can I go?' she **begged**.*

asleep ADJECTIVE

*Grandfather was **asleep** in front of the fire.*

sleeping
dozing
resting
slumbering
snoozing
having a nap

OPPOSITE **awake**

assistant NOUN

*The magician had an **assistant**.*

a helper
a colleague

astonish VERB

*She **astonished** us with her skilful tricks.*

to amaze
to astound

astonished ADJECTIVE

*I was **astonished** when he told me how much his bike cost.*

amazed
staggered
flabbergasted *(informal)*
stunned

ate VERB *(past tense of* eat*)*

athlete NOUN

WORD WEB

Some types of **athletes**:

a sportsman
a sportswoman
a runner
a sprinter
a high jumper
a long jumper

athletics NOUN

WORD WEB

Some types of events in **athletics**:

running
sprinting
hurdles
the high jump
the long jump
the triple jump
cross-country
the marathon
the relay race
the javelin

attach *VERB*
*You must **attach** the string firmly to the kite.*
to fix
to fasten
to join
to connect
to tie
to stick
to glue

attack *VERB*
*The two robbers **attacked** them.*
to assault
to set upon

To **ambush** someone means to jump out from a hiding place and attack them: *Robbers hide in the hills and **ambush** travellers.*

To **mug** someone means to attack and rob them in the street: *Two men tried to **mug** an old lady in the street.*

attitude *NOUN*
*She has a very positive **attitude** towards school.*
an approach
an outlook
a view *She has a very positive **view** of school.*

attractive *ADJECTIVE*
1 *She's a very **attractive** girl.*
beautiful
pretty
lovely
gorgeous
OPPOSITES **unattractive, ugly**

2 *He's an **attractive** boy.*
handsome
good-looking
gorgeous
OPPOSITES **unattractive, ugly**

avoid *VERB*
1 *I'm allergic to cats, so I try to **avoid** them.*
to keep away from
to steer clear of

2 *He always tries to **avoid** doing the washing up.*
to get out of
to escape
to dodge

award *NOUN*
*He got a special **award** for his bravery.*
a prize
a reward
a trophy
a cup
a medal

awful *ADJECTIVE*
*What an **awful** smell!*
terrible
dreadful
horrible
unpleasant
disgusting
appalling

awkward *ADJECTIVE*
1 *The box was an **awkward** shape.*
difficult
bulky
unwieldy

2 *They arrived at a very **awkward** time.*
inconvenient
tricky
OPPOSITE **convenient**

baby *NOUN*
a child
an infant

A **newborn** is a baby that has just been born.

A **toddler** is a baby that is just learning to walk.

back *NOUN*

1 *We sat at the **back** of the hall.*
the rear

2 *I was at the **back** of the bus.*
the end
the rear
the tail end
the far end
OPPOSITE **front**

bad *ADJECTIVE*

OVERUSED WORD

Try to use a more interesting word when you want to say **bad**. Here are some other words you can use instead:

1 *He's a **bad** man.*

Use **wicked** for a very bad person: *The country was ruled by a **wicked** king.*

Use **evil** for something that is very bad and frightening: *I sensed that there was something **evil** in that cave.*

Use **cruel** for someone who is very unkind and enjoys hurting people: *The two horses were bought by a **cruel** master who did not treat them well.*

Use **nasty** for someone who is mean or unkind: *He's a mean and **nasty** boy!*

2 *You **bad** dog!*

Use **naughty** or **disobedient** for a person or animal who doesn't do as they are told: *He was a very **naughty** boy who did not do as he was told.*

3 *There has been a **bad** accident and people have been hurt.*
terrible
awful
dreadful
horrible
shocking
serious

4 *I'm very **bad** at maths.*
hopeless
useless
poor
terrible
weak
incompetent

5 *Your writing is very **bad** —you should take more care with it.*
poor
careless
sloppy
shoddy

6 *Sara's got a **bad** knee.*
sore
injured
painful

7 *Food goes **bad** if you don't keep it in the fridge.*

Use **off** for meat and fish: *Don't eat the meat as it has gone **off**.*

Use **rotten** for fruit: *The apples were brown and **rotten**.*

Use **mouldy** for cheese: *The cheese was **mouldy** and smelly.*

Use **sour** for milk or cream: *This milk has gone **sour**.*
OPPOSITE **good**

bag *NOUN*
She packed her books into her ***bag****.*

WORD WEB

Some types of **bag**:

a backpack
a beach bag
a briefcase
a carrier bag
a handbag
a holdall
a rucksack
a satchel
a school bag
a sports bag
a suitcase
a trunk

a beach bag

a rucksack

a handbag

a sports bag

ball *NOUN*
She threw the ***ball*** *into the air.*
a sphere
a globe

ban *VERB*
Our school has ***banned*** *mobile phones.*

Use **forbid** when a person tells someone not to do something: *The teacher* ***has forbidden*** *us to talk.*

Use **prohibit** when something is not allowed because of a rule or law: *Smoking in public places is now* ***prohibited****.*

band *NOUN*
I play the drums in the school ***band****.*

A **group** is any band, especially one that plays pop music.

A **brass band** is a group playing trumpets and other brass instruments.

An **orchestra** is a large group of musicians playing classical music.

bang *NOUN*
We heard a loud ***bang*** *outside.*
a crash
a thud
a thump
a boom
a blast
an explosion

bang *VERB*
1 *He* ***banged*** *on the door with his fists.*

To **rap** or **tap** means to bang lightly: *She* ***tapped*** *gently on the window.*

To **hammer** means to bang loudly: *He* ***hammered*** *loudly on the door.*

2 *I fell and* ***banged*** *my head.*
to bump
to knock
to hit
to bash

bar *NOUN*

❶ *There were iron **bars** on the windows to stop people from escaping.*

a pole
a rail
a stick
a rod

❷ *Mum gave me a **bar** of chocolate.*

a block
a slab

Use **a cake** for a bar of soap.

bare *ADJECTIVE*

❶ *The baby was **bare**.*

naked
undressed
nude

❷ *The room was **bare**.*

empty
unfurnished

barely *ADVERB*

*There was **barely** any food left.*

hardly
scarcely

base *NOUN*

❶ *Plants grew along the **base** of the wall.*

the bottom
the foot

❷ *The soldiers returned to their **base**.*

a headquarters
a camp

basic *ADJECTIVE*

*You must learn the **basic** skills before trying anything complicated.*

main
key
essential
elementary
chief

bat *NOUN*

WORD WEB

Some types of **bat**:

a badminton racket
a baseball bat
a cricket bat
a golf club
a hockey stick
a shinty stick
a tennis racket

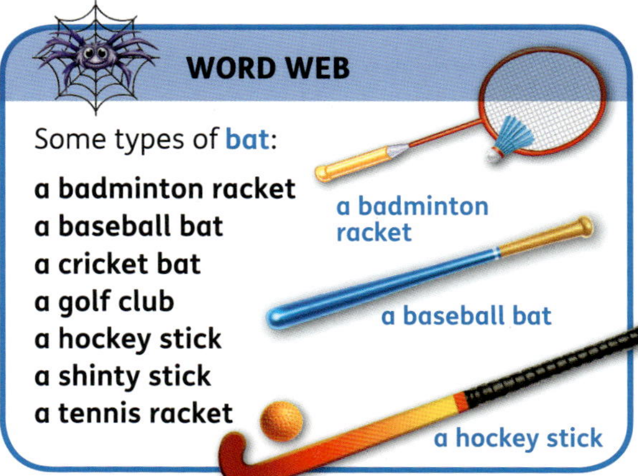

battle *NOUN*

*Many soldiers were killed in the **battle**.*

a fight
an attack
a clash

beach *NOUN*

*The children played on the **beach**.*

the sand
the seaside
the seashore
the shore

Shingle is a pebbly beach: *We walked over the **shingle**, looking for colourful pebbles.*

beam *NOUN*

*A **beam** of light shone through the window.*

a ray
a shaft

bean *NOUN*

WORD WEB

Some types of **bean**:

a broad bean
a green bean
a kidney bean
a runner bean
a soya bean

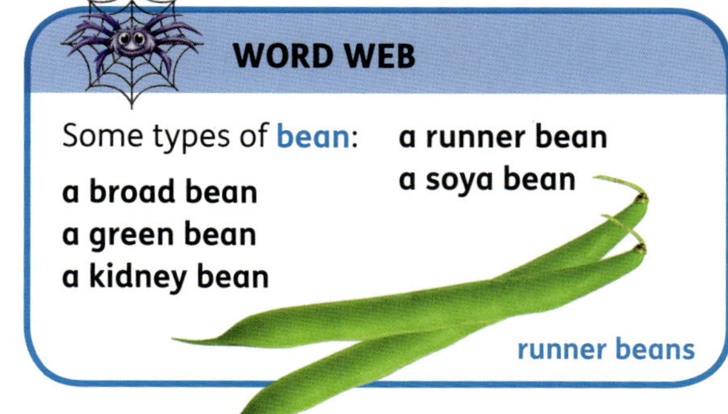

bear *VERB* bears, bearing, bore, borne

1 *The ice may not **bear** your weight.*

to support
to hold

2 *I can't **bear** loud music!*

to stand
to put up with
to tolerate
to endure

beast *NOUN*

*A huge **beast** roamed the forest.*

a creature
a monster
a brute
a wild animal

beat *VERB* beats, beating, beat, beaten

1 *We **beat** the other team one nil.*

to defeat
to vanquish

To **thrash** someone means to beat them very easily: *They **thrashed** us 6–0.*

2 *It's cruel to **beat** animals.*

to hit
to thrash
to whip
to strike
to flog

3 ***Beat** the eggs and sugar together.*

to mix
to blend
to stir
to whip
to whisk

beautiful *ADJECTIVE*

OVERUSED WORD

Here are some more interesting words for **beautiful**:

1 *He married the **beautiful** princess.*

lovely
pretty
fair
attractive

Use **gorgeous**, **stunning** or **enchanting** if someone is very beautiful: *You look absolutely **stunning** in that dress!*

Use **glamorous** if someone looks beautiful and rich: *She looked like a **glamorous** actress.*

OPPOSITE **ugly**

2 *What a **beautiful** view!*

glorious
magnificent
spectacular
stunning

3 *The weather was **beautiful** for sports day.*

lovely
gorgeous
wonderful
fantastic

OPPOSITE **awful**

beauty *NOUN*

1 *The princess was famous for her **beauty**.*

loveliness
prettiness
attractiveness

Use **glamour** if someone looks beautiful and rich: *The actress was famous for her **glamour**.*

OPPOSITE **ugliness**

2 *I was amazed by the **beauty** of the scenery.*

loveliness
splendour
magnificence

become *VERB* becomes, becoming, became, become

❶ *A tadpole will **become** a frog.*
to change into
to grow into
to turn into
to develop into

❷ *He **became** angry.*
to get
to grow
to turn

bed *NOUN*

WORD WEB

Some types of **bed**:

A berth is a bed on a ship.
A bunk is one of two beds on top of each other.
A cot, cradle or **crib** is a bed with sides for a baby.
A four-poster bed is a bed with curtains around it.
A hammock is a piece of cloth that you hang up and use as a bed.

beg *VERB*

*We **begged** him to let us go.*
to ask
to plead with *We **pleaded with** him to let us go.*
to implore *We **implored** him to let us go.*

begin *VERB* begins, beginning, began, begun

❶ *The little girl **began** to laugh.*
to start

❷ *At what time does the concert **begin**?*
to start
to commence
OPPOSITE **end**

beginning *NOUN*

*I was scared at the **beginning** of the story, and hid under the covers.*
the start
the opening
OPPOSITE **ending**

behave *VERB*

❶ *She was **behaving** rather strangely and I asked her if she was OK.*
to act
to react

❷ *Make sure you **behave** at the party.*
to be good
to behave yourself
to be on your best behaviour

behaviour *NOUN*

*The children's **behaviour** was excellent.*
conduct
attitude
manners *The children's **manners** were excellent.*

belief *NOUN*

*People have different religious **beliefs**.*
a faith
a principle
a conviction
an opinion
a view

believe *VERB*

❶ *I don't **believe** what you are saying to me.*
to trust
to accept

❷ *I **believe** that she is innocent.*
to think
to be sure
to be convinced

❸ *The ancient Greeks **believed** in many gods.*
to have faith in
to put your faith in

bell *NOUN*

WRITING TIPS

Here are some useful words for writing about **bells**:

- *The school bell **rings** at ten to nine.*
- *The grandfather clock in the hall **chimes** every hour.*
- *The sleigh bells **jingled** as we rode along in the snow.*
- *The tiny bells on the Christmas tree **tinkled** as I walked past.*
- *The huge church bell began to **toll**.*
- *The ship's bell **clanged** loudly.*
- *At that moment an alarm bell **sounded**.*
- *They heard the **peal** of bells from the cathedral.*

belly *NOUN (informal)*

*I've eaten too much and now my **belly** hurts.*

a tummy *(informal)*
a stomach

belong *VERB*

❶ *This game **belongs** to me.*

to be owned by

❷ *Ali **belongs** to the running club.*

to be a member of
to be in *Ali **is in** the football club.*

❸ *These pencils **belong** in the cupboard.*

to go

belongings *NOUN*

*Be sure to take your **belongings** when you get off the train.*

possessions
property
things

beloved *ADJECTIVE*

*She couldn't wait to get home to her **beloved** kitten.*

darling
dear
adored
precious

bend *NOUN*

*There are a lot of sharp **bends** in this road.*

a corner
a turn
a twist
a curve

bend *VERB* bends, bending, bent

❶ *He **bent** the wire into the correct shape.*

to twist
to curve
to curl
to coil
to wind
to fold
OPPOSITE **straighten**

❷ *She **bent** down to tie her shoelaces.*

to stoop
to crouch
to duck
to lean

bent *ADJECTIVE*

*The back wheel of the bicycle was **bent**.*

twisted
crooked
distorted
OPPOSITE **straight**

berry *NOUN*

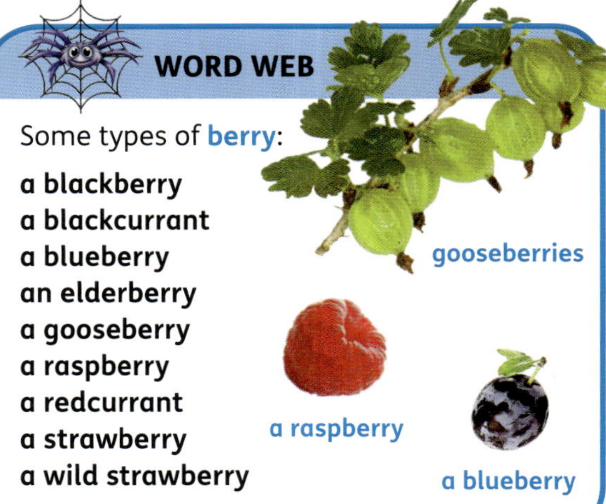

WORD WEB

Some types of **berry**:

a blackberry
a blackcurrant
a blueberry
an elderberry
a gooseberry
a raspberry
a redcurrant
a strawberry
a wild strawberry

gooseberries

a raspberry

a blueberry

besides *ADVERB*

It's too cold to go to the park. ***Besides****, we haven't got a ball.*

also
in addition
additionally
what's more

best *ADJECTIVE*

She is the ***best*** *swimmer in the world.*

finest
greatest
number-one
top

OPPOSITE **worst**

bet *VERB* bets, betting, bet

I ***bet*** *he won't come.*

to feel sure
to be certain
to be positive

better *ADJECTIVE*

Tom has been ill, but he's ***better*** *now.*

all right
recovered
cured
well

beware *VERB*

Beware *of the dog.*

to be careful of
to watch out for

bicycle *NOUN*

a bike
a cycle

WORD WEB

Some types of **bicycle**:

a mountain bike
a road bike
a racing bike
A hybrid bike is a cross between a road and a mountain bike.
A tandem is for two people.
A tricycle has three wheels.
A unicycle has one wheel.

a unicycle

a tandem

a mountain bike

big *ADJECTIVE*

OVERUSED WORD

Try to use a more interesting word when you want to say **big**. Here are some other words you can use instead:

1 *He put the books into a **big** box.*

Use **large** when you want to say that something is quite big: *There was a **large**, wooden crate in the middle of the room.*

Use **bulky** for something that is big and difficult to move: *That bag is too **bulky** to fit in my locker.*

Use **huge** or **enormous** for something that is very big: *We had to climb over some **huge** rocks.*

Use **massive**, **gigantic**, **colossal**, **vast** or **immense** for something that is very big indeed: *In the sky was a **colossal**, black cloud.*

Use **mighty** for something that is very big and powerful: *The dragon swept the ship aside with one of its **mighty** claws.*

2 *There are lots of **big** buildings in the city centre.*
large
tall
high

3 Use **spacious** for houses and flats that have plenty of space inside: *Inside, the flat was quite **spacious**.*

Use **vast** for very big buildings, rooms or ships: *Underneath the house was a **vast** cellar.*

Use **grand** or **magnificent** for things that are big and beautiful: *We were amazed by the **magnificent** mountains.*

4 *Tom is quite **big** for his age.*
tall

Use **broad** or **well-built** for someone who looks strong and not thin: *He was a strong, **well-built** boy.*

5 *This T-shirt is too **big** for me.*
long
loose
baggy

6 *Mice are a **big** problem for farmers.*
important
serious
significant

OPPOSITE **small**

A Bb C D E F G H I J K L M N O P Q R S T U V W X Y Z

bird *NOUN*

WORD WEB

Some familiar British **birds**:

blackbird
blue tit
chaffinch
crow
cuckoo
dove
house martin
lark
magpie
pigeon
robin
raven
sparrow
starling
swallow
thrush
woodpecker
wren

Some **birds** of prey:

buzzard
eagle
falcon
hawk
kestrel
kite
owl
peregrine falcon
vulture

Some farm **birds**:

chicken
duck
goose
turkey

Some water **birds**:

coot
curlew
duck
flamingo
heron
kingfisher
moorhen
pelican
penguin
swan
stork

Some sea **birds**:

albatross
puffin
seagull

Some tropical **birds**:

budgerigar
canary
cockatoo
macaw
mynah bird
parakeet
parrot
toucan
peacock

a macaw

a duck

a puffin

a blue tit

a kingfisher

a kestrel

WRITING TIPS

Here are some useful words for writing about **birds**. Some describe movement, and others sound.

- *A strange-looking bird* ***flew*** *past me.*
- *The eagle* ***soared*** *high in the sky.*
- *I watched the large bird* ***hover*** *and* ***glide****, then* ***swoop*** *down on its prey.*
- *Some sparrows* ***fluttered*** *about in the trees.*
- *A robin* ***hopped*** *onto the branch next to me.*
- *I could hear birds* ***singing*** *early in the morning.*
- *The little birds* ***twittered*** *and* ***chirped*** *in trees.*
- *Owls* ***screeched*** *and* ***hooted*** *in the wood.*
- *Sea birds* ***nest*** *in the cliffs.*
- *Birds* ***flitted*** *in and out of the hedgerows.*

Then one day, a truly magnificent bird flew down out of the sky and landed on the monkey cage.—THE TWITS, Roald Dahl

biscuit *NOUN*
a cookie

A **cracker** is a dry biscuit for eating with cheese.

A **wafer** is a very thin biscuit.

bit *NOUN*

OVERUSED WORD

Here are some more interesting words for **bit**:

Use **piece** with exactly the same meaning as bit: *I've lost a **piece** of my jigsaw.*

Use **chunk**, **lump**, **block** or **slab** for a big bit of something: *A big **lump** of rock was blocking the road.*

Use **fragment** for a small bit of something: *We found some tiny **fragments** of Roman pottery.*

Use **slice** or **sliver** for a thin bit of something: *Would you like a **slice** of birthday cake?*

Use **crumb** for a small bit of something dry: *All that was left of the sandwiches were a few **crumbs**.*

Use **scrap** for a small bit of paper or cloth: *I wrote the address down on a **scrap** of paper.*

Use **shred** for a small bit torn off something: *There was a **shred** of cloth caught on the branch.*

Use **chip** for a small bit that has broken off something: *He found a **chip** of glass on the floor.*

Use **speck** for a small bit of dust or dirt: ***Specks** of dust glittered in the light.*

Use **bite**, **mouthful**, **nibble**, **morsel** or **taste** for a small bit of something you eat: *Can I have a **bite** of your biscuit?*

bite *VERB* **bites, biting, bit, bitten**
1 *Be careful that horse doesn't **bite** you.*
to nip
to snap at

2 *My dog **bit** a hole in my shoe.*
to chew
to gnaw
to nibble

bitter *ADJECTIVE*
*The medicine had a **bitter** taste.*
sour
sharp
acid
OPPOSITE **sweet**

black *ADJECTIVE*
1 *It was a cold, **black** night.*
dark
pitch black
moonless
starless

2 *She had **black** hair.*
dark
jet black
ebony
raven

blame *VERB*
*The teacher **blamed** me for breaking the window.*
to accuse *The teacher **accused** me of breaking the window.*
to tell off *The teacher **told** me **off** for breaking the window.*
to scold *The teacher **scolded** me for breaking the window.*

blanket *NOUN*
*The baby was wrapped in a **blanket**.*
a bedspread
a cover
a quilt
a rug

blew *VERB* (*past tense of* blow)

blob *NOUN*
There was a ***blob*** *of jam on the table.*
a lump
a dollop
a drop

block *NOUN*
They covered the hole with a ***block*** *of concrete.*
a piece
a lump
a slab

block *VERB*
A huge lorry had ***blocked*** *the road.*
to obstruct
to clog up

blow *VERB* blows, blowing, blew, blown
He ***blew*** *on his food to cool it down.*
to breathe
to puff

blue *ADJECTIVE*
navy blue
sky-blue
royal blue
turquoise
azure
bright blue

blush *VERB*
She ***blushed*** *a bright red whenever the teacher spoke to her.*
to go red
to redden
to flush

boast *VERB*
She's always ***boasting*** *about how good she is at netball.*
to brag
to show off
to gloat

boat *NOUN*
We need a ***boat*** *to get across the lake.*
a ship
a vessel
a craft

WORD WEB

Some types of **boat**:

an aircraft carrier
a barge
a battleship
a canoe
a dinghy
a ferry
a fishing boat
a kayak
a lifeboat
a motor boat
a raft
a rowing boat
a sailing boat
a speedboat
a tanker
a trawler
a warship
a yacht

WRITING TIPS

Here are some useful words for writing about **boats**:

- *The little fishing boat* ***bobbed up and down*** *in the water.*
- *The dinghy* ***drifted*** *slowly out to sea.*
- *We* ***floated*** *down the river on our raft.*
- *The barge* ***chugged*** *slowly along the canal.*
- *The speedboat* ***sped*** *quickly through the water.*
- *We* ***sailed*** *the yacht into the harbour and* ***moored*** *it to the jetty.*
- *We were worried our little rowing boat would* ***capsize*** *in the storm.*

He leant back in his seat and surveyed the cushions, the oars, the rowlocks, and all the fascinating fittings, and felt the boat sway lightly under him.—THE WIND IN THE WILLOWS, Kenneth Grahame

bob *VERB*
The toy boat ***bobbed*** *on the water.*
to float
to bounce

body *NOUN*

WORD WEB

Some parts of your **body**:

ankle
arm
armpit
calf
cheek
chest
chin
ear
elbow
eye
finger
foot
forehead
hand
head
heel
hip
knee
leg
lip
mouth
navel
neck
nose
shin
shoulder
skin
stomach
thigh
throat
thumb
toe
waist
wrist

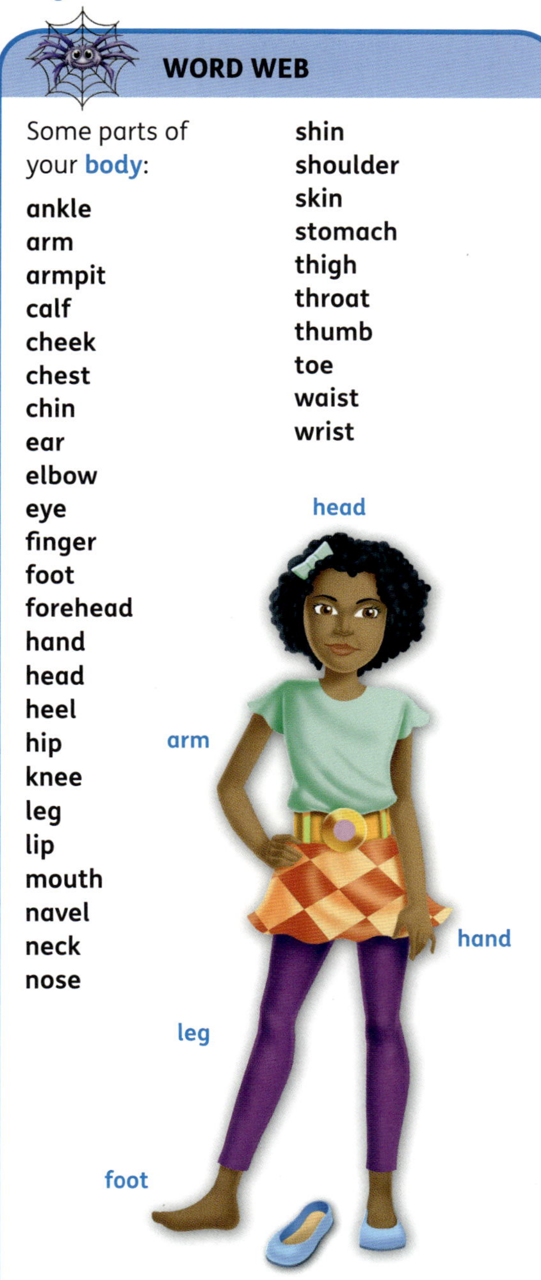

bog *NOUN*
He was sinking into the ***bog****.*
a marsh
a swamp

boil *VERB*
The water had started to ***boil****.*
to bubble
to simmer

boiling *ADJECTIVE*
1 *Can we open a window? It's* ***boiling*** *in here.*
baking
scorching
sweltering
OPPOSITE **freezing**

2 *The soup was* ***boiling*** *hot and I couldn't eat it.*
scalding
piping hot
OPPOSITE **cold**

bolt *VERB*
1 *He* ***bolts*** *the door at night.*
to lock
to fasten

2 *The horse* ***bolted*** *from the stable.*
to run away
to flee

3 *She* ***bolted*** *her food as she was so hungry.*
to gobble down
to guzzle
to wolf

bone *NOUN*

WORD WEB

Some **bones** in your body:

a backbone or **a spine**
A collarbone is the bone from your shoulder to your neck.
A pelvis is the bone across your hips.
ribs
a shoulder blade
a skull

book NOUN

WORD WEB

Some types of **book**:

an annual
an atlas
a brochure
a catalogue
a comic
a dictionary
a directory
an encyclopedia
an e-book
a non-fiction book
a novel
a picture book
a reference book
a story book
a textbook
a thesaurus

boom VERB
*'Silence!' **boomed** the voice.*
to shout
to bellow
to roar
to thunder

bore VERB *(past tense of* **bear***)*

bored ADJECTIVE
1 *I had nothing to do and I felt **bored**.*
uninterested
dreary
at a loose end

2 *I'm **bored** with this game.*
fed up
tired *I'm **tired** of this game.*

boring ADJECTIVE
*This book is really **boring**!*
dull
tedious
dreary

Use **uneventful** or **unexciting** when nothing interesting happens: *It was a very **uneventful** day.*

Use **monotonous** to describe a boring voice: *The doctor spoke in a low, **monotonous** voice.*
OPPOSITE **interesting**

borne VERB *(past participle of* **bear***)*

borrow VERB
*Can I **borrow** your pen for a minute, please?*
to use
to take

boss NOUN *(informal)*
1 *Who's the **boss** here?*
the person in charge
the leader
the chief
the head

2 *Her **boss** said she could have the day off.*
an employer
a manager
a supervisor
a director

bossy ADJECTIVE
*He can be **bossy** sometimes.*
domineering
bullying
controlling

bother VERB
1 *Is the loud music **bothering** you?*
to annoy
to disturb
to upset
to irritate

2 *They didn't **bother** to clear up their mess.*
to make the effort
to take the trouble

bottom NOUN
1 *We'll wait at the **bottom** of the hill.*
the foot
the base
OPPOSITE **top**

2 *She fell and landed on her **bottom**.*
backside
rear
behind
buttocks

bought VERB (*past tense and past participle of* buy)

bounce VERB

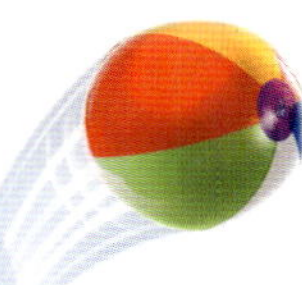

*The ball **bounced** off the wall.*
to rebound
to ricochet

bound VERB (*past participle of* bind)

bowl NOUN
*She put the fruit into a **bowl**.*
a dish
a basin

box NOUN
1 *I bought a **box** of cereal.*
a packet
a carton

2 *We packed the books into a **box**.*
a case
a crate
a chest
a trunk

boy NOUN
a lad
a kid (*informal*)
a child
a youngster
a youth
a teenager

brain NOUN
*He's got a very good **brain**.*
a mind
intelligence
sense

branch NOUN
*A large **branch** had fallen off the tree.*
a bough

brave ADJECTIVE
*Are you **brave** enough to fight the dragon?*
courageous
bold
daring

Use **fearless** if someone seems to feel no fear: *The captain was **fearless** in battle.*

Use **heroic** if someone helps another person in a very brave way: *The firemen were rewarded for their **heroic** rescue of the children.*

Use **adventurous** if someone is brave enough to start a new adventure: *Are you **adventurous** enough to do this challenge?*
OPPOSITE **cowardly**

bravery NOUN
*He got a medal for his **bravery**.*
courage
heroism
valour
OPPOSITE **cowardice**

break VERB breaks, breaking, broke, broken
1 *I dropped a cup and it **broke**.*
to crack

Use **chip** when a small piece breaks off something: *I **chipped** my favourite mug.*

Use **smash**, **shatter** and **splinter** when something breaks into a lot of sharp pieces: *The glass **shattered** into hundreds of tiny pieces.*

Use **crumble** when something breaks into many small pieces: *The biscuit **crumbled** everywhere.*

2 *The stick **broke** into two pieces.*
to snap
to split

3 *The bridge will **break** if there is too much weight on it.*
to collapse
to fall down
to fall apart

4 *My brother **broke** my phone.*
to damage
to ruin
to wreck

5 *She fell and **broke** her wrist.*
to fracture

6 *You will be punished if you **break** the rules.*
to disobey

break NOUN

1 *We climbed through a **break** in the hedge.*
a gap
a hole
an opening

2 *There was a **break** in the oil pipe.*
a crack
a split
a hole

3 *Let's stop for a short **break**.*
a rest
a pause

4 *There will be a fifteen-minute **break** halfway through the show.*
an interval
an intermission

breathe VERB

*I could hear my brother **breathing** in the top bunk.*

To inhale is to breathe in.

To exhale is to breathe out.

Use **pant** when someone is breathing heavily or fast: *I was **panting** after the race.*

bridge NOUN

WORD WEB

Some types of **bridge**:

A flyover goes over a road.
A footbridge is for people.
A railway bridge goes over a rail track.
A viaduct goes over a river or valley.

bright ADJECTIVE

1 *We saw a **bright** light in the sky as the aeroplane flew over.*
shining
gleaming

Use **dazzling** and **brilliant** for a light that is very bright: *We watched the **dazzling** firework display.*

Use **glaring** and **blinding** for a light that is so bright you cannot look at it: *We turned away from the **blinding** headlights.*

Use **glowing** and **gleaming** for a soft, gentle light: *We could see the **glowing** light of the fire in the distance.*

OPPOSITE **dull**

2 *I like wearing **bright** colours.*
vivid
strong
rich

OPPOSITE **dull**

3 *He's a very **bright** boy, who is good at English, maths and music.*
clever
intelligent
brainy
quick
sharp
smart

OPPOSITE **stupid**

4 *It was a lovely **bright** day.*
clear
fine
sunny

Use **brilliant** for a very bright day: *The next morning was a **brilliant** day of blue skies and hot sun.*

OPPOSITE **gloomy**

brilliant ADJECTIVE

1 *She is a **brilliant** scientist.*
intelligent
clever
talented

OPPOSITE **stupid**

2 *It's a **brilliant** movie.*
great
excellent
wonderful
fantastic
marvellous
OPPOSITE **terrible**

bring VERB brings, bringing, brought

1 *I'll **bring** the shopping in.*
to carry

2 *Please **bring** me a drink.*
to get
to fetch

broad ADJECTIVE

*The stream is quite **broad** here.*
wide
big
OPPOSITE **narrow**

broke VERB (past tense of break)

broken VERB (past participle of break)

broken ADJECTIVE

1 *I think my phone's **broken**. It won't come on.*
not working
faulty
out of order
damaged
OPPOSITE **working**

2 *I saw a **broken** window.*
smashed
destroyed
in pieces *The mirror was **in pieces**.*

brought VERB (past tense and past participle of bring)

brown ADJECTIVE

*He was wearing **brown** trousers.*
beige
fawn
khaki
chocolate brown

brush VERB

*We had to **brush** the floor.*
to sweep
to clean

bubble NOUN

*The water was full of **bubbles**.*
Use **foam** or **froth** for bubbles on top of a liquid.
Use **lather** for soap bubbles.
Use **fizz** or **effervescence** for bubbles in a drink.

bug NOUN

1 *You can find lots of interesting **bugs** in your garden.*
an insect
a creepy-crawly *(informal)*

a spider

a caterpillar

2 *She has been off school with a **bug**.*
a virus
a germ
an illness

3 *The computer program had a **bug** in it.*
a fault
an error
a virus

buggy NOUN

*I pushed my baby sister along in her **buggy**.*
a stroller
a pushchair

Use **a pram** for a buggy in which a baby lies flat.

build VERB builds, building, built

*It can take about six months to **build** a new house.*
to construct
to put up
to create

building *NOUN*

WORD WEB

Some **buildings** where people live:

an apartment
a bungalow
a castle
a cottage
a farmhouse
a flat
a house
a mansion
a palace
a skyscraper
a tower
a villa

Some **buildings** where people worship:

a cathedral
a chapel
a church
a gurdwara
a monastery
a mosque
a synagogue
a temple

Other types of **building**:

a cafe
a cinema
a doctor's surgery
a factory
a fire station
a garage
a hospital
a hotel
a library
a mill
a movie theatre
a museum
an office
a police station
a post office
a prison
a school
a shop
a theatre

bully *VERB*

Some of the older boys were ***bullying*** *him.*

to tease
to torment
to threaten

Use **terrorise** and **persecute** when someone bullies a person badly: *He used to* ***terrorise*** *the younger children and take all their money off them.*

bump *NOUN*

1 *The book fell to the ground with a* ***bump****.*

a bang
a crash
a thud
a thump

2 *She's got a nasty* ***bump*** *on her head.*

a lump
a swelling

bump *VERB*

I fell and ***bumped*** *my head.*

to bang
to knock
to hit
to bash
to strike *He* ***struck*** *his head on the corner of the table.*

bumpy *ADJECTIVE*

1 *We drove along the* ***bumpy*** *road.*

rough
uneven

2 *It was a very* ***bumpy*** *ride.*

jerky
jolting
bouncy

OPPOSITE **smooth**

bunch *NOUN*

1 *He bought me a **bunch** of flowers.*
a bouquet
a posy
a spray

2 *She handed me a large **bunch** of keys.*
a collection
a set
a quantity

3 *I went to the park with a **bunch** of friends.*
a group
a crowd
a gang

burn *VERB* burns, burning, burned *or* burnt

1 *Paper **burns** easily.*
to catch fire
to catch light
to burst into flames

2 *A fire was **burning** in the grate.*

Use **blaze** when a fire burns quickly, with a lot of heat: *A warm fire **blazed** in the corner of the room.*

Use **glow** or **smoulder** when a fire burns slowly, without big flames: *Last night's bonfire was still **smouldering** in the garden.*

Use **flicker** when a fire burns with small flames: *The camp fire **flickered** merrily.*

3 *We can **burn** all this rubbish.*
to set fire to
to set alight
to incinerate

4 *He **burnt** his shirt on the iron.*
to scorch
to singe

burst *VERB* bursts, bursting, burst

*My balloon's **burst**!*
to pop
to go bang
to split
to puncture

bus *NOUN*

a coach
a minibus

bush *NOUN*

*We hid in the **bushes**.*
a shrub

business *NOUN*

1 *His parents run their own **business**.*
a company
a firm
an organisation

2 *Her mum works in **business**.*
commerce
industry
trade

busy *ADJECTIVE*

1 *Dad was **busy** in the garden.*
occupied
working
OPPOSITE **idle**

2 *I've had a very **busy** morning.*
active
energetic
OPPOSITE **idle**

3 *London is a very **busy** place.*
crowded
bustling
lively
OPPOSITE **peaceful**

buy *VERB* buys, buying, bought

1 *Where's the best place to **buy** a bike?*
to get
to purchase
to obtain

2 *My friend **bought** me an ice cream.*
to get *My friend **got** me an ice cream.*
to treat someone to *My friend **treated** me **to** an ice cream.*
to pay for *My friend **paid for** an ice cream for me.*
OPPOSITE **sell**

cafe *NOUN*
*We went to a **cafe** for lunch.*
a restaurant
a snack bar
a coffee bar
a tearoom
a cafeteria

cage *NOUN*

WORD WEB

Some types of **cage**:

A hutch is for rabbits.
An enclosure is in a zoo.
An aviary is for birds.
A pen is for farm animals.

call *VERB*
1 *'Hello,' she **called**.*
to shout
to yell
to cry

2 *We've decided to **call** the puppy Lucky.*
to name

3 *I'll **call** you when I get home.*
to phone
to ring
to telephone

calm *ADJECTIVE*
1 *The little village was very **calm**.*
peaceful
quiet
OPPOSITE **noisy**

2 *The sea was **calm** after the storm.*
flat
smooth
still
OPPOSITE **stormy**

3 *It was a lovely **calm** day, and not a leaf moved on the trees.*
still
windless
OPPOSITE **windy**

4 *She asked the children to keep **calm**.*
quiet
relaxed
cool
patient
OPPOSITE **excited**

came *VERB (past tense and past participle of come)*

car *NOUN*

WRITING TIPS

Here are some useful words for writing about **cars**:

- *The little car **accelerated** down the hill then **slowed down** and stopped at the traffic lights.*
- *The sports car was **speeding** along.*
- *Cars **zoomed** past us on the road.*
- *The taxi **raced** away towards the airport.*
- *The old estate car **crawled along** at 40 kilometres per hour.*

'Your sons flew that car to Harry's house and back last night,' shouted Mrs Weasley. 'What have you got to say about that, eh?' 'Did you really?' said Mr Weasley eagerly.
—HARRY POTTER AND THE CHAMBER OF SECRETS, J. K. Rowling

WORD WEB

Some types of **car**:

a convertible
an estate car
an electric car
a four-wheel drive (4x4)
a hatchback
a limousine
an MPV
a people carrier
a racing car
a saloon
a sports car
an SUV
a taxi
a van
a vintage car

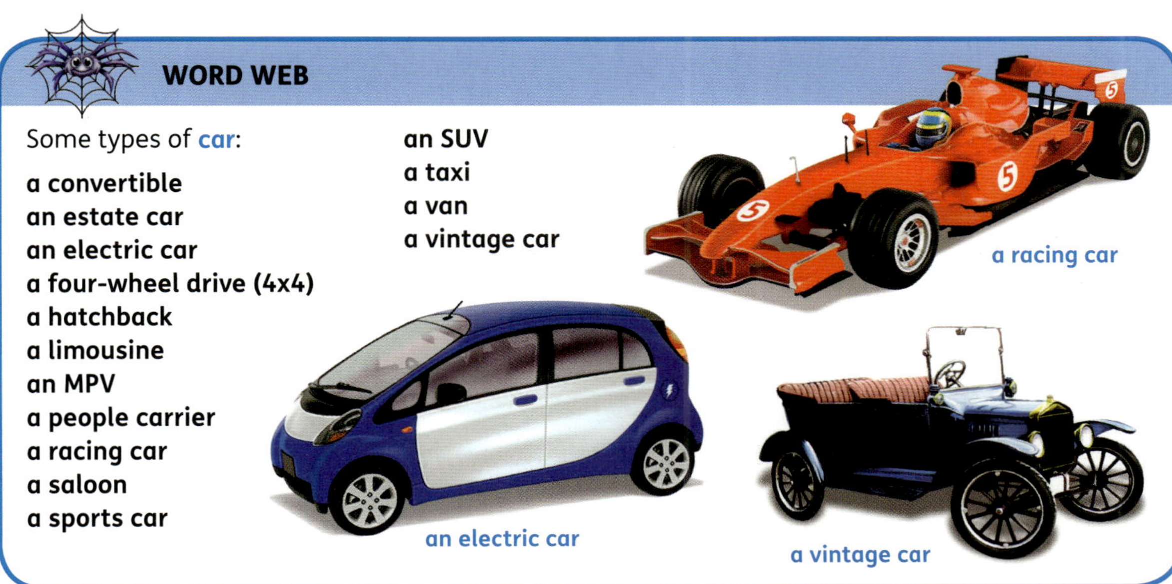
a racing car
an electric car
a vintage car

care VERB

*I don't **care** who wins the game.*

to mind *I don't **mind** who wins.*
to be bothered *I'm not **bothered** who wins.*
to be concerned *I'm not **concerned** about who wins.*

careful ADJECTIVE

1 *Be **careful** when you cross the busy road.*

cautious
alert
attentive
watchful
wary

2 *This is good, **careful** work.*

neat
thorough
conscientious
accurate

OPPOSITE **careless**

careless ADJECTIVE

1 *This work is untidy and **careless**!*

messy
untidy
sloppy
shoddy

2 *She was **careless** and left the door open.*

silly
foolish
thoughtless
irresponsible
reckless

OPPOSITE **careful**

carry VERB

*We **carried** the boxes into the house.*

to lift
to move
to bring
to take
to transport

➤ **carry on**

*The children **carried on** talking after they had been told to be quiet.*

to continue
to keep on
to go on

castle *NOUN*
a fort
a fortress
a stronghold

casual *ADJECTIVE*
*You can wear **casual** clothes for the trip, like jeans and a hoodie.*
relaxed
informal
OPPOSITE **formal**

cat *NOUN*
A **kitten** is a young cat.

A **tomcat** or **tom** is a male cat.

WORD WEB

Some types of domestic **cat**:

a Manx cat
a Persian cat
a Siamese cat
a tabby cat
a tortoiseshell cat

Some types of wild **cat**:

a cheetah
a leopard
a lion
a lynx
an ocelot
a panther
a puma
a tiger
a wildcat

WRITING TIPS

Here are some useful words for writing about **cats**:

- *Cats can **creep** or **slink** along very quietly.*
- *They **prowl** around when they are looking for food, then they **crouch down** and **spring** on their prey.*
- *Cats **miaow** or **mew** when they are hungry.*
- *They **purr** when they are happy, and they **hiss** and **spit** when they are angry.*

'Well! I've often seen a cat without a grin,' thought Alice; 'but a grin without a cat! It's the most curious thing I ever saw in all my life!'—ALICE'S ADVENTURES IN WONDERLAND, Lewis Carroll

catch *VERB* catches, catching, caught
1 *The police have **caught** the thieves.*
to capture
to arrest
to take prisoner *The police have taken the thieves prisoner.*

2 *We **caught** mice in the house and released them into the garden.*
to trap
to snare

3 *I've **caught** a fish!*
to hook
to net

4 *Try to **catch** the ball.*
to get hold of
to take hold of
to hold
to grip
to grab

5 *She **caught** chickenpox.*
to get
to come down with
to go down with
to be infected with

cause *VERB*
*The heavy rain **caused** a lot of flooding.*
to bring about
to lead to
to result in
to produce

celebration *NOUN*
*There was a huge **celebration** when the new king was crowned.*
a party
a feast
a carnival

centre *NOUN*
1 *There was a fire in the **centre** of the room that kept the whole house warm.*
the middle

2 *They live right in the **centre** of the city.*
the middle
the heart

3 *The **centre** of the planet is very hot.*
the core
the middle
the interior

certain *ADJECTIVE*
*I'm **certain** I saw her in town.*
sure
positive
convinced
OPPOSITE **uncertain**

certainly *ADVERB*
1 *It **certainly** wasn't my fault.*
definitely
unquestionably
undoubtedly

2 *'Can I come?' '**Certainly**.'*
of course
naturally
absolutely
sure

chair *NOUN*
*He sat in his usual **chair** by the fire.*
a seat
a place

WORD WEB

Some types of **chair**:

an armchair	**a kitchen chair**
a bench	**a rocking chair**
a couch	**a settee**
a deckchair	**a sofa**
a dining chair	**a stool**

chance *NOUN*
1 *This is our last **chance** to escape.*
an opportunity

2 *There is a **chance** that we will fail.*
a possibility
a risk

3 *We met by **chance**.*
luck
coincidence
fate

change *VERB*
1 *Our school has **changed** a lot in the last five years.*
to alter

2 *I **changed** my design because it didn't work.*
to alter
to modify
to adjust
to revise

3 *Tadpoles **change** into frogs.*
to turn into
to grow into
to develop into
to become

4 *I took the dress back to the shop and **changed** it.*
to exchange
to swap

A B Cc D E F G H I J K L M N O P Q R S T U V W X Y Z

character *NOUN*

1 *Which **character** would you like to play in the school play?*
a part
a role

2 *Tom has got a lovely **character**.*
a personality
a nature
a temperament

charge *NOUN*

*There is no **charge** to go into the museum.*
a fee
a payment

charge *VERB*

1 *How much do they **charge** for orange juice?*
to ask

2 *The bull was about to **charge**.*
to attack
to rush
to stampede

charming *ADJECTIVE*

*What a **charming** little dog!*
lovely
pretty
beautiful
delightful
cute

chart *NOUN*

*We drew a **chart** to show the results of the school's sponsored swim.*
a graph
a diagram
a table

chase *VERB*

1 *The policeman **chased** the thief down the road.*
to run after
to follow
to pursue

2 *It is natural for **cats** to chase birds.*
to hunt
to track
to catch

chat *VERB*

*Stop **chatting** and get on with your work!*
to talk
to chatter
to natter

To **gossip** means to talk about other people: *I thought all the other children were **gossiping** about me.*

cheat *VERB*

1 *The other team won, but we all thought they had **cheated**!*
to break the rules
to not play fair

2 *They **cheated** me out of my money.*
to trick
to swindle
to fool

check *VERB*

1 *Always **check** your spellings.*
to look at
to examine
to double-check

2 ***Check** that the door is locked.*
to make sure
to ensure
to verify

3 *All the cars are carefully **checked** before they are sold.*
to inspect
to test

cheeky *ADJECTIVE*

*Don't be **cheeky** to your parents!*
rude
impertinent
impudent
insolent

disrespectful
OPPOSITE **respectful**

cheer *VERB*
*Everyone **cheered** when our team scored.*
to shout
to applaud

cheerful *ADJECTIVE*
*He seems very **cheerful** today.*
happy
smiling
joyful
light-hearted
OPPOSITE **sad**

chew *VERB*
1 *She was **chewing** on an apple.*

Use **to bite** when you sink your teeth into something: *I **bit** into the warm pie.*

Use **to crunch** when something is crispy or hard: *Ben **crunched** the crispy apple.*

Use **to suck** when you pull liquid into your mouth: *Samir **sucked** his ice lolly.*

Use **to munch** when someone is really enjoying what they are eating: *Alice **munched** on her peanut butter sandwich.*

Use **to nibble** when someone is eating something with small bites: *The rabbit **nibbled** on the lettuce.*

2 *Mice had **chewed** through the wires.*
to bite
to gnaw
to nibble

chicken *NOUN*
A hen is a female chicken.
A rooster is a male chicken.
A chick is a young chicken.
Poultry are chickens and other birds kept for food.

childish *ADJECTIVE*
*This behaviour is very **childish**!*
silly
immature
juvenile
babyish
OPPOSITE **mature**

chilly *ADJECTIVE*
*It's a **chilly** evening so wear a jacket.*
cold
cool
nippy
fresh
frosty
OPPOSITE **warm**

chip *NOUN*
*A **chip** of paint fell off the wall.*
a bit
a piece
a scrap
a fragment

Use **a splinter** or **a sliver** for a thin, sharp piece: *A **splinter** of wood stuck out from the door.*

Use **a flake** for a very thin piece: ***Flakes** of rust were coming off the old bike.*

choke *VERB*
1 *The thick smoke was **choking** us.*
to suffocate
to asphyxiate

2 *The tight collar was **choking** him.*
to strangle
to throttle

choose *VERB* chooses, choosing, chose, chosen
1 *Which cake shall I **choose**?*
to pick
to select
to decide on

2 *We need to **choose** a new class representative.*
to elect
to vote for
to name

A B Cc D E F G H I J K L M N O P Q R S T U V W X Y Z

chop VERB
My dad was ***chopping*** *wood.*
to cut
to saw
to split

chose VERB *(past tense of* **choose***)*

chosen VERB *(past participle of* **choose***)*

chunk NOUN
He gave me a slice of bread and a ***chunk*** *of cheese.*
a piece
a lump
a block
a slab
a wedge

circle NOUN
We all sat in a ***circle****.*
a ring
a round
A disc is a flat circle: *Cut out a* ***disc*** *of paper.*

claim VERB
She walked up to ***claim*** *her prize.*
to ask for
to collect
to request
to demand

clap VERB
The audience ***clapped*** *when the music finished.*
to applaud
to cheer

class NOUN
Which ***class*** *are you in?*
a form
a group
a set

clean ADJECTIVE
1 *After two hours the whole house was* ***clean****.*
spotless
sparkling
tidy
spick and span
OPPOSITE **dirty**

2 *The water in this river is very* ***clean****.*
fresh
pure
clear
unpolluted
OPPOSITE **polluted**

3 *Start again on a* ***clean*** *sheet of paper.*
blank
unused
new

clean VERB
1 *They had to stay and* ***clean*** *the floors.*
to brush
to sweep
to hoover
to vacuum
to wash
to mop

2 *Whose job is it to* ***clean*** *the windows?*
to dust
to wipe
to polish

3 *Go and* ***clean*** *your hands.*
to wash
to scrub
to rinse

4 *Don't forget to* ***clean*** *your teeth.*
to brush

clear ADJECTIVE
1 *Make sure you write nice* ***clear*** *instructions.*
simple
plain
understandable

2 *Her voice was loud and* ***clear****.*
audible
distinct
understandable

3 *It was* ***clear*** *that he was very angry.*
obvious
evident

4 *Windows are usually made of* ***clear*** *glass.*
see-through
transparent
OPPOSITE **opaque**

5 *The water in the lake was lovely and* ***clear****.*
clean
pure
OPPOSITE **dirty**

6 *The next morning the sky was* ***clear****.*
blue
sunny
cloudless
bright
OPPOSITE **cloudy**

clear *VERB*
We need to ***clear*** *these chairs out of the way.*
to move
to remove
to take away

clever *ADJECTIVE*
1 *You're so* ***clever****!*
intelligent
bright
brainy
quick
sharp
smart
gifted

2 *That's a very* ***clever*** *idea.*
good
brilliant
sensible
ingenious

3 *The old fox was very* ***clever****.*
cunning
crafty
OPPOSITE **stupid**

cliff *NOUN*
Don't go near the edge of the ***cliff****.*
a crag
a rock face

climb *VERB*
1 *He* ***climbed*** *up the stairs.*
to go up
to run up

2 *The plane* ***climbed*** *into the air.*
to rise
to ascend
to go up

3 *They* ***climbed*** *over the rocks.*
to clamber
to scramble

clock *NOUN*

WORD WEB

Some types of **clock**:

an alarm clock
a cuckoo clock
a digital clock
a grandfather clock
a watch
a wind-up clock

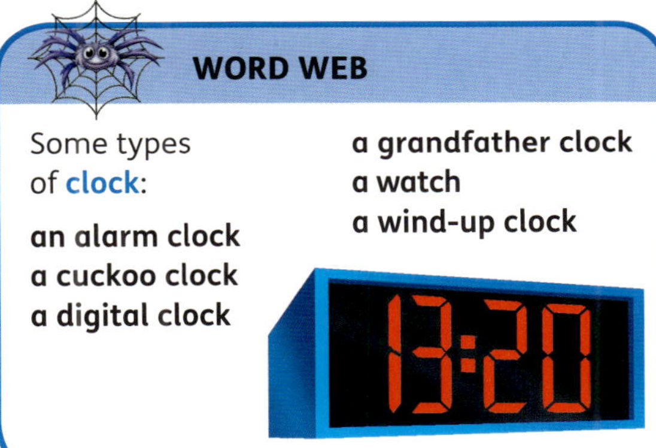

close (*say* **klohss**) *ADJECTIVE*
1 *He sat* ***close*** *to the fire.*
near to
next to
beside
OPPOSITE **far away**

2 *I took a* ***close*** *look at the map.*
careful
detailed

close (*say* **klohz**) *VERB*
Please ***close*** *the door.*
to shut
to lock

Use **slam** when someone closes a door very noisily: *She* ***slammed*** *the door angrily.*
OPPOSITE **open**

clothes *NOUN*

He was dressed in old-fashioned ***clothes****.*

clothing
attire
dress
garments
an outfit

A costume is clothes you wear to look like a particular type of person: *For the play I wore a king's* ***costume****.*

WORD WEB

Some **clothes** for warm weather:

a blouse
a dress
a shirt
shorts
a skirt
a sunhat
trousers
a T-shirt

Some **clothes** for cold weather:

an anorak
a beanie hat
a cardigan
a cloak
a coat
a fleece
gloves
a jumper
mittens
a parka
a pullover
a raincoat
a scarf
a sweater
a sweatshirt
a woolly hat

Some smart **clothes**:

a blazer
an evening gown
a jacket
a suit
a tie
a uniform
a waistcoat

Some informal **clothes**:

a hoodie
jeans
jogging bottoms
a polo shirt
a sweatshirt
a tracksuit

Some **clothes** from around the world:

a djellaba
a hijab
a kimono
a salwar kameez
a sari
a sarong

cloud *NOUN*
*There were **clouds** of smoke.*
a puff
a haze

cloudy *ADJECTIVE*
*It was a **cloudy** day.*
grey
dull
overcast
gloomy
OPPOSITE **clear**

club *NOUN*
*She joined her local drama **club**.*
a society
a group
an association

clue *NOUN*
*Shall I give you a **clue**?*
a hint
a suggestion
a tip

clumsy *ADJECTIVE*
*I can be quite **clumsy** sometimes.*
careless
accident-prone

cold *ADJECTIVE*
1 *It's quite **cold** outside today.*

Use **chilly**, **cool** and **nippy** for weather that is slightly cold: *I put my sweatshirt on because it was getting a bit **chilly**.*

Use **freezing** or **bitter** for weather that is very cold: *It was a **bitter** winter's day and there was snow on the ground.*

Use **frosty**, **icy**, **snowy** or **wintry** when there is frost, ice or snow: *It was a lovely **frosty** morning.*

2 *I'm **cold**!*
chilly
freezing
frozen

Use **chilly** when you feel slightly cold: *I was feeling a bit **chilly** after my swim.*

Use **freezing** or **frozen** when you feel very cold: *After two hours in the snow, I was absolutely **frozen**.*
OPPOSITE **hot**

collapse *VERB*
1 *Some of the old buildings **collapsed** in the storm.*
to fall down
to cave in

2 *Some people **collapsed** in the heat.*
to faint
to pass out
to fall down

collect *VERB*
1 *I **collect** old coins as a hobby.*
to keep
to save

2 *We have **collected** a lot of things for our nature table.*
to accumulate
to bring together
to gather together
to assemble

3 *My mum **collected** me from school.*
to fetch
to pick up

collection *NOUN*
*He's got a huge **collection** of games.*
a set
a hoard
an assortment
a pile

colourful *ADJECTIVE*

*Everyone was wearing **colourful** clothes.*

bright
multicoloured
OPPOSITE **dull**

WORD WEB

Some shades of red:

crimson
maroon
purple
ruby
scarlet

Some shades of blue:

aquamarine
azure
navy blue
royal blue
sapphire
sky blue
turquoise

Some shades of green:

bottle green
emerald
lime green

Some shades of yellow:

gold
lemon
mustard
primrose

Some shades of black:

ebony
jet black

Some shades of white:

cream
ivory
snow white

Some shades of grey:

charcoal grey
dove grey
silver

Some shades of brown:

beige
bronze
chocolate
fawn
khaki
tan

combine *VERB*

1 ***Combine** all the ingredients in a bowl.*

to put together
to mix together
to add together
to blend

2 *The two groups **combined** to make one big group.*

to come together
to join together
to unite
to merge

come *VERB* comes, coming, came

1 *We saw a car **coming** towards us.*

to move
to approach *We saw a car **approaching** us.*
to draw near *We saw a car **drawing near** to us.*

2 *Would you like to **come** to my house?*

to visit

3 *A letter **came** this morning.*

to arrive
to turn up
to appear

comfort *VERB*

*I **comforted** Arun because he was upset.*

to reassure
to calm someone down
to cheer someone up

comfortable *ADJECTIVE*

1 *This chair is very **comfortable**.*

soft
cosy
relaxing

2 *I was very **comfortable** in bed.*

relaxed
cosy
warm
happy
snug
contented

OPPOSITE **uncomfortable**

comment *NOUN*

*One of the boys kept making silly **comments**.*

a remark
an observation

common *ADJECTIVE*

1 *These birds are quite **common** in Europe.*

widespread

2 *Earthquakes are **common** in this part of the world.*

frequent

3 *Having a tooth taken out is a **common** operation.*

routine
standard
everyday

4 *It is very **common** for children to feel nervous before injections.*

ordinary
usual
normal

OPPOSITE **rare**

company *NOUN*

1 *They run a **company** that makes apple juice.*

a business
a firm
a factory

2 *I was lonely and wished I had some **company**.*

friendship
companionship

competition *NOUN*

1 *Let's have a **competition** to see who's the best.*

a contest
a game
a race

2 *Our team won the **competition**.*

a tournament
a championship

complain *VERB*

*Everyone **complained** about the tastless food.*

to moan
to grumble
to whinge

complete *ADJECTIVE*

1 *I haven't got a **complete** set of cards.*

full
whole
entire

OPPOSITE **incomplete**

2 *At last the work was **complete**.*

finished

OPPOSITE **unfinished**

3 *The show was a **complete** disaster.*

total
absolute
utter

completely *ADVERB*

*I'm **completely** exhausted!*

totally
utterly
absolutely

complicated *ADJECTIVE*

❶ *This is a very **complicated** machine.*

complex
sophisticated
intricate

❷ *We had to do some **complicated** sums.*

difficult
hard

OPPOSITE **simple**

computer *NOUN*

WORD WEB

Some types of **computer**:

a desktop
a laptop
a PC or **a personal computer**
a tablet

Some parts of a **computer**:

a mouse
a keyboard
a screen
a touch screen
a monitor

a keyboard

Some things you do with a **computer**:

to search
to upload
to download
to surf the Internet
to save
to open or **close** a **window** or a **document**
to click on something
to select
to copy and paste

concentrate *VERB*

*There was so much noise that I couldn't **concentrate**.*

to think
to work
to pay attention
to focus

concerned *ADJECTIVE*

*We were all very **concerned** about you.*

worried
anxious

confess *VERB*

*Sarah **confessed** that she ate the cake.*

to admit
to own up
to tell the truth

confidence *NOUN*

*Amira has so much **confidence**. She always wants to be the leader.*

self-confidence
self-assurance
assertiveness

confident *ADJECTIVE*

❶ *She looked very calm and **confident**.*

self-assured
unafraid
assertive

❷ *We are **confident** that we can win.*

sure
certain
convinced
positive

confuse *VERB*

*The instructions for the game **confused** me.*

to puzzle
to baffle
to bewilder
to perplex

confused *ADJECTIVE*

*I was feeling very **confused**.*

puzzled
bewildered
baffled

confusion *NOUN*
*Everyone looked at me in **confusion** when I tried to explain.*
bewilderment
bafflement
puzzlement

connect *VERB*
*You need to **connect** this wire to the battery.*
to join
to attach
to fix

considerate *ADJECTIVE*
*Please try to be more **considerate** of other people.*
thoughtful
kind
helpful
unselfish
OPPOSITE **selfish**

constant *ADJECTIVE*
*I'm fed up with the **constant** noise.*
incessant
continuous
relentless
never-ending

constantly *ADVERB*
*He **constantly** complains about his brother.*
always
incessantly
continuously
non-stop *He complains **non-stop** about his brother.*

contact *VERB*
*You should **contact** the school if you are ill.*
to get in touch with
to get in contact with
to speak to
to call

contest *NOUN*
*We're having a jumping **contest**.*
a competition
a match
a championship

continue *VERB*
1 ***Continue** reading until the end of the chapter.*
to go on
to keep on
to carry on

2 *The rain **continued** all afternoon.*
to last
to go on
to carry on

contribute *VERB*
1 *They **contributed** to the school fund.*
to give
to donate
to make a donation *They **made a donation** to the school fund.*

2 *He **contributed** ideas to the class discussion.*
to add
to put forward
to volunteer

control *VERB*
*The pilot uses these levers to **control** the aeroplane.*
to guide
to move
to direct

conversation *NOUN*
*We had a long **conversation** about sport.*
a talk
a discussion
a chat

convinced *ADJECTIVE*
*I'm **convinced** that he is lying.*
sure
certain
confident
positive

cook *VERB*

WORD WEB

Some ways to **cook** bread or cakes:

to bake
to toast

bake

Some ways to **cook** meat:

to barbecue
to casserole
to fry
to grill
to roast
to stew

Some ways to **cook** vegetables:

to bake
to boil
to fry
to roast
to simmer
to steam
to stir-fry

stir-fry

Some ways to **cook** eggs:

to boil
to fry
to poach
to scramble

cooker *NOUN*

*The kitchen sink is next to the **cooker**.*
a stove

An oven is the part of a cooker that you put food inside: *There was a cake in the **oven**.*

A grill is the part of a cooker that you grill food under: *I put some burgers under the **grill**.*

A hob is one of the hot surfaces on top of a cooker: *I put a frying pan on the **hob.***

cooking *NOUN*

*He loves **cooking** and he wants to be a chef.*
cookery

Use **baking** when you are cooking bread, cakes or pies in the oven.

Use **catering** when someone cooks for big groups of people as a job: *They need someone to do the **catering** for their wedding.*

cool *ADJECTIVE*

1 *It's quite **cool** outside today.*
cold
chilly
nippy

2 *I could do with a nice **cool** drink.*
cold
ice-cold
OPPOSITE **hot**

copy *VERB*

1 *See if you can **copy** this picture.*
to reproduce
to make a copy of

2 *Sam can **copy** his teacher's voice.*
to imitate
to mimic
to impersonate

correct *ADJECTIVE*

1 *That is the **correct** answer.*
right

2 *Make sure all your sums are **correct**.*
accurate
exact
right
OPPOSITE **wrong**

correct *VERB*

*Shall I **correct** my mistakes?*
to put right
to rectify

correctly *ADVERB*
*Make sure you spell the word **correctly**.*
right
in the right way
accurately
OPPOSITE **wrongly**

costume *NOUN*
*We had to wear special **costumes** for the play.*
clothes
a disguise
fancy dress
an outfit

cosy *ADJECTIVE*
*The room was small and **cosy**.*
comfortable
snug
warm

count *VERB*
*Can you **count** how many people there are altogether?*
to add up
to calculate
to work out
to tally up

country *NOUN*
1 *Australia is a big **country**.*
a land
a nation

2 *Do you live in the **country** or in a town?*
the countryside

courage *NOUN*
*We were all impressed with Ben's **courage**.*
bravery
heroism
valour

cover *VERB*
1 *Ben pulled his sleeve down to **cover** the scar on his arm.*
to hide
to conceal
to mask

2 *She **covered** him with a blanket as he slept.*
to wrap *She **wrapped** him in a blanket.*

crack *NOUN*
1 *Anna handed me an old cup with a **crack** in it.*
a break
a chip

2 *There was a **crack** in the wall.*
a hole
a gap
a split
a crevice

crack *VERB*
*Watch you don't **crack** the glass.*
to break
to chip

Use **smash** or **shatter** when something cracks and breaks into lots of pieces: *The mirror **smashed** into tiny pieces.*

crafty *ADJECTIVE*
*Foxes are **crafty** animals.*
clever
cunning
sly
sneaky
wily

crash *NOUN*
1 *The two cars had a **crash** on the road.*
an accident
a smash
a collision

A B Cc D E F G H I J K L M N O P Q R S T U V W X Y Z

A **pile-up** is a crash with a lot of cars: *There was a huge **pile-up** on the road.*

❷ *The tree fell down with a loud **crash**.*
a bang
a thud
a clatter
a bump
a thump

crash *VERB*
❶ *The car **crashed** into a wall.*
to smash into
to bang into
to hit *The car **hit** a wall.*

❷ *Two lorries **crashed** in the carpark.*
to collide
to have an accident

❸ *My computer has just **crashed**.*
to go down
to freeze

crawl *VERB*
*We **crawled** through the tunnel.*
to creep
to climb

To **slither** means to crawl along on your stomach, like a snake: *He **slithered** under the gate.*

To **wriggle** means to squeeze through a very small space: *I managed to **wriggle** through a gap in the hedge.*

creamy *ADJECTIVE*
*We had delicious, **creamy** ice cream.*
rich
thick
smooth
velvety

create *VERB*
*I **created** a model of a spaceship.*
to make
to build
to construct
to produce

Use **to invent** when you create something that nobody has thought of before: *I **invented** a new game.*

creation *NOUN*
*This costume is my own **creation**.*
a concept
an invention

creature *NOUN*
*He came face to face with a strange **creature**.*
an animal
a being

Use **a beast** for a wild or strange creature.

Use **a monster** for a scary and imaginary creature.

creep *VERB* creeps, creeping, crept
❶ *We **crept** out through the window and climbed down the tree.*
to crawl
to climb

Use **slither** when you creep along on your stomach, like a snake: *Sam **slithered** under the side of the tent.*

Use **wriggle** when you squeeze through a very small space: *Emma managed to **wriggle** through the gap in the fence.*

❷ *He **crept** away when no one was looking.*
to sneak
to slip
to steal

To **tiptoe** means to creep quietly on your toes: *I **tiptoed** past the sleeping guards.*

creepy *ADJECTIVE*
*I think it's very **creepy** in the cellar.*
frightening
scary
sinister

Use **eerie** or **spooky** when you think there might be ghosts: *It was a **spooky** old mansion.*

crept *VERB (past tense and past participle of creep)*

cried *VERB (past tense and past participle of cry)*

cries *VERB (see cry)*

criminal *NOUN*
*These **criminals** must be caught before they commit any more crimes.*
a crook
a villain
a wrongdoer
an offender

crisp *ADJECTIVE*
*She bit into the **crisp** toast.*
crunchy
hard
OPPOSITE **soft**

crooked *ADJECTIVE*
1 *We sat down by an old, **crooked** tree.*
bent
twisted
misshapen
warped

2 *They climbed up the **crooked** path.*
winding
twisting
bendy
OPPOSITE **straight**

cross *ADJECTIVE*
*My mum was really **cross** with me.*
angry
annoyed

Use **irritated** when someone is slightly cross: *My sister wouldn't shut up, and I was beginning to get a bit **irritated** with her.*

Use **furious**, **livid** or **enraged** when someone is very cross: *My brother was absolutely **furious** when I broke his phone.*
OPPOSITE **pleased**

crouch *VERB*
*She **crouched** down to pick up a shell.*
to bend
to stoop
to squat

crowd *NOUN*
*A **crowd** of people was waiting outside the theatre.*
a group
a mass
a horde

Use **mob** and **rabble** to talk about a noisy or violent crowd: *There was a **rabble** of boys outside the museum.*

crowded *ADJECTIVE*
*The airport was very **crowded** on the first day of the holidays.*
busy
full
packed
swarming with people
teeming with people
OPPOSITE **empty**

cruel *ADJECTIVE*
1 *The king was a **cruel** man and his subjects were terrified of him.*
wicked
heartless
cold-hearted
brutal

2 *Some people think bullfighting is a **cruel** sport.*
barbaric
inhumane
OPPOSITE **kind**

crunch *VERB*
*He **crunched** his apple noisily.*
to chew
to munch
to chomp

a b Cc d e f g h i j k l m n o p q r s t u v w x y z

crush *VERB*
*Mind you don't **crush** the flowers.*
to squash
to flatten
to damage
to break

Use **crumple** or **screw up** for paper or cloth: *He **screwed up** the letter and threw it in the bin.*

cry *VERB* **cries, crying, cried**
1 *Some of the children were **crying**.*

Use **weep** if someone is crying quietly: *A young girl was **weeping** in the garden.*

Use **wail**, **howl** or **sob** if someone is crying noisily, or speaking as they are crying: *'What shall I do now?' she **wailed**.*

Use **whimper** if someone is crying with a low trembling sound: *He was **whimpering** with fear.*

Use **snivel** or **blubber** if someone is crying in a noisy way that you find annoying: *'Crying won't do any good, so stop **snivelling**!' he said.*

2 *'Look out!' she **cried**.*
to shout
to yell
to call

Use **scream** or **shriek** when someone shouts something in a loud high voice because they are frightened or annoyed: *'Help!' they all **screamed** in fright.*

Use **exclaim** when someone is surprised or excited: *'How wonderful!' she **exclaimed**.*

cunning *ADJECTIVE*
*He thought of a **cunning** plan to escape.*
clever
crafty
ingenious
sneaky

cup *NOUN*

WORD WEB

Some types of **cup**:
a beaker
a glass
a goblet
a mug
a teacup
a tumbler

curiosity *NOUN*
*They were full of **curiosity** about what was in the package.*
inquisitiveness
interest

Use **nosiness** when someone is curious about other people's business: *I'm fed up with his **nosiness** and all his questions.*

curious *ADJECTIVE*
1 *We were all very **curious** about the new teacher.*
inquisitive

Use **nosy** when someone is curious about other people's business: *Don't be so **nosy**! It's a secret!*

❷ *There was a **curious** smell in the kitchen and I couldn't work out what it was.*
strange
funny
odd
peculiar

curl *VERB*
*The cat's tail **curled** around my leg.*
to wind
to twist
to coil
to curve

curly *ADJECTIVE*
*She has **curly** brown hair.*

Use **wavy** for hair that is slightly curly.

Use **frizzy** for hair that has small tight curls.

Use **tousled** for hair that has untidy curls.
OPPOSITE **straight**

curve *NOUN*
❶ *There was a **curve** in the road ahead of us.*
a bend
a turn

❷ *We can make a pattern using straight lines and **curves**.*
a loop
a curl
a swirl
an arc

cut *NOUN*
*She had a **cut** on her arm.*
a wound
a graze

A **nick** is a small cut: *Sasha had a little **nick** on her finger.*

A **gash** is a big cut: *Blood was pouring from the **gash** on his leg.*

cut *VERB* cuts, cutting, cut
❶ *I fell over and **cut** my knee.*

Use **graze** or **scratch** when you cut yourself not very badly: *I'm OK. I've just **grazed** my knee a bit.*

Use **wound** or **gash** when you cut yourself badly: *He **gashed** his leg and had to have stitches.*

❷ ***Cut** the meat into small pieces.*
to chop
to chop up

Use **slice** when you cut something into thin pieces: *She **sliced** the bread and put it on a plate.*

Use **dice** when you cut something into small square pieces: ***Dice** the carrot.*

Use **mince** when you cut something into tiny pieces: *For this recipe you need **minced** beef.*

❸ *The hairdresser **cut** my hair.*
to trim
to snip

❹ *My uncle **cut** some wood.*
to chop
to saw

Use **carve** when you cut wood into a special shape: *He **carved** a statue from the block of wood.*

❺ *We need to **cut** the lawn.*
to mow

❻ *Mum **cut** the hedge.*
to prune
to trim
to clip

cute *ADJECTIVE*
*The kittens were so **cute**!*
sweet
adorable
lovable

A B C **Dd** E F G H I J K L M N O P Q R S T U V W X Y Z

Dd

damage *VERB*

1 *Please don't bend the books in case you* ***damage*** *them.*
to spoil

Use **ruin** when you damage something badly: *I dropped my mobile in the bath and* ***ruined*** *it.*

2 *She dropped the box and* ***damaged*** *some of the plates.*
to break

Use **chip** when you break a little bit off something: *I* ***chipped*** *the paint on my new bike.*

Use **scratch** when you leave a mark on something: *You'll* ***scratch*** *the dining room table if you dump your school bag on it.*

Use **smash** when you break something into pieces: *I dropped the vase and* ***smashed*** *it.*

3 *The explosion* ***damaged*** *several buildings.*
to destroy

4 *The crash* ***damaged*** *our car quite badly.*
to dent
to wreck

5 *Someone has deliberately* ***damaged*** *the new fence.*
to vandalise

dance *VERB*

1 *Everyone was* ***dancing*** *to the music.*
to jig about
to leap about

2 *The younger children were all* ***dancing*** *about with excitement.*
to skip about
to jump about
to leap about
to prance about

dance *NOUN*

He did a little ***dance****.*
a jig

WORD WEB

Some types of **dance**:

ballet
ballroom dancing
breakdancing
country dancing
disco dancing
folk dancing
Irish dancing
line dancing
rock and roll
salsa
Scottish country dancing
the tango
tap dancing
the waltz

breakdancing

ballet

danger *NOUN*

1 *The animals could sense* ***danger****.*

trouble

2 *There is a* ***danger*** *that you might fall.*

a risk
a chance
a possibility

dangerous *ADJECTIVE*

1 *It's* ***dangerous*** *to play with matches.*

risky
unsafe

OPPOSITE **safe**

2 *A knife is a* ***dangerous*** *weapon.*

lethal
deadly

3 *These are* ***dangerous*** *chemicals.*

harmful
poisonous
toxic
hazardous

4 *The police were searching for a* ***dangerous*** *criminal.*

violent

Use **threatening** or **menacing** if someone seems to want to harm you: *He came towards us in a* ***threatening*** *way.*

dare *VERB*

1 *Come and catch me, if you* ***dare****!*

to be brave enough
to have the courage
to have the nerve

2 *I* ***dare*** *you to climb that tree.*

to challenge

daring *ADJECTIVE*

Which of you is the most ***daring****?*

brave
bold
courageous
fearless
adventurous

OPPOSITE **timid**

dark *ADJECTIVE*

1 *It was very* ***dark*** *outside last night.*

black

Use **pitch-black** if it is completely dark: *It was* ***pitch-black*** *in the tunnel.*

OPPOSITE **light**

2 *No one was in; the house was* ***dark****.*

Use **gloomy**, **murky** or **dingy** if a place is dark and unpleasant: *The cellar was damp and* ***gloomy*** *and slightly spooky.*

Use **dim** if a place is rather dark: *It was too* ***dim*** *to read.*

Use **unlit** if there are no lights in a room: *We walked along a long* ***unlit*** *corridor.*

OPPOSITE **bright**

3 *They walked through the* ***dark*** *woods.*

Use **shady** if a place is nice and cool: *We found a lovely* ***shady*** *spot under some trees for our picnic.*

Use **shadowy** if there are lots of big shadows: *I couldn't see into the* ***shadowy*** *corners.*

OPPOSITE **bright**

4 *Sarah has* ***dark*** *hair.*

black
brown

Use **ebony** or **jet-black** if someone's hair is very dark: *She had beautiful* ***jet-black*** *hair.*

OPPOSITE **light**

darkness *NOUN*

We couldn't see anything in the ***darkness****.*

blackness
gloom

OPPOSITE **light**

dash *VERB*

She ***dashed*** *out of the room.*

to run
to rush
to sprint
to fly
to dart
to hurry

dawdle VERB
They were late for the party because they had ***dawdled*** *along the road.*
to stroll
to amble
to wander

day NOUN
Some animals sleep during the ***day****.*
daytime

Daylight is the time during the day when it is light: *When he woke up it was* ***daylight****.*
OPPOSITE **night**

dazzle VERB
The bright car lights ***dazzled*** *me.*
daze
blind

dead ADJECTIVE
1 *My grandmother is* ***dead*** *now.*
deceased
passed away *My grandmother has* ***passed away****.*

2 *We found the* ***dead*** *body of a mouse.*
lifeless

deadly ADJECTIVE
Don't touch that bottle, it is poison and is ***deadly****.*
lethal
fatal
OPPOSITE **harmless**

dear ADJECTIVE
He was delighted to see his ***dear*** *daughter again.*
beloved
darling

decide VERB
1 *He* ***decided*** *to leave.*
to make up your mind *He* ***made up his mind*** *to tell his parents everything.*
to resolve *He* ***resolved*** *to tell his parents everything.*

2 *I can't* ***decide*** *which cake to have.*
to choose

declare VERB
The teacher ***declared*** *that our team had won.*
to announce
to state

decorate VERB
They ***decorated*** *the Christmas tree with tinsel.*
to adorn
to beautify

decoration NOUN
We put some ***decorations*** *on the cake.*
a trimming
an adornment
An **ornament** is an object used as a decoration: *My aunt has lots of* ***ornaments*** *on her shelves.*

deep ADJECTIVE
The treasure was hidden in a ***deep*** *hole.*
bottomless
OPPOSITE **shallow**

defeat VERB
1 *They finally* ***defeated*** *their enemies.*
to beat
to overcome
to conquer

2 *We* ***defeated*** *the other team in the final.*
to beat

Use **thrash** if you defeat someone easily: *We* ***thrashed*** *the other team 9–0.*

defend VERB
The soldiers stayed behind to ***defend*** *the city.*
to protect
to guard

definite ADJECTIVE
1 *The party will probably be next Saturday, but it's not* ***definite*** *yet.*
certain
fixed
settled

❷ *I can see a **definite** improvement in your work.*
clear
obvious
positive

delay VERB

❶ *The bad weather **delayed** us.*
to hold someone up *The bad weather **held** us **up**.*
to make someone late *The bad weather **made** us **late**.*

❷ *We had to **delay** the start of the race.*
to postpone
to put off
to put back

deliberate ADJECTIVE

*He said it was a **deliberate** mistake to see if anyone noticed.*
intentional
conscious
planned
OPPOSITE **accidental**

deliberately ADVERB

*Alex **deliberately** left the gate open.*
on purpose
intentionally
knowingly
consciously
OPPOSITE **accidentally**

delicious ADJECTIVE

*This food is **delicious**!*
lovely

Use **tasty**, **scrumptious**, **gorgeous** or **succulent** if food tastes delicious: *Mmm, this cake is **gorgeous**!*

Use **mouthwatering** if food looks delicious: *The table was covered with **mouthwatering** food.*
OPPOSITE **horrible**

delighted ADJECTIVE

*I was **delighted** with my present.*
pleased
thrilled
overjoyed
ecstatic

delightful ADJECTIVE

*It was a **delightful** surprise.*
wonderful
lovely
charming

deliver VERB

*We will **deliver** the new computer to your house tomorrow.*
to bring
to take
to transport

demand VERB

*She **demanded** an explanation for his behaviour.*
to insist on
to ask for
to request

demolish VERB

*They are going to **demolish** the old school building.*
to knock down
to pull down
to bulldoze
to flatten

demonstrate VERB

*Lucy **demonstrated** how her model worked.*
to show
to illustrate
to display

department NOUN
*The shop has a big toy **department** on the second floor.*
a section
a division

depend VERB
➤ **depend on**
*The young chicks **depend on** their mother for food.*
to need
to rely on

describe VERB
❶ *She **described** the animal she had seen in the park.*
to give a description of *She **gave a description of** the animal.*

❷ *Ria **described** the amazing things she'd seen on the school trip.*
to explain
to relate
to recount

design VERB
*They have **designed** a new type of engine.*
to create
to make
to invent
to devise
to plan

designer NOUN
*He wants to be a clothes **designer**.*
a creator
an inventor
a maker

despair NOUN
*I was full of **despair** when I saw how badly damaged my bike was.*
desperation
gloom
misery
hopelessness
OPPOSITE **hope**

desperate ADJECTIVE
❶ *They were in a **desperate** situation.*
hopeless
dreadful
serious
dire

❷ *I was **desperate** to go home.*
longing
anxious
frantic

despite ADVERB
*We played football **despite** the rain.*
in spite of
regardless of *We played football **regardless of** the rain.*

destroy VERB
❶ *The hurricane **destroyed** several buildings.*
to demolish
to flatten
to crush

❷ *The storm **destroyed** their small boat.*
to smash
to wreck

❸ *The fire **destroyed** many old books.*
to ruin

destruction NOUN
*The storm caused a lot of **destruction**.*
devastation
damage
OPPOSITE **creation**

determination *NOUN*
*If you have enough **determination** you will succeed.*
resolve
commitment
dedication
will-power

determined *ADJECTIVE*
1 *We are **determined** to win the race.*
resolved

2 *You have to be very **determined** if you want to succeed.*
single-minded
strong-willed

device *NOUN*
1 *They use a special **device** for opening the bottles.*
a gadget
a tool
an implement

2 *You can download the app onto your **device**.*

Some electronic **devices**:

a mobile phone or a mobile
a tablet
a laptop

diagram *NOUN*
*We drew a **diagram** of the machine.*
a plan
a drawing
a sketch

diary *NOUN*
*I am keeping a **diary** of what we do on our holiday.*
a journal
a daily record
A blog is a diary you write on the Internet: *I wrote about the holiday on my **blog**.*
A vlog is a video diary on the Internet .

did *VERB (past tense of* do*)*

die *VERB* dies, dying, died
1 *My grandfather **died** last year.*
to pass away

2 *They were very glad that no one had **died** in the fire.*
to perish
to be killed *No one was **killed** in the fire.*

3 *The plants **died** because I forgot to water them.*
to shrivel
to wither

different *ADJECTIVE*
1 *Your book is **different** from mine.*
dissimilar
unlike
OPPOSITE **similar**

2 *I have ten pencils in **different** colours.*
assorted
various

3 *Each one of the puppies is slightly **different**.*
special
distinctive
individual
unique

4 *We always go shopping on Saturday. Let's do something **different** for a change!*
new
exciting
unusual
extraordinary

5 *Our new neighbours are certainly **different**!*
strange
peculiar
odd
unusual
bizarre

difficult *ADJECTIVE*
*The teacher gave us some very **difficult** work to do.*
hard
tough
tricky
complicated
OPPOSITE **easy**

dig *VERB* digs, digging, dug
1 *We **dug** a hole in the garden.*
to make
to excavate

2 *We'll have to **dig** our way out of here!*
to tunnel
to burrow

3 *They **dig** stone out of the ground here.*

You **quarry** stone and **mine** coal: *Coal has been **mined** here for 200 years.*

dip *VERB*
*She **dipped** her hand into the water.*
to lower
to drop
to plunge
to immerse

direction *NOUN*
*Will you show us the right **direction**?*
way
route

Use **course** for the direction in which a ship or plane travels: *The ship took a **course** to the west.*

dirt *NOUN*
*Their clothes were covered in **dirt**.*
mud
muck
dust
grime
filth

dirty *ADJECTIVE*
1 *Why are your clothes so **dirty**?*

Use **mucky** or **grubby** if something is slightly dirty: *His sweatshirt was old and slightly **grubby**.*

Use **muddy** if something is covered in mud: *Take your **muddy** boots off!*

Use **greasy** if something is covered in oil or grease: *He handed me a horrible **greasy** spoon.*

Use **filthy** or **grimy** if something is very dirty: *Go and wash your hands.They're **filthy**!*

Use **stained** if something has dirty marks on it: *His shirt was **stained** with ink.*

2 *The room was very **dirty**.*
dusty
messy
filthy

3 *The water in some rivers is too **dirty** to drink.*
polluted
foul
OPPOSITE **clean**

disagree *VERB*
*Lucy and Adam **disagree** about everything.*
to argue
to quarrel
to have different opinions
OPPOSITE **agree**

disappear *VERB*
*The cat **disappeared** into the bushes.*
to vanish
OPPOSITE **appear**

disappointed *ADJECTIVE*
*I was very **disappointed** when the trip was cancelled.*
upset
sad
dejected
downcast

disaster *NOUN*
*The warehouse fire was a terrible **disaster**.*
a tragedy
a catastrophe
a calamity

discover *VERB*
*We **discovered** an old map in the attic.*
to find
to come across
to uncover
to unearth

discovery *NOUN*
*The law of gravity was an important **discovery**.*
a find
a breakthrough

An **invention** is a new machine or device nobody has thought of before: *The car engine was an important **invention**.*

discussion *NOUN*
*We had a **discussion** about which vegetables to plant in the garden.*
a talk
a conversation
a debate

disease *NOUN*
*The scientists found a cure for the **disease**.*
an illness
a complaint
a sickness
an infection

disguise *VERB*
1 *I tried to **disguise** the dirty mark on the carpet.*
to conceal
to cover up
to hide
to camouflage

2 *He was **disguised** as a guard.*
to dress up *He was **dressed up** as a guard.*

disgusting *ADJECTIVE*
*This food is **disgusting** and I can't eat it!*
horrible
revolting
foul
OPPOSITE **lovely**

dish *NOUN*
*She put the vegetables in a deep **dish**.*
a bowl
a plate
a platter

display *NOUN*
*We made a **display** of our paintings.*
an exhibition
a presentation

display *VERB*
*We will **display** the best pictures in the hall.*
to show
to hang up
to exhibit

distance *NOUN*
*We measured the **distance** between the two posts.*
the space
the gap
the length
the width

A B C **Dd** E F G H I J K L M N O P Q R S T U V W X Y Z

distant *ADJECTIVE*

They travelled to many ***distant*** *lands.*

faraway
far off
remote

distract *VERB*

I'm trying to concentrate and you're ***distracting*** *me.*

to disturb
to interrupt
to bother
to put off *You're* ***putting*** *me* ***off****.*

disturb *VERB*

1 *I'm working, so please don't* ***disturb*** *me.*

to interrupt
to bother

To **pester** or **hassle** someone means to keep disturbing them: *My little brother has been* ***pestering*** *me all morning!*

2 *Seeing the house so dark* ***disturbed*** *me.*

to worry
to trouble
to alarm
to upset
to distress

dive *VERB*

He ***dived*** *into the water.*

to plunge
to leap
to jump

divide *VERB*

1 *We can* ***divide*** *the grapes between us.*

to share
to split

2 *She* ***divided*** *the lasagne into ten pieces.*

to cut
to split
to separate

dizzy *ADJECTIVE*

I felt weak and ***dizzy****.*

giddy
faint
light-headed
unsteady

do *VERB* does, doing, did, done

OVERUSED WORD

Try to use a more interesting word when you want to say **do**. Here are some other words you can use instead:

1 *I usually try to* ***do*** *my work quickly.*

to get on with
to finish
to complete

2 *We're going to* ***do*** *an experiment.*

to carry out
to conduct

3 *I can't* ***do*** *this sum.*

to work out
to calculate
to solve
to answer

4 *What are you* ***doing*** *just now?*

to be up to *What are you up to?*

5 *They are in danger—we must* ***do*** *something!*

to take action
to act

6 *You have* ***done*** *very well.*

to get on
to perform

doctor *NOUN*

WORD WEB

Some types of **doctor**:

A general practitioner or **GP** is a doctor who looks after families and treats all kinds of illness.
A consultant is a doctor in a hospital.
A surgeon is a doctor who performs operations.
A specialist is a doctor who knows a lot about one type of illness.
A paediatrician is a specialist who looks after children.

dog *NOUN*

a hound
A bitch is a female dog.
A puppy is a young dog.

WORD WEB

Some types of **dog**:

a beagle
a boxer
a bulldog
a chihuahua
a collie
a dachshund
a Dalmatian
a German Shepherd
a Great Dane
a greyhound
a Labrador
A mongrel is a mixture of different breeds.
a poodle
a retriever
a sheepdog
a spaniel
a terrier

WRITING TIPS

Here are some useful words for writing about **dogs**:

- *The dogs **barked** and **yapped** excitedly when they heard us coming.*
- *Our dog always **whines** by the kitchen door when she wants to go out.*
- *The little dog **yelped** when I accidentally trod on his tail.*
- *The guard dog **growled** and **snarled** at us.*
- *The dog was **panting** in the heat.*

Pongo stood on his hind legs and kissed the wet dog on the nose.—ONE HUNDRED AND ONE DALMATIONS, Dodie Smith

done *VERB* *(past participle of* do*)*

doomed *ADJECTIVE*

*Their mission was **doomed**.*
cursed
jinxed
ill-fated

doubt *NOUN*

*There is **doubt** about his fitness for the match.*
concern
worry
anxiety
uncertainty

doubt *VERB*

*I **doubt** that I'll get to the concert on time.*
to question
to wonder
to be uncertain about

drag *VERB*

*We **dragged** the box out into the hall.*
to pull
to haul
to tug
to draw
to tow

draw VERB **draws, drawing, drew, drawn**

1 *Are you good at **drawing** pictures?*

to sketch
to paint
to trace
to doodle

2 *She **drew** the curtains.*

to close
to open
to pull back

3 *The two teams **drew** in the last game.*

to finish equal
to tie

dreadful ADJECTIVE

1 *The whole house was in a **dreadful** mess.*

terrible
awful
horrible
ghastly
appalling

2 *The situation was really **dreadful**.*

awful
dire
frightening
desperate
serious

dream NOUN

1 *Do you ever remember your **dreams**?*

A bad dream is a horrible dream.
A nightmare is a frightening dream.

2 *Alice's **dream** is to be a vet.*

an ambition
a wish
a goal

A **fantasy** is a dream you have which is unlikely to come true: *Ben has this **fantasy** about being a pop star.*

A **daydream** is something you think about that is not real or true at the moment: *I had a **daydream** about playing in the park.*

dress NOUN

*She was wearing a red **dress**.*

a frock
a gown

dress VERB

1 *Hurry up and get **dressed** or we will be late for school.*

to put clothes on

2 *He was **dressed** in a black suit.*

to be attired in *He was **attired in** a black suit.*
to be wearing *He was **wearing** a black suit.*
to have on *He **had** a black suit **on**.*

drew VERB *(past tense of* draw*)*

drink VERB **drinks, drinking, drank, drunk**

1 *He picked up the glass of milk and **drank** it.*

Use **swallow** when someone drinks something quickly without tasting it: *She took a deep breath and **swallowed** the disgusting medicine.*

Use **sip** when someone drinks slowly: *She **sipped** her apple juice through a straw.*

Use **gulp** or **swig** when someone drinks very quickly: *He was so thirsty that he **gulped** down a whole bottle of water.*

Use **guzzle** or **slurp** when someone drinks quickly and noisily: *She **slurped** the hot tea.*

2 *The dog **drank** its water.*

to lap up

drip VERB
*After the rain, water was **dripping** from the trees above us.*
to drop
to splash
to trickle
to dribble

drive VERB **drives, driving, drove, driven**
1 *She got into her car and **drove** away.*

Use **speed** or **zoom** when someone drives quickly: *They **zoomed** along the road.*

Use **crawl** when someone drives slowly: *We **crawled** along behind the tractor.*

2 *She **drove** the car carefully into the parking space.*
to steer
to guide
to manoeuvre
to control

drop NOUN
*I felt a few **drops** of rain on my face.*
a drip
a spot
a droplet

drop VERB
*He accidentally **dropped** his glass.*
to let go of

dry ADJECTIVE
1 *The ground was very **dry**.*
hard
parched
arid

Use **barren** for dry ground where nothing grows.
OPPOSITE **wet**

2 *They lived on **dry** bread and water.*
hard
stale

duck NOUN
A drake is a male duck.
A duckling is a young duck.

dug VERB *(past tense and past participle of* dig*)*

dull ADJECTIVE
1 *This television show is very **dull**.*
boring
tedious
uninteresting
OPPOSITE **interesting**

2 *She was wearing a **dull** green jumper.*
drab
dark
dreary
dowdy
OPPOSITE **bright**

3 *It was a rather **dull** day.*
grey
cloudy
overcast
dismal
miserable
OPPOSITE **bright**

dump VERB
1 *Someone **dumped** rubbish by the road.*
to leave
to abandon
to throw away
to discard

2 *She **dumped** her bags on the kitchen floor.*
to drop
to throw
to fling

dusty ADJECTIVE
*The room was very **dusty**.*
dirty
mucky
filthy
OPPOSITE **clean**

duty NOUN
*It is your **duty** to look after the younger children.*
a responsibility
a job

dying VERB (see die)

eager *ADJECTIVE*
*We were **eager** to go out and play.*
keen
impatient
anxious
enthusiastic
longing
OPPOSITE **reluctant**

early *ADJECTIVE*
*I was **early** for school today.*
ahead of time
in plenty of time

Use **punctual** or **on time** when someone or something arrives at exactly the right time: *I'm always **punctual** for school.*
OPPOSITE **late**

earn *VERB*
*You can **earn** money by delivering newspapers.*
to make
to get

earth *NOUN*
1 *This is the largest lake on **earth**.*
the world
the globe
the planet

2 *Bulbs will start to grow when you plant them in the **earth**.*
the soil
the ground

easy *ADJECTIVE*
*These sums were **easy** and we did them quickly.*
simple
straightforward
obvious
OPPOSITE **difficult**

eat *VERB* eats, eating, ate, eaten

OVERUSED WORD

Try to use a more interesting word when you want to say **eat**. Here are some other words you can use instead:

Use **guzzle**, **polish off** and **scoff** when someone eats something quickly: *We soon **polished off** the rest of the sandwiches.*

Use **wolf down**, **bolt**, **gobble** and **devour** when someone eats something very quickly and greedily: *The hungry children **wolfed down** the pizza.*

Use **munch**, **crunch** and **chomp** when someone eats noisily: *Anita **munched** noisily on an apple.*

Use **chew** and **suck** when someone eats something without biting it: *She was **sucking** a large ice lolly.*

Use **nibble** when someone eats something by taking small bites: *She was **nibbling** on a piece of cheese.*

Use **gnaw** when someone takes bites of something hard: *The dog was **gnawing** a bone.*

Use **peck** when a bird eats something with its beak: *Chickens **pecked** the ground.*

edge *NOUN*

❶ *I bumped my leg on the **edge** of the table.*
the side

❷ *There was a pattern around the **edge** of the plate.*
the outside
the border

❸ *The **edge** of the cup was cracked.*
the rim
the brim

❹ *We walked right to the **edge** of the field.*
the boundary
the margin

❺ *Keep close to the **edge** of the road when you are walking.*
the side
the verge
the kerb

❻ *We live on the **edge** of the town.*
the outskirts
the suburbs

effect *NOUN*

*What will be the **effect** of the hot sun on these plants?*
the result
the impact
the consequence

effort *NOUN*

❶ *You should put more **effort** into your spellings.*
work
energy

❷ *I made an **effort** to be cheerful.*
an attempt

elect *VERB*

*We **elect** a new school captain each year.*
to choose
to pick
to vote for
to appoint

embarrassed *ADJECTIVE*

*I felt really **embarrassed** about my mistake.*
uncomfortable
awkward
ashamed
shy
self-conscious

empty *ADJECTIVE*

❶ *There was an **empty** bottle on the table.*
unfilled

Use **blank** or **clear** for a page or screen: *Start again with a **blank** piece of paper.*

OPPOSITE **full**

❷ *They've moved away, so their house is **empty**.*

Use **unoccupied** or **vacant** if nobody is living in a house: *The house will be **vacant** next month, so we'll be able to move in.*

Use **bare** or **unfurnished** if there is nothing inside a room or house: *There was no furniture and the room was completely **bare**.*

OPPOSITE **occupied**

❸ *It was raining, so the town centre was **empty**.*
deserted
abandoned

OPPOSITE **crowded**

enchant *VERB*

*A witch had **enchanted** the forest.*
to cast a spell on
to bewitch

encourage *VERB*

❶ *My parents **encouraged** me to learn French.*
to persuade
to urge
to support *My parents **supported** me learning French.*

❷ *We all cheered to **encourage** our team.*
to support
to cheer on
to inspire
to reassure

OPPOSITE **discourage**

end *NOUN*

❶ *We walked right to the **end** of the lane.*
the limit
the boundary

❷ *Please go to the **end** of the line.*
the back
the rear

❸ *He tied a balloon to the **end** of the stick.*
the tip
the top
the bottom

❹ *This book has a happy **end**.*
an ending
a finish
a conclusion

end *VERB*

*When will the concert **end**?*
to stop
to finish
to conclude

Use **cease** when something finally ends, after a long time: *The rain finally **ceased**.*

ending *NOUN*

*I liked the **ending** of the story.*
the conclusion
the end
the close
OPPOSITE **beginning**

enemy *NOUN*

*He fought bravely against his **enemy**.*
an opponent
a foe
a rival
OPPOSITE **friend**

energetic *ADJECTIVE*

*I'm feeling quite **energetic** this morning and I'm going to go for a run.*
active
lively
full of beans

energy *NOUN*

*The children seem to have a lot of **energy** today.*
strength
stamina

enjoy *VERB*

*I really **enjoyed** drinking my smoothie.*
to like
to love
to take pleasure from

enjoyable *ADJECTIVE*

*It was a very **enjoyable** trip.*
pleasant
pleasurable
delightful
OPPOSITE **unpleasant**

enter *VERB*

❶ *She **entered** the house through the back door.*
to go into
to come into
to walk into
to run into
OPPOSITE **leave**

❷ *Are you going to **enter** the competition?*
to go in for
to take part in
to join in

entertain *VERB*

*The clown **entertained** the children.*
to amuse
to delight
to make someone laugh
to please

enthusiastic *ADJECTIVE*

*He is very **enthusiastic** about joining the basketball team.*
keen *He is **keen** to join the basketball team.*
eager *He is **eager** to join the basketball team.*

entrance *NOUN*

1 *We couldn't find the **entrance** to the building.*
the way in
the door
the gate
OPPOSITE **exit**

2 *They stood by the **entrance** to the cave.*
the mouth
the opening

equal *ADJECTIVE*

*We all got an **equal** amount.*
the same *We all got **the same** amount.*
identical
equivalent

equipment *NOUN*

*We keep the games **equipment** in the shed.*
things
gear *(informal)*
tackle
apparatus

escape *VERB*

1 *The police arrived too late and the robbers had **escaped**.*
to get away
to run away
to make your escape
to bolt
to flee *The police arrived too late and the robbers had **fled**.*

To **break free** means to escape when you have been tied up or held: *Two policemen were holding him, but he managed to **break free**.*

To **give someone the slip** means to get away from someone who is following you: *I knew someone was following me, but I managed to **give them the slip**.*

2 *We went indoors to **escape** from the rain.*
to avoid
to get away from

even *ADJECTIVE*

1 *You need an **even** surface for road cycling.*
flat
smooth
level
OPPOSITE **uneven**

2 *Their scores were **even** at half time.*
equal
level
the same
OPPOSITE **different**

evening *NOUN*

*We should be there by **evening**.*
dusk
nightfall
sunset

event *NOUN*

1 *The party will be a big **event**.*
an occasion

2 *Some strange **events** have been happening lately.*
an incident

everyday *ADJECTIVE*

*We wore our **everyday** clothes.*
normal
ordinary
usual
regular

evil *ADJECTIVE*

*An **evil** king ruled over the land.*
wicked
cruel
vile
black-hearted
OPPOSITE **good**

exact *ADJECTIVE*

*Make sure you add the **exact** amount of water.*
right
correct
precise

exactly *ADVERB*
*The total was **exactly** £10.*
precisely
OPPOSITE **approximately**

examine *VERB*
*She **examined** the rock carefully.*
to inspect
to study
to scrutinise

example *NOUN*
*Can you show the other teachers an **example** of your work?*
a sample
a specimen

excellent *ADJECTIVE*
*This is an **excellent** piece of work.*
very good
wonderful
brilliant
first-class
superb
outstanding
OPPOSITE **bad**

exchange *VERB*
*I **exchanged** my old red bike for a new blue one.*
to change
to swap

excited *ADJECTIVE*
*She was very **excited** because it was her birthday.*
happy
thrilled
enthusiastic
OPPOSITE **calm**

excitement *NOUN*
*I like films with a lot of **excitement**.*
action
activity
drama
suspense
thrills

exciting *ADJECTIVE*
1 *We had a very **exciting** day at the zoo.*
thrilling
exhilarating

Use **action-packed** or **eventful** when a lot of different things happen: *We had an **action-packed** holiday.*

2 *I can't put this **exciting** book down.*
gripping

3 *It was a very **exciting** game to watch.*
fast-moving
tense
nail-biting
OPPOSITE **boring**

exclaim *VERB*
*'Wow!' he **exclaimed**.*
to cry
to declare
to call out
to burst out

excuse *VERB*
*Please **excuse** me for being late.*
to forgive
to pardon

exercise *NOUN*
*You should do more **exercise** to keep fit.*
sport
PE
games
running around

exhausted *ADJECTIVE*
*I was **exhausted** after my long run.*
tired
worn out
shattered

exist *VERB*
*Do fairies really **exist**?*
to be alive
to be real
to be found

expect VERB
*I **expect** it will rain later as there are dark clouds in the sky.*
to think
to believe
to suppose

expensive ADJECTIVE
*Those leggings are very **expensive** and I don't think I can afford them.*
dear
costly
OPPOSITE **cheap**

explain VERB
*Ellie **explained** how the machine worked.*
to describe
to show *She **showed** us how the machine worked.*

explode VERB
1 *The firework **exploded** with a shower of stars.*
to go off
to burst
to go bang

2 *Don't put the tin in the microwave as it will **explode**.*
to blow up

explore VERB
*Let's **explore** the cave.*
to look round
to search
to investigate

explorer NOUN
*The **explorers** landed on an island.*
an adventurer
a traveller
a voyager

explosion NOUN
*There was a big **explosion** when the bomb fell.*
a blast
a bang

Use an **eruption** for an explosion from a volcano.

extra ADJECTIVE
*I've brought some **extra** food in case we get hungry.*
more
additional

extraordinary ADJECTIVE
*Standing before us was an **extraordinary** creature.*
strange
bizarre
incredible
remarkable
unusual
amazing
OPPOSITE **ordinary**

extreme ADJECTIVE
*No plants can grow in the **extreme** heat of the desert.*
great
intense
severe

extremely ADJECTIVE
*She was **extremely** annoyed.*
intensely
greatly
severely

A B C D E Ff G H I J K L M N O P Q R S T U V W X Y Z

Ff

face *NOUN*
The little boy had a sad ***face****.*
an expression

fact *NOUN*
We read some interesting ***facts*** *about trees.*
information
data

fade *VERB*
1 *My dress has* ***faded*** *from dark to light blue.*
to become lighter
to bleach

2 *It was evening and the light was beginning to* ***fade****.*
to go
to dwindle
to grow dim

3 *The sound of the engine gradually* ***faded*** *as the car moved further away.*
to become faint
to disappear
to die away
to vanish

fail *VERB*
Our attempt to launch the boat ***failed****.*
to be unsuccessful
to meet with disaster
to be in vain

failure *NOUN*
The magician's trick was a complete ***failure****!*
a disaster
a flop
OPPOSITE **success**

faint *ADJECTIVE*
1 *I heard* ***faint*** *music from next door.*
quiet
weak
muffled
dim
OPPOSITE **loud**

2 *The writing was* ***faint*** *and hard to read.*
unclear
indistinct
faded
OPPOSITE **clear**

faint *VERB*
I ***fainted*** *because it was so hot.*
to pass out
to lose consciousness

fair *ADJECTIVE*
1 *Tom has* ***fair*** *hair.*
light
golden
blonde
pale
OPPOSITE **dark**

2 *It's not* ***fair*** *if she gets more sweets than me.*
right
reasonable
OPPOSITE **unfair**

3 *I don't think the referee was very* ***fair****.*
impartial
unbiased
honest
OPPOSITE **biased**

4 *We've got a* ***fair*** *chance of winning.*
reasonable
good
moderate

fair *NOUN*
Our school is having a summer ***fair****.*
a fete
a festival
a carnival
a gala

fairly ADJECTIVE
*I did **fairly** well in the test.*
quite
moderately
reasonably

fairy NOUN
*I wrote a story about a magic **fairy**.*
a sprite
a spirit
An elf or **an imp** is a mischievous fairy.
A nymph is a beautiful fairy that lives in trees or near water.

faithful ADJECTIVE
*Joshua was his **faithful** friend.*
loyal
devoted
true
reliable
OPPOSITE **unfaithful**

fall VERB **falls, falling, fell, fallen**
1 *Watch you don't **fall** over the step.*

Use **trip** or **stumble** when someone falls because their foot catches on something: *I **tripped** over one of the wires.*

Use **slip** when someone falls on a slippery surface: *I **slipped** on the ice.*

Use **tumble** when someone falls from a height: *He **tumbled** off the wall.*

Use **plunge** when someone falls into water: *She couldn't stop running and **plunged** head first into the pond.*

Use **lose your balance** when someone falls after they have been balancing: *I **lost my balance** and crashed my bike.*

2 *The book **fell** off the table.*
to drop
to tumble

Use **crash** when something makes a loud noise as it falls: *The pile of plates **crashed** to the floor.*

3 *Snow began to **fall**.*
to come down
to descend

4 *The number of children at the school has **fallen**.*
to drop
to go down
to decrease
OPPOSITE **to rise**

false ADJECTIVE
1 *He was wearing a **false** beard and glasses as a disguise.*
fake
artificial
pretend
OPPOSITE **real**

2 *I was given **false** information about the school trip.*
incorrect
misleading
untrue
wrong
OPPOSITE **correct**

family NOUN
*I really enjoy being with my **family** in the holidays.*
relatives
relations

famous ADJECTIVE
*Ben dreams that one day he might be a **famous** pop star.*
well-known
world-famous
celebrated
OPPOSITE **unknown**

fan NOUN
*Are you a hockey **fan**?*
a supporter
a follower
an admirer

a b c d e Ff g h i j k l m n o p q r s t u v w x y z

fancy *ADJECTIVE*
*She made a very **fancy** cake.*
elaborate
decorative
special
OPPOSITE **plain**

fantastic *ADJECTIVE*
*We had a **fantastic** time at the concert.*
wonderful
brilliant
great
fabulous
marvellous
sensational
OPPOSITE **terrible**

farm *NOUN*

WORD WEB

Some types of **farm**:

An arable farm is one that grows crops.
A dairy farm is one that keeps cows.
a fruit farm
A poultry farm is one with chickens, ducks or turkeys.
A ranch is a cattle farm in North America.
A smallholding is a small farm.

fashion *NOUN*
*These blue shoes are the latest **fashion**.*
a style
a trend
a craze
a look

fashionable *ADJECTIVE*
1 *He wears very **fashionable** clothes.*
trendy
stylish

2 *These coats are **fashionable** at the moment.*
popular
in fashion
all the rage *(informal)*
OPPOSITE **unfashionable**

fast *ADJECTIVE*
1 *He's a very **fast** runner.*
quick
speedy
swift

2 *He loves driving **fast** cars.*
powerful

3 *We'll go on the **fast** train.*
high-speed
express

4 *We were walking at quite a **fast** pace.*
brisk
quick
swift
rapid
OPPOSITE **slow**

fast *ADVERB*
*She was walking quite **fast**.*
quickly
rapidly
swiftly

fasten *VERB*
1 *Please remember to **fasten** your seat belt.*
to do up
to buckle

2 *I stopped to **fasten** my shoelaces.*
to tie up
to do up

3 ***Fasten** the badge to your sweatshirt.*
to attach
to fix
to secure

fat *ADJECTIVE*
*The ticket collector was a little **fat** man.*

Use **plump**, **tubby**, **chubby** or **podgy** for someone who is slightly fat in a nice way: *In the pushchair was a **chubby** smiling baby.*

Use **stout** or **portly** for an older person who is quite fat: *My uncle Bill likes his food and as a result he's rather **stout**.*

Use **overweight** or **obese** for someone who is fat in an unhealthy way: *If you don't do enough exercise, you can become **obese**.*
OPPOSITE **thin**

favour *NOUN*
*Please will you do me a **favour**?*
a good turn
a good deed
a kindness

favourite *ADJECTIVE*
*What is your **favourite** book?*
best-loved
number-one

fear *NOUN*
*He didn't want to sing in the concert and I could see **fear** in his eyes.*

Use **terror** for a very strong feeling of fear: *Emily screamed in **terror** as the ogre came towards her.*

Use **panic** for a sudden feeling of fear when you are so frightened that you don't know what to do: *A feeling of **panic** came over me as our little boat began to sink.*

Use **dread** or **horror** for a feeling of fear and disgust: *He watched in **horror** as the huge snake slid towards him.*

fearful *ADJECTIVE*
*The people were **fearful** when they saw the giant.*
afraid
anxious
frightened
full of fear

Use **terrified** or **petrified** if you are very fearful: *Lisa was **terrified** when she saw the lion was so close.*

feel *VERB* **feels, feeling, felt**
1 *She put out her hand and **felt** the puppy's fur.*
to touch
to stroke
to rub

2 *I **felt** that I was in the right.*
to believe
to think
to consider
to judge

feeling *NOUN*
1 *Try to think about other people's **feelings**.*
an emotion

2 *I had a **feeling** that somebody was following me.*
a sensation

felt *VERB* *(past tense and past participle of* feel*)*

festival *NOUN*
*Diwali is a Hindu religious **festival**.*
a celebration

fetch *VERB*
1 *Shall I **fetch** your bag from the cloakroom for you?*
to get
to bring

2 *I'll come and **fetch** from the house you at five o'clock.*
to collect
to pick up

fiction *NOUN*
*I like to read **fiction**.*
stories
tales
myths
legends
fantasies

field NOUN
*The ponies have their own **field** behind the house.*
a paddock
an enclosure
a meadow

fierce ADJECTIVE
*Tigers are very **fierce** animals.*
ferocious
savage
aggressive
dangerous

fiery ADJECTIVE
*We could feel the **fiery** heat of the sun.*
burning
blazing
flaming
raging
fierce

fight VERB fight, fighting, fought
1 *The men began to **fight**.*
to brawl
to wrestle
to grapple

2 *Why are you two children always **fighting**?*
to argue
to quarrel
to bicker
to squabble

fight NOUN
*The two boys had a **fight** after school.*

Use **brawl** or **punch-up** for a small fight without weapons: *The argument between the two boys ended up as a **punch-up**.*

Use **battle** or **clash** for a big fight between a lot of people: *Many **battles** were fought during the war.*

Use **duel** for a fight between two people, usually with pistols or swords: *He challenged his enemy to a **duel**.*

fighter NOUN
1 *The knight was a brave **fighter**.*
a warrior
a soldier

2 *The two **fighters** came into the ring.*
a boxer
a wrestler

fill VERB
1 *We **filled** the boxes with toys.*
to pack
to load
to stuff
to cram

2 *They **filled** the huge balloon with air.*
to inflate
OPPOSITE **empty**

film NOUN
*We watched a **film** on TV last night.*
a movie

WORD WEB

Some types of **film**:
an action film
an adventure film
a cartoon
a comedy
A documentary is a film that gives you information about something.
a horror film
a superhero film
a thriller
A western is a film about cowboys.

filthy ADJECTIVE
1 *The footballers were **filthy** by the end of the game.*
dirty
muddy
mucky

❷ *The room was **filthy** and hadn't been cleaned for months.*
dirty
dusty
messy

❸ *The water in this river is **filthy** and brown.*
polluted
OPPOSITE **clean**

finally *ADVERB*
*We **finally** arrived home at seven o'clock.*
eventually
at last

find *VERB* finds, finding, found
❶ *I can't **find** my homework in my bedroom although I'm sure I put it there.*
to locate
OPPOSITE **lose**

❷ *The children **found** an old map in the attic.*
to discover
to come across
to stumble upon
to notice
to spot

❸ *I lost my cat but **found** her in the neighbour's garden.*
to trace
to track down

❹ *When the archaeologists started digging, they **found** some very interesting things.*
to dig up
to uncover
to unearth
to discover

fine *ADJECTIVE*
❶ *You will need to use a very **fine** thread.*
thin
delicate
light
lightweight
OPPOSITE **thick**

❷ *I hope the weather is **fine** for sports day.*
sunny
dry
bright
clear
cloudless
OPPOSITE **dull**

❸ *I felt ill yesterday, but today I feel **fine**.*
okay
all right
well
OPPOSITE **ill**

❹ *The town hall is a very **fine** building.*
beautiful
magnificent
splendid

finish *VERB*
❶ *What time will the party **finish**?*
to end
to stop

❷ *Have you **finished** your homework?*
to complete
to do

❸ *Hurry up and **finish** your meal.*
to eat
to eat up

❹ *I haven't **finished** my drink.*
to drink
to drink up
OPPOSITE **start**

fire *NOUN*
❶ *We lit a match to start a **fire**.*
A bonfire is a fire outside.

❷ *The explosion caused a huge fire.*
a blaze
an inferno

fire *VERB*
*They were **firing** at a row of bottles on the wall.*
to shoot

firm *ADJECTIVE*
1 *The ladder didn't feel very **firm**.*
stable
secure
steady
solid
OPPOSITE **unsteady**

2 *We patted the sand down until it was **firm**.*
hard
solid
rigid
OPPOSITE **soft**

first *ADJECTIVE*
1 *We were the **first** to arrive at the party.*
earliest
soonest
fastest

2 *Who designed the **first** aeroplane?*
earliest
original

fit *ADJECTIVE*
1 *You have to be **fit** to run a marathon.*
strong
healthy
well
OPPOSITE **unfit**

2 *I don't think this food is **fit** to eat.*
suitable
good enough
OPPOSITE **unsuitable**

fit *VERB* **fits, fitting, fitted**
1 *These shoes **fit** me very well.*
to be the right size *These shoes are **the right size** for me.*

2 *This box won't **fit** in the back of the car.*
to go

fix *VERB*
1 *Mum **fixed** the shelves onto the wall.*
to attach
to tie
to stick
to nail
to fasten
to secure

2 *Our TV is broken and we can't **fix** it.*
to mend
to repair

flap *VERB*
*The loose sails were **flapping** in the wind.*
to flutter
to wave about

flash *VERB*
*We saw a light **flash** in the distance.*
to blink
to wink

Use **sparkle**, **twinkle** and **flicker** if a small light flashes many times: *The diamonds in her crown **sparkled**.*

Use **glint** and **glitter** when something made of metal or glass flashes: *The sword **glinted** in the sunlight.*

flat *ADJECTIVE*
*You need a nice **flat** surface to work on.*
level
even
smooth
horizontal
OPPOSITE **uneven**

flee *VERB* **flees, fleeing, fled**
*They tried to **flee** but the giant chased them.*
to run away
to bolt
to escape
to fly

flew *VERB (past tense of fly)*

flicker *VERB*
*The candle **flickered** in the wind.*
to glimmer
to waver
to flutter

float VERB

*A leaf **floated** down the river.*

to drift
to sail
to bob

flood NOUN

*A big **flood** almost covered the town.*

a deluge
a torrent

flow VERB

*Water was **flowing** along the pipe.*

Use **pour**, **stream**, **gush** and **spurt** when water flows very quickly: *The side of the pool split and water came **gushing** out.*

Use **flood** and **cascade** when a large amount of water flows quickly: *The waterfall **cascades** over the rocks.*

Use **drip** and trickle when water flows very slowly: *Water was **dripping** from the tap.*

Use **leak** when water flows through a small hole in something: *Water was **leaking** into the house through a hole in the roof.*

Use **gurgle**, **burble** and **babble** when water flows noisily over stones: *A little stream **babbled** under the bridge.*

flower NOUN

*We admired the **flowers** on the rose bush.*

a bloom
blossom

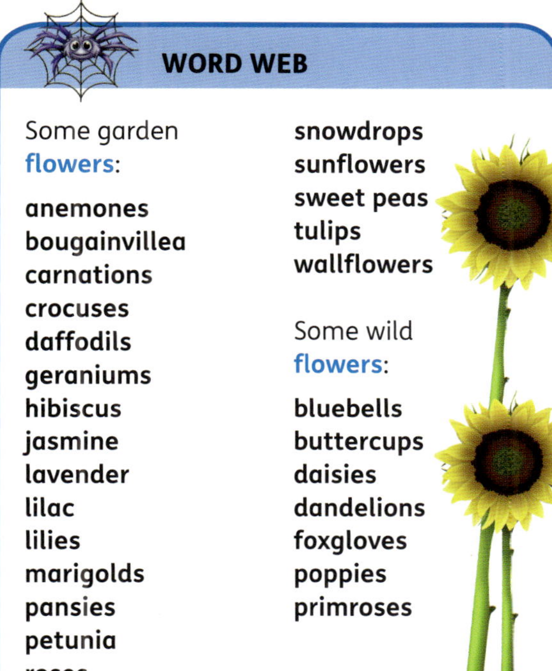

WORD WEB

Some garden **flowers**:

anemones
bougainvillea
carnations
crocuses
daffodils
geraniums
hibiscus
jasmine
lavender
lilac
lilies
marigolds
pansies
petunia
roses
snowdrops
sunflowers
sweet peas
tulips
wallflowers

Some wild **flowers**:

bluebells
buttercups
daisies
dandelions
foxgloves
poppies
primroses

sunflowers

flown VERB (past participle of fly)

fluffy ADJECTIVE

*She picked up the small, **fluffy** kitten.*

furry
soft
woolly

fly VERB flies, flying, flew, flown

*We watched the birds **flying** above us.*

Use **glide** when something moves quietly through the sky: *A balloon **glided** silently past.*

Use **soar** when a bird or plane flies high in the sky: *The eagle **soared** high above us.*

Use **hover** when something stays in the same place in the air: *A helicopter **hovered** over the field.*

A B C D E Ff G H I J K L M N O P Q R S T U V W X Y Z

Use **flutter**, **flit** and **dart** when something flies about quickly: *Bats were **flitting** about in the barn.*

Use **swoop** or **dive** when something flies down towards the ground: *The owl **swooped** down onto its prey.*

fold *VERB*

***Fold** the paper along the dotted line.*
to bend
to crease

follow *VERB*

❶ *Our friends **followed** us to the campsite.*

Use **chase**, **run after** and **pursue** when someone is trying to catch a person: *The police **pursued** the two robbers.*

Use **shadow** and **tail** when someone follows a person secretly: *We **tailed** the teacher as far as the library.*

Use **track** when someone follows the tracks that a person has left: *They brought in dogs to **track** the criminals.*

❷ ***Follow** this road until you come to a crossroads.*
to take
to go along
to continue along

❸ ***Follow** my instructions carefully.*
to pay attention to
to obey

food *NOUN*

❶ *We were all tired, thirsty and in need of **food**.*
something to eat
refreshments
nourishment
grub *(informal)*
a meal

❷ *We've got plenty of **food** for the animals.*
feed
fodder

foot *NOUN*

A **paw** is a dog's or cat's foot.
A **hoof** is a horse's foot.
A **trotter** is a pig's foot.

forbidden *ADJECTIVE*

*Running in the corridors is **forbidden**.*
banned
prohibited
not permitted
not allowed
OPPOSITE **allowed**

force *NOUN*

*We had to use **force** to open the door.*
strength
might
power
violence

force *VERB*

❶ *He **forced** me to give him money.*
to make *He **made** me give him the money.*
to order *He **ordered** me to give him the money.*

❷ *They **forced** the door open.*
to push
to break
to smash

forest *NOUN*

*There are lots of large trees in the **forest**.*
a wood

A **jungle** or **a rainforest** is a tropical forest.

forget *VERB* **forgets, forgetting, forgot, forgotten**

*I **forgot** my PE kit.*
to leave behind *I **left** my PE kit **behind**.*
to not bring *I **haven't brought** my PE kit.*
OPPOSITE **remember**

forgive *VERB* **forgives, forgiving, forgave, forgiven**

*I'm sorry. Please **forgive** my terrible behaviour.*
to excuse
to pardon

form NOUN

❶ *The bicycle is a **form** of transport.*

a type
a sort
a kind

❷ *The magician changes into any **form** he chooses.*

a shape

form VERB

*These rocks **formed** millions of years ago.*

to develop
to be made *These rocks **were made** millions of years ago.*

fought VERB *(past tense and past participle of* fight*)*

foul ADJECTIVE

*There was a **foul** smell in the kitchen.*

horrible
disgusting
nasty
revolting
repulsive

found VERB *(past tense and past participle of* find*)*

fragile ADJECTIVE

*Be careful, these glasses are **fragile**.*

delicate
flimsy
breakable
brittle
OPPOSITE **strong**

free ADJECTIVE

❶ *At last he was **free**!*

at liberty
out of prison

❷ *If you buy a book, you get a **free** pencil case.*

for nothing
complimentary

free VERB

*Ben was **freed** from detention at 4 o'clock.*

to release
to liberate
to set free

freedom NOUN

*At weekends we have more **freedom** to do what we want.*

liberty
independence

freezing ADJECTIVE

*It's **freezing** outside, so wear a hat.*

bitterly cold
frosty
icy
wintry
OPPOSITE **boiling**

fresh ADJECTIVE

❶ *Start each answer on a **fresh** page.*

clean
new
different

❷ *I love the taste of **fresh** strawberries.*

freshly picked

❸ *We had **fresh** bread for tea.*

warm
freshly baked

❹ *The **fresh** air at the seaside will do you good.*

clean
clear
pure
bracing

❺ *I felt lovely and **fresh** after my swim.*

lively
energetic
refreshed
invigorated

friend NOUN

A **mate** or **pal** are quite informal ways of saying a friend: *Who's your best **mate**?*

A **companion** is someone you travel with or do things with: *I wanted a travelling **companion**.*

A **partner** or **colleague** is someone you work with: *I always choose Sam as my **partner** in class.*

A B C D E Ff G H I J K L M N O P Q R S T U V W X Y Z

A **playmate** is a friend you play with: *The new boy next door will make a good **playmate** for you.*

An **ally** is someone who helps you in a fight: *He needed an **ally** against his enemies.*

friendly *ADJECTIVE*

1 *Olly is **friendly** and nice to everyone.*
kind
nice
pleasant
amiable
affectionate
welcoming

2 *Don't worry, our dog is very **friendly**.*
good-natured
gentle

3 *Tina and I are quite **friendly** now.*
pally *(informal)*
matey *(informal)*
close
OPPOSITE **unfriendly**

friendship *NOUN*

*Our **friendship** is very important to me.*
closeness
affection
attachment
fellowship

frighten *VERB*

*The noise downstairs **frightened** us.*
to scare
to alarm

Use **startle**, **shock** or **make someone jump** if something frightens you suddenly: *Sam **startled** me when he jumped out from behind a bush.*

Use **terrify** if something frightens you a lot: *That story used to **terrify** me when I was young.*

frightened *ADJECTIVE*

*Are you **frightened** of spiders?*
afraid
scared
alarmed

Use **startled** if you are frightened by something sudden: *I was **startled** when the door suddenly opened.*

Use **terrified** or **petrified** if you are very frightened: *James was **petrified** when he saw the lion.*

frightening *ADJECTIVE*

*The movie was quite **frightening** and I was too scared to sleep after watching it.*
scary
alarming

Use **terrifying** for something that is very frightening: *It was **terrifying** going on such a big roller coaster.*

front *NOUN*

*At last we got to the **front** of the queue.*
the beginning
the head
OPPOSITE **back**

fruit *NOUN*

WORD WEB

Some fruits:

an apple
an apricot
a banana
blackberries
cherries
a fig
gooseberries
a grapefruit
a guava
a kiwi fruit
a lemon
lychees
a mango
a melon
a nectarine
an orange
a papaya
a peach
a pear
a pineapple
a plum
raspberries
rhubarb
strawberries
a tangerine
a tomato
a watermelon

kiwi fruit

full ADJECTIVE

❶ *We poured water into the bucket until it was **full**.*
full to the brim
overflowing

❷ *The school hall was **full**.*
packed
full to capacity

❸ *The room was **full** of people.*
crowded
packed

❹ *The basket was **full** of good things to eat.*
packed with
crammed with
bursting with
bulging with
OPPOSITE **empty**

fun NOUN

*We had lots of **fun** on the beach.*
enjoyment
pleasure
amusement
entertainment

funny ADJECTIVE

❶ *He told us a very **funny** joke and we laughed for ages.*
amusing

Use **hilarious** for something that is very funny: *The comedian was absolutely **hilarious**.*

Use **witty** for something that is funny and clever: *Joe's very good at making **witty** remarks.*

OPPOSITE **serious**

❷ *We had to write a **funny** poem.*
humorous

❸ *You look really **funny** in that hat.*
comical
ridiculous

❹ *This sauce tastes **funny**.*
strange
peculiar
odd
curious

furious ADJECTIVE

*My dad was **furious** when he saw the mess.*
livid
fuming
enraged

furry ADJECTIVE

*The bear's **furry** coat looked soft.*
fluffy
woolly
soft
fuzzy

fussy ADJECTIVE

❶ *Some children are quite **fussy** about their food.*
choosy
picky
hard to please

❷ *My sister is very **fussy** about keeping her room neat and tidy.*
particular
fastidious

game *NOUN*
*The children were playing a **game** of hopscotch.*
a match
a tournament
a competition
a contest

gang *NOUN*
*Do you want to join our **gang**?*
a group
a crowd
a band

gap *NOUN*
*We climbed through a **gap** in the hedge.*
a hole
an opening
a space

gasp *VERB*
*Everybody was **gasping** after the race.*
to pant
to puff
to breathe heavily

gather *VERB*
1. *People **gathered** round to listen.*
to crowd round
to come together
to assemble
to flock

2. *We **gathered** blackberries from the fields.*
to pick
to collect

3. *I need to **gather** some information for my project.*
to collect
to find
to put together

gave *VERB (past tense of* give*)*

general *ADJECTIVE*
*Our **general** opinion is that school is fun.*
common
popular
widespread
accepted
usual

generous *ADJECTIVE*
*My grandma is very **generous**.*
kind
unselfish
big-hearted
OPPOSITE **selfish**

genius *NOUN*
*Tara is a **genius** at maths.*
a mastermind
a wizard
an expert

gentle *ADJECTIVE*
1. *Anna is very **gentle** with the baby.*
kind
quiet
good-tempered
sweet-tempered
loving
tender

2. *I gave her a **gentle** tap on the shoulder.*
light
soft
OPPOSITE **rough**

get VERB gets, getting, got

OVERUSED WORD

Here are some more interesting words you can use instead of **get**:

1. *I **got** a new bike for my birthday.*
to receive
to be given

2. *Where can I **get** some paper?*
to find
to obtain

3. *We're going to the shop to **get** some food.*
to buy
to purchase

4. *How much money do you **get** for doing the paper round?*
to earn
to receive

5. *I wonder who will **get** the first prize.*
to win

6. *Our team **got** fifteen points.*
to score

7. *I'll go and **get** the drinks.*
to fetch
to bring

8. *I **got** chickenpox last winter.*
to catch

9. *What time will we **get** home?*
to arrive
to reach
to come

10. *It's **getting** colder.*
to become
to grow
to turn

ghost NOUN
*Have you ever seen a **ghost**?*
a phantom
an apparition
a spirit
a spook
a spectre

giant ADJECTIVE
*They made a **giant** pizza that could feed the whole class.*
enormous
huge
massive
gigantic
immense
colossal
vast
OPPOSITE **tiny**

gift NOUN
1. *He gave me a birthday **gift**.*
a present

2. *The money was a **gift** for the school.*
a donation
a contribution

giggle VERB
*The children were all **giggling**.*
to snigger
to titter
to chuckle

girl NOUN
a lass
a kid *(informal)*
a child
a youngster
a teenager

A B C D E F Gg H I J K L M N O P Q R S T U V W X Y Z

give VERB gives, giving, gave, given

OVERUSED WORD

Try to use a more interesting word when you want to say **give**. Here are some other words you can use instead:

1 *Mia **gave** me a book.*
to hand
to pass

2 *I'm going to **give** Rebecca a bracelet for her birthday.*
to buy

3 *The school **gives** us pens and paper.*
to provide
to supply

4 *The judges **gave** the first prize to our team.*
to award
to present

5 *We **gave** our old toys to the children's hospital.*
to donate
to contribute

glad ADJECTIVE
*I'm **glad** you got here safely.*
pleased
relieved
happy
delighted

Use **delighted** if you are very glad about something: *We were **delighted** when we won the competition.*

gloomy ADJECTIVE
1 *The room was dark and **gloomy** with the curtains closed.*
dingy
dim
dismal
dreary
OPPOSITE **bright**

2 *I felt **gloomy** because my best friend was moving to a new school.*
unhappy
dejected
glum
down-hearted
miserable
downcast
OPPOSITE **cheerful**

glow VERB
*It was a dark night but a lamp **glowed** in the window.*
to gleam
to glimmer
to shine

Use **smoulder** and **burn** for something that is glowing because it is on fire: *The logs were still **smouldering** on the fire.*

glue NOUN
*Stick the pieces of paper together with **glue**.*
adhesive
gum
paste

go NOUN
*Would you like to have a **go** with my new computer game?*
a try
a turn
an attempt
a chance
an opportunity

go VERB goes, going, gone, went

OVERUSED WORD

Here are some more interesting words you can use instead of go:

1 *Let's **go** along this path.*
to walk

Use **run**, **rush**, **hurry** or **race** when you go very quickly: *I **rushed** home.*

Use **march** or **stride** when you take big steps: *Mr Hill **strode** angrily towards the house.*

Use **saunter** or **stroll** when you go slowly, in a relaxed way: *We **strolled** through the park.*

Use **creep**, **sneak** or **tiptoe** when you go quietly or secretly: *I **sneaked** out of the class.*

2 *We're **going** at six o'clock.*
to leave
to set out
to depart

3 *This road **goes** to London.*
to lead

4 *My bag has **gone**!*
to disappear
to vanish

5 *My watch doesn't **go**.*
to work
to function

6 *All the children **went** quiet.*
to become
to grow

➤ go down
***Go down** the stairs.*
to descend

➤ go into
***Go into** the kitchen.*
to enter

➤ go out of
***Go out of** the house.*
to leave
to exit

➤ go up
***Go up** the stairs.*
to climb
to ascend

good ADJECTIVE

OVERUSED WORD

Here are some more interesting words you can use instead of good:

1 *This is a really **good** book.*

Use **wonderful**, **brilliant**, **excellent**, **fantastic** or **great** to mean very good: *He told us a **wonderful** story.*

Use **enjoyable** or **fun** for something you enjoy: *We had an **enjoyable** day at the park.*

Use **exciting**, **gripping**, **thrilling** or **interesting** for something that interests you: *The book was really **gripping**.*

Use **amusing** or **entertaining** for something that makes you laugh: *It was a very **entertaining** programme.*

2 *Will is a good singer.*
skilful
talented
gifted

3 *I hope the weather is **good** for sports day.*
fine
nice
dry
sunny
warm

4 *Jessica has got a **good** imagination.*
lively
vivid

5 *He gave a **good** description.*
clear
vivid
precise
accurate

6 *You have been a very **good** friend to me.*
kind
caring
loving
loyal

7 *Have you been **good**?*
well-behaved
polite
obedient
OPPOSITE **bad**

got VERB (past tense and past participle of get)

grab VERB

1 *I **grabbed** my coat and ran as I was late.*
to seize
to snatch
to pick up

2 *Tom **grabbed** my arm forcefully.*
to take hold of
to grasp
to clutch
to grip

graceful ADJECTIVE

*She is a very **graceful** dancer.*
elegant
beautiful
smooth
effortless
OPPOSITE **clumsy**

grateful ADJECTIVE

*We are **grateful** for all your help.*
thankful
obliged
appreciative *We are **appreciative** of all your help.*
OPPOSITE **ungrateful**

greasy ADJECTIVE

*These chips are very **greasy**.*
oily
fatty

great ADJECTIVE

1 *The teacher led the children into a **great** hall.*
large
enormous
huge
immense
OPPOSITE **small**

2 *The royal wedding was a **great** occasion.*
grand
magnificent
splendid
OPPOSITE **unimportant**

3 *He was a **great** musician.*
famous
well-known
celebrated
OPPOSITE **terrible**

4 *It's a **great** book!*
wonderful
brilliant
excellent
fantastic
OPPOSITE **terrible**

greedy ADJECTIVE

*Don't be **greedy**—you've had three cakes already!*
piggish
gluttonous
selfish

green ADJECTIVE

*She was wearing a **green** dress.*
emerald
Lime green is bright green.
Bottle green is dark green.

greet VERB

*She went to the door to **greet** her guests.*
to welcome
to hail
to receive

grey ADJECTIVE

1 *The sky was **grey** and it started to rain.*
cloudy
dull
overcast
grim
forbidding

② *They met an old man with **grey** hair.*
white
silver

grin VERB
*He **grinned** at me happily.*
to smile
to beam

grip VERB
*The old lady **gripped** my arm tightly.*
to hold on to
to grasp
to clutch

groan VERB
*We **groaned** mum said it was bedtime.*
to moan
to sigh
to protest

ground NOUN
① *Don't leave your bags on the wet **ground**.*
soil
earth
dirt

② *Who owns that piece of **ground**?*
land
territory

group NOUN
① *There was a large **group** waiting outside.*
a crowd
a throng

Use **mob** for a large, noisy group: *There was an angry **mob** outside the school.*

② *He was showing a **group** of tourists round the museum.*
a party

③ *We met up with a **group** of our friends.*
a bunch
a crowd
a gang

④ *What's your favourite pop **group**?*
a band

group VERB
*We had to **group** the poems together according to their author.*
to arrange
to classify
to sort
to order
to organise

grow VERB grows, growing, grew, grown
① *The sunflowers **grew** very tall this year.*
to get bigger
to get taller
to shoot up

② *The seeds are starting to **grow**.*

Use **germinate** or **sprout** when seeds first start to grow: *After three or four days the seeds will start to **germinate**.*

Use **shoot up** or **spring up** when the plant starts to grow taller: *Weeds were **springing up** all over the garden.*

Use **flourish** when a plant grows well and is healthy: *The tree we planted is **flourishing**.*

③ *The number of children in our school is **growing**.*
to increase
to go up
to rise

④ *We **grow** vegetables in our garden.*
to plant
to produce

growl VERB
*The dog **growled** at me when I opened the gate.*
to snarl

Use **bark** when a dog makes short loud sounds.

Use **roar** when a lion or tiger makes a very loud sound.

grown-up NOUN
*Ask a **grown-up** if you need help.*
an adult

A B C D E F Gg H I J K L M N O P Q R S T U V W X Y Z

grown-up *ADJECTIVE*
*You need to behave in a **grown-up** manner.*
mature
responsible
sensible
OPPOSITE **childish**

grumble *VERB*
*Stop **grumbling** about how much homework you have to do!*
to complain
to moan
to whinge
to whine

grumpy *ADJECTIVE*
*Why are you so **grumpy** today?*
cross
bad-tempered
sulky
moody
irritable
OPPOSITE **good-tempered**

guard *VERB*
1 *Soldiers **guard** the castle against attack.*
to protect
to defend
to watch
to shield

2 *A mother elephant will **guard** her young.*
to look after
to watch over
to protect
to shelter

guard *NOUN*
*There was a **guard** by the door.*
a sentry
a lookout

A security officer is a guard in a bank, office or shop.

guess *VERB*
1 *Can you **guess** how many sweets are in the jars?*
to estimate

2 *Because they were late, I **guessed** that they had missed the bus.*
to think
to suppose
to predict
to suspect
to infer

guide *VERB*
*He **guided** us through the wood to the main road.*
to lead
to steer
to escort
to accompany
to direct

guilty *ADJECTIVE*
*I felt **guilty** because I had been horrible to my sister.*
bad
ashamed
sorry
remorseful
sheepish
OPPOSITE **innocent**

Hh

habit NOUN
*She has a **habit** of playing with her hair.*
a custom
a routine

had VERB (past tense and past participle of have)

hair NOUN
*She had blonde **hair**.*

Use **locks** for long hair and **curls** for curly hair: *She had long golden **locks**.*

WORD WEB

Words to describe hair:	Words to describe the colour of hair:
beautiful	auburn
bobbed	black
cropped	blonde
curly	brown
dishevelled	chestnut
fine	dark
frizzy	ebony
glossy	fair
long	ginger
scruffy	golden
shiny	grey
short	jet black
sleek	mousy
straight	red
thick	sandy
tousled	strawberry blonde
untidy	white
wavy	
windswept	

hairy ADJECTIVE
*They were greeted by a large, **hairy** dog.*
furry
shaggy
woolly

handle VERB
*You **handled** the situation very well.*
to cope with
to deal with
to manage

handsome ADJECTIVE
*He is a very **handsome** man.*
good-looking
attractive

Use **gorgeous** for a man who is very handsome: *He's my favourite actor—he's absolutely **gorgeous**!*

OPPOSITE **ugly**

hang VERB hangs, hanging, hung
1 *A bunch of keys was **hanging** from his belt.*
to dangle
to swing
to be suspended

2 *We **hung** the picture on the wall.*
to attach
to fasten
to fix

3 *He was **hanging** on to the rope.*
to hold on to
to cling on to

happen VERB
*At what time did the power cut **happen**?*
to take place
to occur
to come about
to arise

happy *ADJECTIVE*

OVERUSED WORD

Try to use a more interesting word when you want to say **happy**. Here are some other words you can use instead:

*I'm feeling very **happy** today.*

Use **cheerful**, **contented**, **light-hearted** or **good-humoured** if you are in a good mood and not grumpy or upset about anything: *Sara is a very **cheerful** person who's always smiling.*

Use **pleased** or **glad** if you are happy about something that has happened: *I'll be very **glad** when this adventure is over!*

Use **delighted**, **thrilled** or **overjoyed** if you are very happy: *Everyone was **overjoyed** when the children were found safe and well.*

OPPOSITE **unhappy**

hard *ADJECTIVE*

OVERUSED WORD

Try to use a more interesting word when you want to say **hard**. Here are some other words you can use instead:

1 *The ground was **hard** and frozen.*
firm
solid

Use **rigid** or **stiff** for material that is too hard to bend easily: *This card is too **stiff** to fold.*

OPPOSITE **soft**

2 *The teacher gave us some very **hard** sums to do.*
difficult
complicated
tricky
challenging
tough

OPPOSITE **easy**

3 *Carrying the bricks was very **hard** work.*
tiring
exhausting
strenuous
back-breaking

OPPOSITE **easy**

hardly *ADVERB*

*I was so tired I could **hardly** walk.*
scarcely
barely
only just

harm *VERB*

1 *He would never **harm** anyone.*
to hurt
to injure
to ill-treat

2 *Smoking **harms** your health.*
to damage
to ruin

harmless *ADJECTIVE*

*The liquid is **harmless**.*
safe

Non-toxic means not poisonous.

OPPOSITE **dangerous**

harsh *ADJECTIVE*

1 *The machine made a **harsh** sound.*

Use **rough** or **grating** for a low sound: *The wheel made a loud **grating** sound as it turned.*

Use **shrill** or **piercing** for a high sound: *They heard a **piercing** scream.*

OPPOSITE **gentle**

❷ *That punishment seemed a bit* ***harsh****.*
hard
severe
strict
unkind
cruel
OPPOSITE **lenient**

hasty ADJECTIVE

I was too ***hasty*** *so I got the answer wrong.*
hurried
rushed
quick
speedy
rapid

hat NOUN

WORD WEB

Some types of **hat**:

a baseball cap
a beanie
a beret
a boater
a bonnet
a bowler hat
a cap
a fedora
a fez
a flat cap
a helmet
a panama
a riding hat
a sombrero
a straw hat
a sun hat
a top hat
a turban
a woolly hat
a witch's hat

a bowler hat

a sombrero

a top hat

hate VERB

I ***hate*** *cold weather!*
to dislike
to detest
to loathe
to despise
to not be able to stand *I* ***can't stand*** *cold weather!*
OPPOSITE **love**

have VERB has, having, had

❶ *Our school* ***has*** *a smartboard in every classroom.*
to own
to possess

❷ *I don't need this book now. You can* ***have*** *it.*
to keep

❸ *I* ***had*** *some lovely presents for my birthday.*
to get
to receive

❹ *My brother* ***has*** *chickenpox.*
to be suffering from
to be infected with *He* ***is infected with*** *chickenpox.*

heal VERB

That cut on your arm will soon ***heal****.*
to get better
to mend

healthy ADJECTIVE

❶ *Most of the children here are very* ***healthy*** *and well.*
strong
well
fit
in good shape

❷ *This food is very* ***healthy*** *and delicious.*
nutritious
nourishing
good for you
wholesome
OPPOSITE **unhealthy**

heap *NOUN*
*There was a **heap** of dirty clothes on the floor.*
a pile
a mound
a mass
a stack

hear *VERB* **hears, hearing, heard**
❶ *I couldn't **hear** what she was saying.*
to make out
to catch

❷ *Have you **heard** the band's new single?*
to listen to

heat *NOUN*
*I could feel the **heat** from the fire.*
warmth

heat *VERB*
*We can **heat** up a pizza for lunch.*
to warm up

heavy *ADJECTIVE*
*These bags are very **heavy** and I can't lift them.*
weighty
OPPOSITE **light**

held *VERB (past tense and past participle of* **hold***)*

help *VERB*
❶ *Shall I **help** you with your bags?*
to assist
to lend a hand
to give someone a hand

❷ *The team must all **help** one another.*
to support
to cooperate with

help *NOUN*
*Do you need some **help**?*
assistance
advice
support

helpful *ADJECTIVE*
*She is always very **helpful** in class.*
kind
considerate
willing
thoughtful
OPPOSITE **unhelpful**

helping *NOUN*
*He gave me a huge **helping** of chips.*
a portion
a serving

hesitate *VERB*
*She **hesitated** before diving into the water.*
to pause
to wait
to delay
to dither

hide *VERB* **hides, hiding, hid, hidden**
❶ *We **hid** in the garden shed.*
to keep out of sight

Use **go into hiding** when someone hides for a long time: *The robbers **went into hiding** for several weeks after the theft.*

Use **lie low** when someone tries to avoid certain people: *I knew Mrs Flint would be furious with me, so I decided to **lie low** for a day or two.*

❷ *They **hid** the money in a hollow tree.*
to conceal
to stash

high ADJECTIVE

1 *There are a lot of **high** buildings in the city.*
tall
big
towering

2 *Some shops charge very **high** prices.*
inflated
exorbitant

3 *She spoke in a **high** voice.*
high-pitched
squeaky
piercing

Use **piercing** or **shrill** for a loud, unpleasant high voice: *'Get out!' she cried in a **shrill** voice.*

OPPOSITE **low**

hill NOUN

*We walked up the **hill**.*
a mountain
a slope

hit VERB hit, hitting, hit

1 *You mustn't **hit** people as you might hurt them.*
to strike

To **punch** or **thump** someone means to hit them with your fist: *'Get out of my way or I'll **thump** you!' he shouted.*

To **slap** someone means to hit them with your open hand: *She **slapped** his face.*

To **smack** someone means to hit them as a punishment: *Some parents **smack** their children.*

To **beat** or **thrash** someone means to hit them many times with a stick: *The cruel master used to **beat** the horses.*

2 *I fell and **hit** my elbow on the pavement.*
to knock
to bang
to bash
to bump

3 *The car went out of control and **hit** a wall.*
to bump into
to run into
to crash into
to smash into
to collide with

4 *He **hit** the ball as hard as he could.*
to strike
to whack

hoarse ADJECTIVE

*Dad's voice was **hoarse** because he had a cold.*
croaking
husky
rough
gruff

hobby NOUN

*Skateboarding is my favourite **hobby**.*
a pastime
an interest
an activity
a leisure activity

hold VERB holds, holding, held

1 *Can I **hold** the baby?*
to carry
to cuddle
to hug
to cradle
to embrace

2 *She **held** the handrail tightly.*
to grip
to grasp
to clutch

3 *One of the boys was **holding** a stick.*
to brandish
to wield

4 *This box **holds** twenty pencils.*
to take
to contain
to carry
to have space for *This box **has space for** twenty pencils.*

hole *NOUN*

1 *We climbed through a **hole** in the hedge.*
an opening
a gap
a space

2 *There was a big **hole** in the ground.*
a pit
a crater
a chasm
a pothole

3 *I could see them through a **hole** in the wall.*
a crack
a slit
a chink

4 *There's a **hole** in my shirt.*
a split
a rip
a tear

5 *There was a **hole** in one of the water pipes.*
a crack
a leak

6 *One of my bicycle tyres has a **hole** in it.*
a puncture

7 *The tiny animal escaped back into its **hole**.*
a burrow
a den
a nest

holiday *NOUN*

*We are going to have a **holiday** by the seaside.*
a vacation
a break
time off

home *NOUN*

*This is my **home**, where I have lived for four years.*
a residence
a house
a flat
an apartment

honest *ADJECTIVE*

1 *I'm sure he is an **honest** boy who never lies.*
good
trustworthy
law-abiding
OPPOSITE **dishonest**

2 *Did you enjoy the film? Be **honest**.*
truthful
sincere
frank

hope *VERB*

*I **hope** my parents get me a bike for my birthday.*
to want *I **want** my parents to get me a bike for my birthday.*
to wish *I **wish** for a bike for my birthday.*

hope *NOUN*

*My **hope** was that we would win.*
a dream
a wish
an ambition

hopeful *ADJECTIVE*

*I feel **hopeful** about the football match.*
optimistic
positive
confident
upbeat
OPPOSITE **pessimistic**

hopeless *ADJECTIVE*

1 *The situation is **hopeless**.*
desperate
impossible

2 *I'm **hopeless** at swimming.*
bad
no good
terrible
useless
incompetent
OPPOSITE **good**

horrible *ADJECTIVE*

❶ *Don't be **horrible**! You'll upset him.*

nasty
unpleasant
mean
unkind
obnoxious
horrid

❷ *I can't eat this food. It's **horrible**.*

revolting
disgusting
tasteless
inedible

❸ *I don't like that **horrible** jumper!*

vile
hideous
repulsive

❹ *The weather was **horrible** and we stayed in.*

awful
dreadful
terrible
appalling

❺ *I had a dream about a **horrible** monster.*

terrible
frightening
terrifying

OPPOSITE **pleasant**

horrify *VERB*

*The sight of the ugly monster **horrified** them.*

to appal
to shock
to alarm
to sicken
to terrify

horror *NOUN*

*The sight of the beast filled me with **horror**.*

fear
terror
dread

horse *NOUN*

a pony

A **nag** is an old horse.
A **mare** is a female horse.
A **stallion** is a male horse.
A **foal** is a baby horse.
A **colt** is a young horse.

WORD WEB

Some types of **horse**:

a carthorse
a racehorse
a Shetland pony
a Shire horse

Some words to describe the colour of a **horse**:

black
white
chestnut
dapple grey

A **bay** is reddish brown.
A **roan** is brown or black, with some white hairs.
A **palomino** has a gold coat with a white mane.
A **piebald** horse has patches of different colours.
A **skewbald** horse has patches of white and another colour.

WRITING TIPS

Here are some useful words for writing about **horses**:

- *The little pony **trotted** down the lane.*
- *The stallion **cantered** across the field.*
- *The racehorse **galloped** towards the finishing line.*
- *The foal **neighed** excitedly.*

They urged their horses into a canter over the bridge.—OLAF THE VIKING PIG WHO WOULD BE KING, Martin Conway

hot *ADJECTIVE*

1 *The weather will be **hot** next week.*

Use **warm** when the weather is quite hot: *It was a lovely **warm** spring morning.*

Use **boiling hot**, **baking hot** and **scorching hot** when it is very hot: *It was a **baking hot** summer's day.*

Use **sweltering** when it is too hot: *We couldn't do anything in the afternoon because it was **sweltering**.*

OPPOSITE **cold**

2 *Be careful with that pan—it's **hot**.*

Use **red hot** or **burning hot** for something that is very hot: *The coals on the barbecue were **red hot**.*

OPPOSITE **cold**

3 *Don't spill that **hot** water over yourself.*

Use **boiling** for a liquid that is hot enough to boil: *You make tea with **boiling** water.*

Use **scalding** or **scalding hot** for a liquid that is hot enough to burn your skin: *Don't get into the bath yet—the water's **scalding hot**.*

Use **piping hot** for food or drink that is nice and hot: *She brought us a bowl of **piping hot** soup.*

OPPOSITE **cold**

4 *We sat down in front of the **hot** fire.*

warm
blazing
roaring

OPPOSITE **cold**

5 *We add chillies to food to make it **hot**.*

spicy
peppery

OPPOSITE **mild**

house *NOUN*

a home
a dwelling

WORD WEB

Some types of **house**:

a bungalow
a castle
a cottage
a farmhouse
a mansion
a palace
a shack
a villa

howl *VERB*

*I heard something **howling** in the wood.*

to cry
to shriek
to wail
to yowl

hug *VERB*

*She **hugged** me and told me not to cry.*

to cuddle
to hold
to embrace

huge *ADJECTIVE*

*The **huge** creature came after them.*

great
enormous
gigantic
massive

OPPOSITE **tiny**

hung *VERB (past tense and past participle of* hang*)*

hunger *NOUN*

***Hunger** was making me grumpy so Mum gave me a sandwich.*

appetite

Use **starvation** or **famine** for hunger that is bad enough to make someone ill or die: *The animals were suffering from **starvation**.*

hungry *ADJECTIVE*

1 *I'm glad it's lunchtime because I'm **hungry**.*

Use **starving**, **famished** or **ravenous** if you are very hungry: *I was absolutely **starving** after swimming.*

Use **peckish** if you are slightly hungry: *Have an apple if you're **peckish**.*

2 *The people have no food and their children are **hungry**.*
starving
underfed
undernourished

hunt *VERB*

1 *Lions **hunt** deer and other animals.*
to chase
to kill

2 *Will you help me **hunt** for my purse?*
to look for
to search for

hurry *VERB*

1 *Come on, **hurry** up!*
to be quick *Come on, **be quick**!*
to get a move on *(informal)*

2 *He **hurried** out of the room.*
to rush
to dash
to run
to race
to fly
to scurry

hurt *VERB* **hurts, hurting, hurt**

1 *You mustn't **hurt** animals.*
to injure
to harm

2 *I fell and **hurt** my leg.*
to injure
to cut
to graze
to bruise
to sprain
to twist
to dislocate
to break

3 *My head was **hurting** after I bumped it.*
to be sore
to be painful

Use **ache** to describe a pain that continues for a long time: *My poor head was **aching**.*

Use **pound** or **throb** to describe a banging pain: *My toothache was **throbbing** terribly.*

Use **sting** or **smart** to describe a sharp pain: *The salt water made my eyes **sting**.*

4 *It **hurt** me when they laughed at my picture.*
to upset
to offend
to distress
to sadden

hut *NOUN*

*We slept in a little **hut** in the wood.*
a shack
a cabin
a shelter
a shed

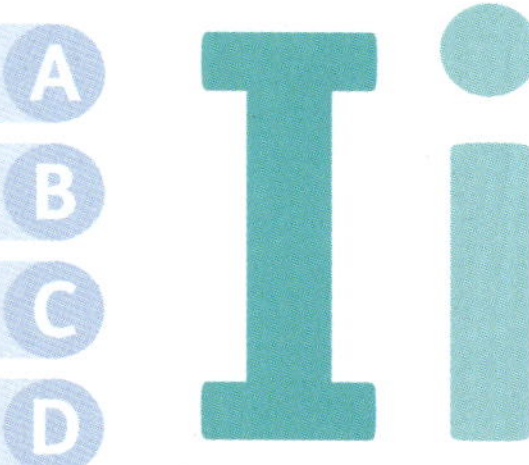

A B C D E F G H Ii J K L M N O P Q R S T U V W X Y Z

idea *NOUN*

1 *I've got an **idea** about what to do today.*
a suggestion
a plan
a thought
A **brainwave** is a very good idea that you suddenly think of: *We were wondering what to do, then Dora suddenly had a **brainwave**.*

2 *I don't always agree with your **ideas**.*
an opinion
a belief

3 *The film gave us an **idea** of life in wartime.*
an impression
a picture

ignore *VERB*

*I said hello to them, but they **ignored** me.*
to take no notice of *They **took no notice of** me.*
to pay no attention to *They **paid no attention to** me.*

ill *ADJECTIVE*

*I felt too **ill** to go to school.*
unwell
poorly
sick

Use **queasy** when you feel as if you are going to be sick: *I was feeling a bit **queasy** after eating all that chocolate.*
OPPOSITE **well**

illegal *ADJECTIVE*

*It is **illegal** to steal.*
against the law
unlawful
forbidden
prohibited
OPPOSITE **legal**

illness *NOUN*

*She is suffering from a nasty **illness**.*

Use **ailment** or **complaint** for any illness: *Stomach ache is a very common **complaint**.*

Use **disease** for a serious illness: *Cancer is a very serious **disease**.*

Use **infection** or **bug** for an illness that you catch from other people: *I think I've caught a **bug** from someone at school.*

imaginary *ADJECTIVE*

1 *Dragons are **imaginary** animals.*
mythical
fictional
fictitious
legendary
unreal

2 *We played on our **imaginary** island.*
pretend
invented
made-up
OPPOSITE **real**

imagine *VERB*

1 *I tried to **imagine** what life was like in Roman times.*
to think about
to picture
to visualise
to envisage

❷ *It didn't really happen. You only **imagined** it.*
to dream

immediately *ADVERB*
*We need to leave **immediately** or we'll be late.*
at once
straight away
this minute
instantly

impatient *ADJECTIVE*
*Lunch took a long time and I was starting to get **impatient**.*
frustrated
irritated
infuriated
restless
anxious
OPPOSITE **patient**

important *ADJECTIVE*
❶ *There is one **important** thing you must remember.*
vital
crucial
essential
basic
main
necessary

❷ *The World Cup is a very **important** sporting event.*
big
major
special
significant

❸ *I was nervous about meeting such an **important** person.*
famous
distinguished
prominent
high-ranking
leading
OPPOSITE **unimportant**

impossible *ADJECTIVE*
*I can't do that—it's **impossible**!*
not possible
not humanly possible
not feasible
OPPOSITE **possible**

impressed *ADJECTIVE*
*The teacher said she was **impressed** with our work.*
struck
pleased
excited
OPPOSITE **unimpressed**

impressive *ADJECTIVE*
*The model car he made was really **impressive**.*
striking
spectacular
magnificent
remarkable
admirable
OPPOSITE **unimpressive**

improve *VERB*
❶ *Your maths is **improving** every week.*
to get better
to come on

❷ *Try to **improve** your handwriting as I can't read it.*
to make progress with

include *VERB*
*The book **includes** lots of pictures and maps.*
to contain
to incorporate

increase *VERB*
❶ *Our class has **increased** in size.*
to get bigger
to grow
to expand

❷ *The noise gradually **increased**.*
to get louder
to build up

❸ *The price of tickets has* ***increased*** *from five to ten pounds.*
to go up
to rise
To double is to become twice as much.
OPPOSITE **decrease**

incredible *ADJECTIVE*

❶ *It seems* ***incredible*** *that someone could survive for so long in the desert.*
unbelievable
extraordinary
unlikely
unimaginable

❷ *This is such an* ***incredible*** *book that I can't put it down!*
great
excellent
brilliant
wonderful
fantastic
amazing

informal *ADJECTIVE*

It was a very ***informal*** *party.*
relaxed
casual
easy-going
friendly
OPPOSITE **formal**

information *NOUN*

We are collecting ***information*** *about rainforests.*
facts
details
data
material

injure *VERB*

❶ *He fell and* ***injured*** *his leg.*
to hurt
to cut
to bruise

Use **graze** when you don't cut yourself very badly: *I* ***grazed*** *my arm slightly when I fell.*

Use **gash** when you cut yourself very badly: *He* ***gashed*** *his leg on a sharp rock.*

❷ *I landed on my wrist and* ***injured*** *it.*
to sprain
to twist
to dislocate
to break

injury *NOUN*

The captain couldn't play because he had an ***injury****.*
a wound
a cut
a bruise
a burn
A graze is a small cut.
A gash is a big cut.

innocent *ADJECTIVE*

The jury decided that he was ***innocent****.*
not guilty
blameless
OPPOSITE **guilty**

insect *NOUN*

Henry is fascinated by ***insects****.*
a bug
a creepy-crawly

WORD WEB

Some types of insect:

an ant
a bee
a beetle
a bluebottle
a bumble bee
a butterfly
a cricket
a daddy-long-legs
a dragonfly
a fly
a grasshopper
a honey bee
a ladybird
a locust
a midge
a mosquito
a moth
a stick insect
a wasp
a woodlouse

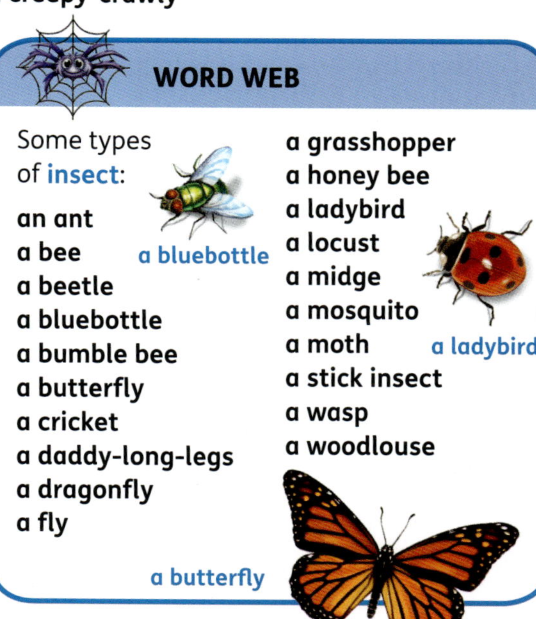

a bluebottle

a ladybird

a butterfly

WRITING TIPS

Here are some useful words for writing about **insects**:

- *The ladybird **flew** away.*
- *A wasp was **buzzing** around the kitchen.*
- *Bees come together and **swarm** when they are looking for a new hive.*
- *A fly **crawled** up my leg.*
- *The beetle **scuttled** away.*
- *Ants were **scurrying** around looking for food.*

an ant

Insects were swarming all over the earthen mound inside the container.—COLONY, J. A. Henderson

inspect *VERB*

*He **inspected** the cup to see if it was cracked.*
to examine
to check
to look at

instant *ADJECTIVE*

*The film was an **instant** success.*
immediate
instantaneous

instruct *VERB*

1 *The judo teacher **instructs** us on how to move safely.*
to coach
to teach
to train

2 *The fire chief **instructed** everyone to leave the building.*
to order
to command
to tell

instructions *NOUN*

*Read the **instructions** on the packet carefully.*
directions
guidelines

intelligent *ADJECTIVE*

*He's **intelligent** and does well at school.*
clever
bright
brainy
quick
sharp
smart
brilliant
OPPOSITE **stupid**

intend *VERB*

1 *I didn't **intend** to upset her.*
to mean
to want
to plan

2 *We **intend** to set up a school drama club next year.*
to plan
to propose
to aim

interested *ADJECTIVE*

*I'm very **interested** in old coins.*
fascinated *I'm **fascinated** by old coins.*

interesting *ADJECTIVE*

*This is a really **interesting** book.*
fascinating
intriguing
exciting
entertaining
gripping
OPPOSITE **boring**

interrupt *VERB*

*Please don't **interrupt** when I'm talking.*
to butt in
to barge in
to interject

interval *NOUN*

*You can have an ice cream during the **interval**.*
a break
an interlude
an intermission

a b c d e f g h Ii j k l m n o p q r s t u v w x y z

A B C D E F G H Ii J K L M N O P Q R S T U V W X Y Z

introduce *VERB*

1 *The teacher* ***introduced*** *the new boy to the class.*

to present

2 *They've* ***introduced*** *a new school uniform.*

to bring in
to establish
to start
to initiate

invade *VERB*

The Romans ***invaded*** *Britain.*

to attack
to occupy
to march into

invent *VERB*

Who ***invented*** *the first computer?*

to design
to develop
to create
to devise

inventor *NOUN*

He was the ***inventor*** *of the telephone.*

the creator
the developer
the designer

investigate *VERB*

For our homework, we had to ***investigate*** *how the Romans lived.*

to explore
to look into
to research
to study

invisible *ADJECTIVE*

Ivy had grown over the old door and made it ***invisible****.*

hidden
concealed

Use **microscopic** for something that is invisible because it is very small: *The leaf is covered with* ***microscopic*** *hairs.*

OPPOSITE **visible**

invite *VERB*

I've ***invited*** *all my friends to the party.*

to ask

irritate *VERB*

My little brother keeps ***irritating*** *me by playing with my toys.*

to annoy
to pester
to bother
to get on someone's nerves (*informal*) *My little brother is* ***getting on my nerves****.*

irritated *ADJECTIVE*

I was beginning to feel ***irritated*** *by the girl's questions.*

cross
annoyed
angry
exasperated
infuriated

irritating *ADJECTIVE*

He has some very ***irritating*** *habits.*

annoying
infuriating
maddening
exasperating

item *NOUN*

How many ***items*** *did you buy?*

a thing
an object
an article

jail *NOUN*
*He was locked up in **jail**.*
prison
a cell
a dungeon

jealous *ADJECTIVE*
*I felt a little bit **jealous** when I saw her new bike.*
envious
resentful

jewel *NOUN*
*We found a box full of diamonds and other **jewels**.*
a gem
a gemstone
a precious stone

WORD WEB

Some types of **jewel**:

a diamond
an emerald
jet
an opal
a pearl
a ruby
a sapphire

Some types of **jewellery**:

a bangle
a bracelet
a brooch
a crown
earrings
a necklace
a ring
a tiara

a brooch

rings

job *NOUN*
1 *I want to have an interesting **job**.*
an occupation
a profession
a career
work
employment

2 *I had to do a couple of **jobs** for my mum.*
a chore
a task
an errand

WORD WEB

Some **jobs** people do:

an architect
an artist
a blacksmith
a builder
a carpenter
a chef
a cook
a dentist
a detective
a doctor
a dustman
an electrician
an engineer
a farmer
a firefighter
a hairdresser
a journalist
a lawyer
a lecturer
a librarian
a mechanic
a musician
a nurse
an office worker
a photographer
a pilot
an optician
a plumber
a policeman
or policewoman
a postman
or postwoman
a professor
a reporter
a sailor
a scientist
a secretary
a shopkeeper
a teacher
a vet
a waiter or **waitress**

a police officer

join VERB

1 *Join the two wires together.*
to fix
to fasten
to attach
to connect
to tie
to stick
to glue

2 *Why don't you **join** your local drama group?*
to become a member of
to enrol in

joke NOUN

1 *He told us some funny **jokes**.*
a funny story
a witticism

2 *She hid my school bag as a **joke**.*
a trick
a prank

journey NOUN

*He set out on his **journey**.*
a trip

An **expedition** is a long journey: *They are planning an **expedition** to the North Pole.*

A **voyage** is a journey by sea: *The **voyage** was long and very rough.*

A **flight** is a journey by air: *Our **flight** took two hours.*

A **ride** is a journey in a vehicle, on a bike or on an animal: *It was a long bus **ride** to the airport.*

A **drive** is a journey by car: *It's a long **drive** from London to Inverness.*

A **trek** or **hike** is a long journey on foot: *The three-day **trek** through the mountains was exhausting.*

An **excursion** is a journey for pleasure: *They went on an **excursion** to the beach.*

jump VERB

1 *He **jumped** into the air and caught the ball.*
to leap
to spring

2 *The cat **jumped** on the mouse.*
to pounce
to spring

3 *The kangaroo **jumped** off into the distance.*
to hop
to bound
to bounce

4 *She was **jumping** for joy.*
to leap about
to prance about
to skip about

5 *Sammy **jumped** over the fence.*
to leap over
to vault over

Use **hurdle** when you jump over something while you are running: *He **hurdled** the gate.*

Use **clear** when you jump over something easily, without touching it at all: *The horse **cleared** the last fence in the race.*

6 *She **jumped** into the water.*
to leap
to dive
to plunge

7 *The sudden noise made me **jump**.*
to start
to flinch

just ADVERB

1 *This is **just** what I wanted.*
exactly
precisely

2 *The classroom is **just** big enough for all the children.*
hardly
barely
scarcely

keen *ADJECTIVE*

1 *All the children are **keen** on going to the park.*
enthusiastic about
fond of

2 *She was **keen** to go with her sisters.*
eager
anxious

3 *I am a **keen** reader.*
avid
enthusiastic
passionate

keep *VERB* **keeps, keeping, kept**

1 *You don't have to give the book back to me. You can **keep** it.*
to have
to hold on to

2 ***Keep** still!*
to stay
to remain

3 *They **keep** chickens on their farm.*
to have
to look after

4 *I told him to be quiet, but he **kept** talking.*
to continue
to carry on

kill *VERB*

1 *The knight **killed** the mighty dragon.*
to slay

2 *Someone has threatened to **kill** him.*
to murder

Use **assassinate** when someone kills a very important person: *Someone has **assassinated** the king!*

Use **execute** when people kill someone as a punishment: *In some countries, they **execute** criminals instead of sending them to prison.*

3 *The soldiers **killed** hundreds of innocent people.*
to slaughter
to massacre

4 *A butcher **kills** animals and sells their meat.*
to slaughter

5 *Sometimes a vet has to **kill** an animal if it is badly injured.*
to destroy
to put down
to put to sleep

kind *ADJECTIVE*

1 *He's a very **kind** boy.*
gentle
good-natured
kind-hearted
caring
thoughtful
considerate

2 *It was very **kind** of you to give so much money to the school.*
generous
unselfish
helpful
OPPOSITE **unkind**

kind *NOUN*

1 *A dictionary is a **kind** of book.*
a type
a sort

2 *A terrier is a **kind** of dog.*
a breed

3 *A ladybird is a **kind** of beetle.*
a species

4 *What **kind** of trainers do you want to buy?*
a brand
a make

kindness *NOUN*
He shows a lot of ***kindness*** *to his little sister.*
goodness
kind-heartedness
gentleness
care
OPPOSITE **unkindness**

king *NOUN*
He was crowned as the new ***king****.*
a monarch
a sovereign
a ruler

knew (*past tense of* know)

knob *NOUN*
1 *He turned the door* ***knob****.*
a handle

2 *She started fiddling with the* ***knobs*** *on the machine.*
a switch
a button
a control

knock *VERB*
1 *I* ***knocked*** *on the door as there was no bell.*

Use **rap** or **tap** when someone knocks not very loudly: *She* ***rapped*** *lightly on the window.*

Use **bang** or **hammer** when someone knocks loudly: *He* ***hammered*** *on the door with the brass knocker.*

2 *I fell and* ***knocked*** *my head against the table.*
to bang
to bump
to hit
to bash

know *VERB* **knows, knowing, knew, known**
1 *Do you* ***know*** *how a car works?*
to understand
to remember
to see

2 *I didn't* ***know*** *the answer to that question.*
to be sure of
to be certain of *I wasn't* ***certain*** *of the answer.*

3 *I* ***knew*** *that someone was watching me.*
to sense
to realise
to be aware *I was* ***aware*** *that someone was watching me.*

4 *As soon as I saw the man, I* ***knew*** *who he was.*
to recognise
to identify

5 *Do you* ***know*** *my sister?*
to have met *Have you* ***met*** *my sister?*
to be acquainted with *Are you* ***acquainted*** *with my sister?*

knowledge *NOUN*
She has a lot of ***knowledge*** *about animals.*
learning
understanding
information
education

Ll

label NOUN
*Read the **label** on the packet.*
a tag
a sticker
a ticket

laid VERB *(past tense and past participle of lay)*

lake NOUN
*We went for a paddle in the **lake.***
a pond
a pool
A lagoon is a salt-water lake.
A loch is a lake in Scotland.

land NOUN
1 *This is good **land** for growing crops.*
ground
earth
soil

2 *He has travelled to many faraway **lands**.*
a country
a nation
a region

A kingdom is a land with a king or queen.

land VERB
1 *The plane should **land** at seven o'clock.*
to touch down
to come down
to arrive

2 *They rowed towards the island and **landed** on a small beach.*
to come ashore
to go ashore

3 *The bird **landed** on a small branch.*
to alight
to fly down onto
to come to rest on

large ADJECTIVE
1 *He was carrying a **large**, heavy box.*
big

Use **huge** or **enormous** for something that is very large: *He came out with the most **enormous** sandwich I had ever seen.*

Use **massive** or **gigantic** for something that is very large indeed: *Some dinosaurs were so **massive** that they couldn't run very fast.*

2 *There are some very **large** buildings in the city centre.*
big
tall

Use **spacious** for buildings that have plenty of space inside: *Our new flat is bright and **spacious**.*

Use **grand** or **magnificent** for things that are very large and beautiful: *The prince lived in a **magnificent** palace.*

3 *She gave me a **large** portion of chips.*
big
generous
sizeable
OPPOSITE **small**

last ADJECTIVE

*Z is the **last** letter of the alphabet.*

final
concluding
ultimate
OPPOSITE **first**

last VERB

*The party **lasted** for two hours.*

to continue
to carry on
to go on

late ADJECTIVE

*We were going to miss the concert as the bus was **late**.*

delayed
overdue
OPPOSITE **early**

later ADVERB

*Do you want to go to the park **later**?*

afterwards
in a while
in due course
OPPOSITE **earlier**

laugh VERB

*All the children started **laughing**.*

Use **chuckle** when someone laughs quietly to themselves: *The professor read the letter and **chuckled** to himself.*

Use **giggle**, **titter** or **snigger** when someone laughs in a slightly silly way: *The girls **giggled** as he walked past.*

Use **cackle** when someone laughs in a nasty way: *The old witch **cackled** with laughter.*

Use **guffaw**, **roar with laughter** or **shriek with laughter** when someone laughs very loudly: *He threw back his head and **guffawed** loudly.*

Use **burst out laughing** when someone suddenly starts to laugh: *We all **burst out laughing** when we saw his new hat.*

laughter NOUN

*We could hear a lot of **laughter** coming from the playground.*

laughing
hilarity
amusement

launch VERB

*They **launched** a rocket to the moon.*

to fire
to blast off
to send
to set off

law NOUN

*Everyone must obey the **laws** of the country.*

a rule
a regulation

lay VERB lays, laying, laid

*I **laid** the clothes on my bed so I could decide what to wear.*

to put
to place
to spread
to set out

layer NOUN

1 *There was a thick **layer** of dust on the old books.*

a coating
a covering
a film
a blanket

2 *The pond was covered in a **layer** of ice.*

a sheet

lazy ADJECTIVE

*Get up! Don't be so **lazy**!*

idle
indolent

lead VERB leads, leading, led

1 *He **led** us to the secret cave.*

to take
to guide

❷ *Who is going to **lead** the expedition?*
to command
to be in charge of

❸ *Our team was **leading** at the end of the first round.*
to be winning
to be in the lead *Our team was **in the lead**.*

leader NOUN
*Who is the **leader** of your gang?*
the boss
the chief
the captain
the commander

leak VERB
*Water was **leaking** out of the pipe.*
to drip
to trickle
to seep
to spill

leak NOUN
*There was a **leak** in the pipe.*
a hole
a crack
a puncture

lean VERB leans, leaning, leaned *or* leant
❶ *She **leaned** forward to look out of the window.*
to stretch
to bend

❷ *The old building **leans** to one side.*
to slant
to tilt

❸ *He was **leaning** against the wall.*
to recline

❹ *He **leaned** his bicycle against the wall.*
to prop
to rest

leap VERB leaps, leaping, leaped *or* leapt
❶ *The cat **leaped** into the air.*
to jump
to spring

❷ *She **leaped** over the fence.*
to hurdle *She **hurdled** the fence.*
to clear *She **cleared** the fence.*

❸ *She **leaped** into the water.*
to jump
to dive
to plunge

learn VERB learns, learning, learned *or* learnt
*We are **learning** about the Vikings at school.*
to find out
to discover

leave VERB leaves, leaving, left
❶ *What time does the train **leave**?*
to go
to set off
to depart
OPPOSITE **arrive**

❷ *The ship **leaves** at nine o'clock.*
to sail
to set sail
to depart

❸ *The plane **leaves** at eleven thirty.*
to take off
to depart

❹ *She **left** the party quietly when no one was looking.*
to sneak off
to slip away
to creep off

❺ *He **left** in a terrible temper.*
to go off
to storm off
to stomp off

❻ *Where did you **leave** your bag?*
to put

❼ *All my friends went away and **left** me alone and now I'm here on my own!*
to desert
to abandon

a b c d e f g h i j k Ll m n o p q r s t u v w x y z

A B C D E F G H I J K Ll M N O P Q R S T U V W X Y Z

led *VERB (past tense and past participle of* **lead***)*

left *VERB (past tense and past participle of* **leave***)*

let *VERB* **let, letting, let**
Will you ***let*** *me ride your bike?*
to allow *Will you* ***allow*** *me to ride your bike?*
to give someone permission *Will you* ***give me permission*** *to ride your bike?*

letter *NOUN*
1 *What* ***letter*** *does your name start with?*
a character
a symbol
A vowel is one of the letters A, E, I, O or U.
A consonant is one of the letters that is not a vowel.

2 *The school sent our parents a* ***letter****.*
a note
a message

level *ADJECTIVE*
1 *Put your laptop on a* ***level*** *surface.*
flat
even
smooth
horizontal
OPPOSITE **uneven**

2 *Their scores were* ***level*** *at half time.*
even
equal
the same
OPPOSITE **different**

lid *NOUN*
Put the ***lid*** *back on the jar.*
a top
a cap
a cover

lie *NOUN*
Don't tell ***lies*** *as someone will find you out.*
a fib *(informal)*
an untruth

lie *VERB* **lie, lying, lied**
1 *She was* ***lying*** *on the sofa.*
to rest
to lounge
to recline
to sprawl
to stretch out

2 *I don't believe him—I think he's* ***lying****.*
to fib *(informal)*
to tell lies
to bluff

lift *NOUN*
1 *We took the* ***lift*** *up to the fifth floor.*
an elevator

2 *He gave us a* ***lift*** *in his new car.*
a ride

lift *VERB*
He ***lifted*** *the trophy proudly.*
to raise
to hoist
to pick up

light *ADJECTIVE*
1 *My suitcase is quite* ***light****.*
not very heavy
OPPOSITE **heavy**

2 *Our classroom is nice and* ***light****.*
bright
well-lit
airy
OPPOSITE **dim**

3 *She was wearing a* ***light*** *blue T-shirt.*
pale
pastel
Use **fair** for light coloured hair.
OPPOSITE **dark**

light NOUN

1 *There wasn't enough **light** to see.*
daylight
sunlight
brightness

2 *Please could you switch the **light** on?*

WORD WEB

Some types of **light**:

Floodlights are lights at a sports ground.
A headlight is a light on a car.
a lamp
A searchlight is a powerful torch.
A spotlight is a light on a stage.
a street light
a torch

WRITING TIPS

Here are some useful words for writing about **light**:

- *I could see a light **shining** through the trees.*
- *A pale light **glowed** beneath the water.*
- *The fairy lights **gleamed** and **glimmered** in the darkness.*
- *The water **glistened** and **sparkled** in the sunlight.*
- *Stars **twinkled** above us.*
- *The light from the lighthouse **flashed**.*
- *Searchlights **flickered** in the distance.*
- *The headlights **glared** in the darkness.*

Just then a flash of lightning came and lighted up the country around for a moment.—PRINCE AND ROVER OF CLOVERFIELD FARM, Helen Fuller Orton

like PREPOSITION

Your pencil case is like mine.
the same as
similar to

like VERB

OVERUSED WORD

Here are some more interesting words you can use instead of **like**:

1 *I **like** our new teacher.*
to get on well with
to be fond of

Use **love**, **adore** or **idolise** if you like someone a lot: *She **idolises** her grandad!*

2 *Tom **likes** playing video games.*
to be keen on
to enjoy

Use **love**, **adore** or **be mad about** if you like something a lot: *She **is mad about** horses!*

3 *I think that boy **likes** you!*
to fancy
OPPOSITE **dislike**

likely ADJECTIVE

*It's quite **likely** that it will rain later.*
possible
probable
OPPOSITE **unlikely**

line NOUN

1 *Draw a **line** across the top of the page.*
a mark

2 *Her old face was covered in **lines**.*
wrinkles

3 *We all stood in a **line**.*
a row
a queue

listen VERB

*Please **listen** to what I am going to say.*
to pay attention
to attend *Please **attend** to what I am going to say.*

litter *NOUN*

*The playground was covered in **litter**.*

rubbish

mess

little *ADJECTIVE*

OVERUSED WORD

Try to use a more interesting word when you want to say **little**. Here are some other words you can use instead:

1. *They live in a **little** house on the edge of the village.*

small

Use **tiny** or **titchy** in an informal situation for something that is very small: *The mouse began to dig with its **titchy** paws.*

Use **cramped** or **poky** for a house or room that is too small: *They lived in a **cramped** one-room flat.*

2. *He's only a **little** boy.*

young

3. *It's only a **little** problem.*

small

slight

minor

4. *We had a **little** chat.*

short

brief

OPPOSITE **big**

live *VERB*

1. *Plants cannot **live** without water.*

to exist

to survive

to remain alive

2. *We live in London.*

to reside

lively *ADJECTIVE*

*The puppies were **lively** and lots of fun.*

active

busy

energetic

boisterous

playful

frisky

OPPOSITE **quiet**

load *VERB*

1. *We **loaded** the suitcases into the car.*

to put

to lift

2. *We **loaded** the trolley with food.*

to fill

to pack

to pile up

lock *NOUN*

*We need to put a **lock** on the shed door.*

a bolt

a padlock

lock *VERB*

*Don't forget to **lock** the door.*

to shut

to fasten

to bolt

to secure

lonely ADJECTIVE

❶ *I felt **lonely** when all my friends had left.*
alone
isolated
friendless
forlorn

❷ *They live in a **lonely** part of the country.*

Use **remote** or **isolated** for a place that is far away from towns and cities: *They live in a **remote** village in the mountains.*

Use **solitary** for a place that is on its own far from other places: *On top of the hill is a **solitary** farmhouse.*

Use **secluded** for a place that not many people can see: *Behind the house is a **secluded** garden.*

Use **uninhabited** for a place where no one lives: *The northern side of the island is **uninhabited**.*

long ADJECTIVE

❶ *It's quite a **long** movie and is very boring.*
lengthy

❷ *We had to sit and listen to his **long** speech.*
endless
interminable
long-drawn-out
OPPOSITE **short**

look VERB

OVERUSED WORD

Try to use a more interesting word when you want to say **look**. Here are some other words you can use instead:

❶ *I'm **looking** at a squirrel in the garden.*
to watch
to observe
to study

❷ *She **looked** at the picture.*

Use **glance** or **peep** when you look at something quickly: *I **glanced** at the clock to see what time it was.*

Use **stare** or **gaze** when you look at something for a long time: *We **gazed** at the beautiful view.*

Use **peer** or **squint** when you look at something carefully because you cannot see it very well: *We **peered** through the window into the dark room.*

❸ *I could see that Lucy was **looking** at me.*

Use **stare** if you look at someone for a long time: *Why are you **staring** at me?*

Use **glare**, **glower** or **scowl** if you look at someone angrily: *Mum **glared** at me angrily.*

❹ *That dog doesn't **look** very friendly.*
to seem
to appear

➤ **look after**
*I have to **look after** my little brother.*
to take care of
to care for
to mind
to keep an eye on

➤ **look for**
*I'll help you **look for** your gloves.*
to search for
to hunt for
to try to find

➤ **look out**
*He told us to **look out** for snakes.*
to watch out
to beware *He told us to **beware** of snakes.*
to be on your guard *He told us to **be on our guard** for snakes.*

loose *ADJECTIVE*

1 *One of my teeth is **loose**.*
wobbly
shaky
OPPOSITE **secure**

2 *The rope was a bit **loose** and didn't feel safe.*
slack
OPPOSITE **tight**

3 *I like to wear **loose** clothes.*
baggy
big
oversized
OPPOSITE **tight**

lose *VERB* loses, losing, lost

1 *I've **lost** my phone somewhere in the house.*
to mislay
to misplace
OPPOSITE **find**

2 *Our team **lost** the game.*
to be defeated
OPPOSITE **win**

loud *ADJECTIVE*

1 *We heard a **loud** bang.*
noisy
deafening
ear-splitting

2 *I don't like **loud** music.*
blaring

3 *He spoke in a **loud** voice.*

Use **booming** or **thunderous** for a deep voice: *'Come here!' he shouted in a **booming** voice.*

Use **shrill** or **piercing** for a high voice: *'Get away from me,' she shrieked in a **shrill** voice.*

OPPOSITE **quiet**

love *VERB*

1 *Anita **loves** her dog.*
to be very fond of
to adore

Use **worship** or **idolise** if you love someone and admire them a lot: *He **idolises** his older brother who is very good at football.*

2 *Sarah **loves** sport.*
to enjoy
to be very keen on
to be obsessed with
to be mad about
OPPOSITE **hate**

lovely *ADJECTIVE*

OVERUSED WORD

Here are some more interesting words you can use instead of **lovely**:

❶ *What a **lovely** picture!*
beautiful
gorgeous
delightful

❷ *You look **lovely** today.*
pretty
beautiful
attractive

Use **gorgeous** or **stunning** if someone is very lovely: *She looks absolutely **stunning** in that dress!*

Use **glamorous** if someone looks beautiful and rich: *The film stars all looked very **glamorous**.*

❸ *The food was **lovely**.*
delicious
tasty

❹ *These flowers smell **lovely**.*
beautiful
fragrant
perfumed

❺ *He's a **lovely** boy.*
kind
pleasant
charming
polite

❻ *It was a **lovely** day for sports day.*
beautiful
warm
sunny
glorious
wonderful

❼ *We had a **lovely** time on holiday.*
enjoyable
wonderful
fantastic
OPPOSITE **horrible**

low *ADJECTIVE*

❶ *We sat on a **low** bench under the tree.*
small

❷ *We shop there because their prices are **low**.*
reasonable
reduced

❸ *He spoke in a **low** voice.*
soft
deep
OPPOSITE **high**

luck *NOUN*

*It was just by **luck** that Sophie phoned me when she did.*
chance
accident
coincidence

luckily *ADVERB*

***Luckily** I caught the cup before it hit the floor.*
fortunately
by good luck

lucky *ADJECTIVE*

*We were **lucky** it didn't rain.*
fortunate
in luck
OPPOSITE **unlucky**

luggage *NOUN*

*We put all our **luggage** on the train.*
bags
suitcases
baggage

lump *NOUN*

❶ *She gave him a **lump** of cheese.*
a piece
a chunk
a block
a wedge

❷ *I've got a **lump** on my head where I hit it.*
a bump
a swelling
a bulge

machine *NOUN*
*They have a special **machine** for cutting the metal.*
an appliance
a contraption
a tool
a device

magic *NOUN*
1 *He said he could do **magic** to make rain fall.*
sorcery
witchcraft
wizardry

2 *There was a conjurer at the party who performed some **magic**.*
conjuring
tricks

magician *NOUN*
1 *He was taken prisoner by an evil **magician**.*
a wizard
a sorcerer
an enchanter

2 *The children watched the **magician** doing magic tricks.*
a conjuror

magnificent *ADJECTIVE*
*The king lived in a **magnificent** palace.*
grand
splendid
wonderful

main *ADJECTIVE*
*The **main** ingredient of bread is flour.*
most important
principal
chief
essential
basic
major

mainly *ADVERB*
*Spiders **mainly** eat insects.*
chiefly
mostly
principally
primarily

make *VERB* **makes, making, made**
1 *We managed to **make** a shelter out of some old pieces of wood.*
to build
to form
to construct
to create
to put together

2 *They **make** cars in that factory.*
to produce
to manufacture
to assemble

3 *The heat of the sun can be used to **make** electricity.*
to generate
to produce
to create

4 *We **made** some cakes and biscuits for the party.*
to bake
to cook
to prepare

5 *You can **make** this old dish into a bird bath.*
to change
to turn
to transform

6 *Please don't **make** too much mess.*
to create
to cause

7 *They **made** me clean the floor although I didn't have time.*
to force
to order *They **ordered** me to clean the floor.*

man *NOUN*
*I'll ask the **man** in the ticket office.*
a gentleman
a bloke *(informal)*
a guy *(informal)*
a chap *(informal)*
A **bachelor** is an unmarried man.
A **husband** is a married man.
A **father** is a man who has children.
A **widower** is a man whose wife has died.

manage *VERB*
1 *I finally **managed** to open the door.*
to succeed in *I finally **succeeded** in opening the door.*
2 *His father **manages** a shop.*
to run
to be in charge of
to look after

manager *NOUN*
*My mum is the **manager** of an office.*
the director
the head
the chief

map *NOUN*
*He drew a **map** to show us how to get to the school.*
a plan
a diagram

mark *NOUN*
1 *There were dirty **marks** all over the wall.*
a stain
a spot
a smear
a smudge
a streak
2 *The deer had left **marks** in the snow on the ground.*
tracks
footprints
a trail

mark *VERB*
1 *The mud has **marked** the carpet.*
to stain
to dirty
to blot
2 *The teacher **marked** our spelling tests.*
to correct
to grade

market *NOUN*
*You can buy all sorts of things at the **market**.*
a bazaar
a street market
a car boot sale

marvellous *ADJECTIVE*
*We had a **marvellous** holiday and were sad to come home.*
wonderful
brilliant
great
fantastic
perfect

mass *NOUN*
1 *There was a **mass** of rubbish to clear away.*
a heap
a pile
a mound
a stack
2 *There was a **mass** of people in front of the stage.*
a group
a crowd
a horde

massive *ADJECTIVE*
*They live in a **massive** house with seven bedrooms.*
enormous
huge
gigantic
colossal
immense
OPPOSITE **tiny**

match NOUN

❶ *We watched a football **match** on TV.*
a game

❷ *We went to see a boxing **match** at the local gym.*
a contest
a fight

match VERB

❶ *Your T-shirt **matches** your eyes.*
to go with
to tone with
to blend with

❷ *You have to **match** the word to the picture.*
to connect
to put together

material NOUN

❶ *Stone is a good building **material**.*
a substance

❷ *Her skirt was made of bright yellow **material**.*
cloth
fabric

WORD WEB

Some types of **material**:

corduroy
cotton
denim
fleece
linen
lycra™
nylon
polyester
satin
silk
velvet
wool

maybe ADVERB

*I don't know why they're late. **Maybe** they missed the bus.*
perhaps
possibly
OPPOSITE **definitely**

meal NOUN

WORD WEB

Some types of **meal**:

breakfast
brunch
dinner
lunch
tea
supper

A feast is a big meal.
A snack is a small meal.
A picnic is a meal outside.
A barbecue is a meal that you cook outside.
A buffet is a meal where people help themselves to food, usually cold.

mean ADJECTIVE

❶ *That was a really **mean** thing to do and it hurt my feelings.*
unkind
nasty
selfish
cruel
vindictive
OPPOSITE **kind**

❷ *He's really **mean** with his money.*
stingy
tight-fisted
miserly
OPPOSITE **generous**

mean VERB means, meaning, meant

❶ *We **meant** to be home by six but there was a lot of traffic.*
to intend
to aim
to plan

❷ *What does that sign **mean**?*
to signify
to indicate
to say
to stand for

meaning NOUN
*I don't know the **meaning** of that word.*
the significance
the definition
The moral is the meaning of a story: *The **moral** of the story is, think before you act.*

measurement NOUN
*We wrote down the **measurements** of the room.*
the size
the dimensions
the length
the width
the breadth
the height
the depth

medium ADJECTIVE
*I am **medium** height for my age.*
average
normal
ordinary

meet VERB **meets, meeting, met**
1 *We'll **meet** at the swimming pool at 11 a.m.*
to meet up
to get together

2 *Mum will **meet** us at the shops later.*
to join
to see

3 *As I was walking along the lane, I **met** my friend Poppy.*
to encounter
to see
to bump into
to run into
to come across

4 *I haven't **met** our new neighbours yet and they've lived here for a month now.*
to get to know
to be introduced to *I haven't been **introduced** to them yet.*

5 *Two rivers **meet** here.*
to join
to come together
to merge
to converge

meeting NOUN
*The teachers are having a **meeting**.*
a gathering
a discussion
a conference
a get-together

melt VERB
*The ice **melted** in the heat of the sun.*
to thaw
to soften
to unfreeze

memory NOUN
1 *He has a bad **memory**—he forgets everything.*
recall
recollection

2 *I will keep this in my **memory** for ever.*
mind
remembrance

mend VERB
1 *Do you think you can **mend** my bike?*
to repair
to fix

2 *Dad likes **mending** old furniture.*
to do up
to restore
to renovate

3 *I need to **mend** these jeans.*
to sew up
to patch

To darn is to mend socks or knitted clothes.

mention VERB
1 *Nobody **mentioned** the stolen money.*
to talk about
to refer to
to allude to

2 *She **mentioned** that she was hungry.*
to say
to remark

merry ADJECTIVE
*They clapped their hands and sang a **merry** song.*
happy
cheerful
joyful
jolly
OPPOSITE **sad**

mess NOUN
1 *Who's going to clear up all this **mess**?*
clutter
untidiness
litter
disorder

2 *The papers were all in a terrible **mess**.*
a muddle
a jumble

message NOUN
*She sent me a **message** to say that she was ill.*
a letter
a note
an email
a text message

messy ADJECTIVE
*Tidy up this **messy** room!*
untidy
cluttered
dirty
disorganised
OPPOSITE **neat**

met VERB *(past tense and past participle of* meet*)*

method NOUN
*The book shows the **method** for making pancakes.*
the technique
the way
the procedure

middle NOUN
1 *There was a big puddle in the **middle** of the playground.*
the centre
the midpoint

2 *They live right in the **middle** of London.*
the centre
the heart

3 *Is it possible to dig to the **middle** of the earth?*
the core
the centre

mild ADJECTIVE
1 *The soup had a **mild** flavour.*
delicate
subtle
bland
OPPOSITE **strong**

2 *It was only a **mild** illness.*
slight
OPPOSITE **severe**

3 *The weather was quite **mild**.*
warm
pleasant
balmy

mind NOUN
*I can't keep all those facts in my **mind**.*
brain
head
memory

mind VERB
*I don't **mind** if you're a bit late.*
to object
to care
to be bothered

miserable ADJECTIVE
*I felt really **miserable** when all my friends left.*
unhappy
depressed
gloomy
wretched
OPPOSITE **cheerful**

misery *NOUN*
*There was **misery** on everyone's faces as the other team scored again.*
grief
sadness
sorrow
unhappiness
despair
gloom
OPPOSITE **joy**

miss *VERB*
1 *I just **missed** hitting him with my bike.*
to avoid

2 *I tried to catch the ball, but I **missed** it.*
to drop

3 *Hurry or you'll **miss** the bus.*
to be late for

4 *I really **missed** my brother when he was away.*
to long for
to pine for

missing *ADJECTIVE*
*My phone is **missing**.*
lost
nowhere to be found *The phone was **nowhere to be found**.*

mission *NOUN*
*He was sent on a secret **mission** to find the spy.*
a task
a voyage
an expedition
a quest

mist *NOUN*
*They got lost in the **mist**.*
fog
haze

mistake *NOUN*
1 *I knew I had made a **mistake**.*
an error

A **blunder** is a bad mistake: *John knew that he had made a terrible **blunder**.*

A **slip** or a **slip-up** is a small mistake: *If she made even one **slip** she would be caught.*

An **oversight** is a mistake you make when you forget to do something: *My name was missed off the list because of an **oversight**.*

2 *There must be a **mistake** in your calculations.*
an error
an inaccuracy

3 *The teacher corrected my **mistakes**.*
a spelling mistake
a misspelling

mix *VERB*
1 ***Mix** red and yellow to make orange.*
to blend
to combine
to put together

2 ***Mix** all the ingredients together in a bowl.*
to stir
to blend
to beat
to whisk

mixed *ADJECTIVE*
*We had fish with **mixed** vegetables.*
various
assorted
miscellaneous

mixture *NOUN*
1 *She dipped her finger into the cake **mixture**.*
mix

2 *Purple is a **mixture** of blue and yellow.*
a blend
a combination

3 *We had pizza with a **mixture** of different vegetables.*
a variety
an assortment

moan *VERB*
1 *He **moaned** with pain.*
to groan
to wail

A B C D E F G H I J K L Mm N O P Q R S T U V W X Y Z

2 *Stop **moaning** about everything!*
to complain
to grumble
to whinge
to whine

model NOUN
*They made a **model** of a space ship.*
a copy
a replica
a representation

modern ADJECTIVE
1 *She likes to wear very **modern** clothes.*
fashionable
trendy
stylish

2 *The factory is full of very **modern** machinery.*
new
up-to-date
high-tech
state-of-the-art
cutting-edge
OPPOSITE **old-fashioned**

modest ADJECTIVE
1 *She was very **modest** about all her achievements.*
humble
self-effacing
OPPOSITE **conceited**

2 *He was too **modest** to walk around in his swimming trunks.*
shy
bashful
coy

money NOUN
1 *I need some **money** for my bus fare.*
cash
change
coins
silver
coppers
notes
currency

2 *His family has got lots of **money**.*
wealth
riches

3 *He earns **money** by working in a hospital.*
wages
a salary
an income
pay

4 *My parents give me **money** every week.*
pocket money
an allowance

5 *Have you got any **money** in the bank?*
savings
funds

monster NOUN
*A huge **monster** was coming towards them.*
a beast
a creature

WRITING TIPS

Here are some useful words for writing about **monsters**:

- *The **huge**, **ugly** giant was coming towards us.*
- *The ogre was **hideous**, with a **horrible**, **hairy** face.*
- *In the cave lived a **fierce** and **terrible** dragon.*
- *The **terrifying** dragon was **huge**, with green **scaly** skin.*
- *We had heard stories of a **fearsome** werewolf that lived in the forest.*

Griswold Gristle and Judge Cedric were stumbling through the wood, running as if all the monsters in the world were after them.—MEASLE AND THE SLITHERGOUL, Ian Ogilvy

WORD WEB

Some types of **monster**:

a dragon
a giant
an ogre
a troll
a vampire
a werewolf

moody *ADJECTIVE*

*Why are you so **moody** with everyone today?*

bad-tempered
sulky
grumpy
irritable
sullen

OPPOSITE **cheerful**

mountain *NOUN*

*We could see the **mountains** in the distance.*

a hill
a peak

A mountain range is a group of mountains.

move *VERB*

OVERUSED WORD

Here are some more interesting words you can use instead of **move**:

1 *We **moved** the table into the corner.*

to push
to pull
to carry

Use **drag** when something is very heavy: *They **dragged** the heavy crate outside.*

2 *The train **moved** out of the station.*

Use **to speed**, **to hurtle**, **to whizz** or **to zoom** when something moves very quickly: *A sports car **zoomed** past us.*

Use **to dart**, **to dash** or **to race** when a person moves very quickly and suddenly: *He suddenly **darted** out from behind a bush.*

Use **to crawl**, **to creep** or **to trundle** when something moves very slowly: *The train **crawled** along at 25 miles per hour.*

Use **to glide**, **to slide**, **to float** or **to drift** when something moves smoothly and gracefully: *The little boat **drifted** slowly through the water.*

Use **to rise**, **to climb** or **to ascend** when something moves upwards: *The rocket **ascended** into space.*

Use **to fall**, **to descend**, **to drop** or **to sink** when something moves downwards: *The hot-air balloon **sank** gently down to the ground.*

Use **to stir**, **to sway**, **to wave**, **to flap** or **to shake** when something moves about: *The trees **swayed** gently in the breeze.*

Use **to totter**, **to stagger** or **to stumble** when someone moves in an unsteady way as if they are going to fall: *He was **tottering** along carrying a huge pile of plates.*

Use **to spin**, **to turn**, **to rotate**, **to revolve**, **to twirl** or **to whirl** when something moves round and round: *The dancers **whirled** round and round.*

mud *NOUN*

*His boots were covered in **mud**.*

dirt
muck
clay
sludge

muddle *NOUN*

*My school books were in a terrible **muddle**.*

a mess
a jumble

muddy *ADJECTIVE*

*Don't come in here in those **muddy** boots!*

mucky
filthy
dirty

music *NOUN*

WORD WEB

Some types of **music**:

blues
classical
country
folk
jazz
opera
pop
rap
reggae
rock

Some stringed instruments:

a banjo
a cello
a double bass
a guitar
a harp
a mandolin
a sitar
a ukulele
a viola
a violin

Some woodwind instruments:

a bassoon
a clarinet
a flute
an oboe
a piccolo
a recorder

Some brass instruments:

a bugle
a cornet
a horn
a saxophone
a trombone
a trumpet
a tuba

Some keyboard instruments:

an accordion
a harpsichord
a keyboard
an organ
a piano

Some percussion instruments:

cymbals
a drum
a glockenspiel
a tambourine
a triangle
a xylophone

Some types of musician:

a performer
a player
a singer
a composer

mysterious *ADJECTIVE*

*She disappeared in a very **mysterious** way.*

strange
weird
puzzling
baffling
mystifying
curious

mystery *NOUN*

*The police finally solved the **mystery** of the crime.*

a puzzle
a riddle
a secret
an enigma

Nn

name *NOUN*

*What is your **name**?*

a first name
a surname
a family name

nasty *ADJECTIVE*

1 *Don't be **nasty** to your brother.*

horrible
unpleasant
mean
spiteful
unkind
obnoxious
horrid
malevolent
OPPOSITE **nice**

2 *There was a **nasty** smell in the kitchen.*

horrible
unpleasant
revolting
disgusting
foul
repellent
OPPOSITE **nice**

3 *She's got a **nasty** cut on her arm.*

bad
awful
terrible

natural *ADJECTIVE*

1 *This jumper is made of **natural** wool.*

real
genuine
pure
OPPOSITE **artificial**

2 *It's **natural** to feel upset when your pet dies.*

normal
ordinary
usual
OPPOSITE **unnatural**

naughty *ADJECTIVE*

*The children were being really **naughty** and their mum told them off.*

bad
badly behaved
disobedient
mischievous
disruptive
bad-mannered
rude
OPPOSITE **well-behaved**

near *ADJECTIVE*

*Our house is **near** the school.*

close to
next to
beside

nearly *ADVERB*

*I've **nearly** finished my drink.*

almost
virtually
just about
practically

neat *ADJECTIVE*

1 *Her bedroom is always very **neat**.*

tidy
clean
orderly
spick and span

2 *He looked very **neat** in his new uniform.*

smart
elegant
well-turned-out
OPPOSITE **untidy**

necessary *ADJECTIVE*
*It is **necessary** to water plants in dry weather.*
important
essential
vital
crucial
OPPOSITE **unnecessary**

necklace *NOUN*
*She was wearing a lovely **necklace** around her neck.*
a chain
a pendant
beads
A locket is a necklace with a picture in a small case.

need *VERB*
1 *All plants and animals **need** water.*
to require
to depend on
to rely on
to want

2 *You **need** to finish your homework.*
to have to *You **have to** finish your homework.*
should *You **should** finish your homework.*
must *You **must** finish your homework.*

neighbourhood *NOUN*
*There are lots of shops in my **neighbourhood**.*
an area
a district
a community

nervous *ADJECTIVE*
1 *Are you **nervous** about starting school?*
worried
anxious
apprehensive

2 *The horses seemed very **nervous**.*
jumpy
agitated
fearful
panicky
tense
OPPOSITE **calm**

new *ADJECTIVE*
1 *She was wearing a **new** dress.*
brand new

2 *The hospital has got a lot of **new** equipment.*
modern
up-to-date
state-of-the-art
high-tech
cutting-edge
latest *The hospital has got a lot of the **latest** equipment.*

3 *See if you can think of some **new** ideas.*
fresh
different
original
novel
innovative
OPPOSITE **old**

next *ADJECTIVE*
1 *They live in the **next** street.*
nearest
closest
adjacent

2 *They set off the **next** day.*
following

nice *ADJECTIVE*

OVERUSED WORD

Try to use a more interesting word when you want to say **nice**. Here are some other words you can use instead:

❶ *You look very **nice** with your hair short.*

Use **pretty**, **beautiful** or **lovely** to describe a woman or girl. Use **handsome** to describe a boy or man. Use **gorgeous** or **stunning** for someone who looks very nice: *You look absolutely **stunning** in that dress.*

Use **glamorous** for someone who looks rich: *All the pop stars were arriving for the ceremony looking very **glamorous**.*

❷ *She likes wearing **nice** clothes.*
pretty
lovely
beautiful
smart
elegant

Use **fashionable** or **stylish** for clothes that look good and modern: *I saw a pair of really **stylish** shoes that I want to buy.*

❸ *The food was very **nice**.*
delicious
tasty
mouth-watering

❹ *Some of the flowers smell very **nice**.*
pleasant
fragrant
perfumed

❺ *Did you have a **nice** holiday?*
pleasant
lovely
enjoyable
wonderful
fantastic

❻ *He's a very **nice** boy.*
friendly
kind
likeable
pleasant

Use **helpful** or **thoughtful** for someone who thinks about other people or helps other people: *It was very **thoughtful** of you to unpack the shopping for me.*

Use **charming** or **polite** for someone who behaves well and isn't rude to people: *Remember to be **polite** to your aunt and uncle.*

❼ *I hope we have **nice** weather for our trip to the beach.*
fine
lovely
pleasant
beautiful
warm
sunny

Use **glorious** or **wonderful** for weather that is very nice: *It was a **glorious** hot summer's day.*

OPPOSITE **horrible**

night *NOUN*
I woke up during the ***night****.*
night-time

Dark is the time during the night when it is dark: *When I got home it was* ***dark****.*

OPPOSITE **day**

noise *NOUN*

❶ *There's too much* ***noise****!*
commotion
din
racket
row
rumpus
uproar

❷ *I heard a sudden* ***noise****.*
a sound
a bang
a clang
a clank
a scream
a shout

A **screech** is a loud screaming sound: *We heard the* ***screech*** *of the racing cars' tyres.*

A **clatter** is the sound of things banging against each other: *The plates fell to the floor with a* ***clatter****.*

A **thud** or **thump** is the sound of something heavy falling to the floor: *The book fell to the floor with a* ***thud****.*

A **roar** or **rumble** is a long, low sound: *We heard a* ***rumble*** *of thunder in the distance.*

A **squeak** is a very high sound: *The gate opened with a* ***squeak****.*

noisy *ADJECTIVE*

❶ *The car engines are so* ***noisy*** *that we can't hear ourselves speak.*
loud
deafening
ear-splitting

❷ *She asked the children not to be so* ***noisy*** *as she was trying to sleep.*
loud
rowdy
boisterous

OPPOSITE **quiet**

nonsense *NOUN*
*Don't talk **nonsense**!*
rubbish
drivel
gibberish
gobbledegook

normal *ADJECTIVE*
1 *It's quite **normal** to feel tired at the end of the day.*
natural
common
usual
OPPOSITE **abnormal**

2 *It looked like a **normal** car but she'd been told that it was very expensive.*
ordinary
standard
typical
average
everyday
OPPOSITE **special**

normally *ADVERB*
*I **normally** go to bed at eight o'clock.*
usually
generally
as a rule

nosy *ADJECTIVE*
*Don't be so **nosy**!*

Use **inquisitive** or **curious** when someone wants to know about something: *I was **curious** to know why Oscar wasn't at school.*

Use **snooping** or **prying** when someone wants to know too much about something: *I wish those **snooping** kids would mind their own business!*

note *NOUN*
*I found a **note** saying that he would be home for tea.*
a letter
a message
a reminder

notice *NOUN*
*We put up a **notice** to tell people about our play.*
a poster
a sign
an announcement
an advertisement

notice *VERB*
*I **noticed** that there were no lights on in the house.*
to observe
to see
to spot

nuisance *NOUN*
*The rain was a **nuisance**.*
a problem
a pain

Use **inconvenience** for something that causes you a lot of problems: *It was a terrible **inconvenience** when the bus was cancelled.*

Use **pest** for a person or animal that annoys you: *My little sister is such a **pest**!*

number *NOUN*
1 *Can you add up those **numbers**?*
a figure
a digit
a numeral

2 *Make sure you have the right **number** of chairs.*
a quantity

Use **amount** for something you cannot count: *Make sure you add the right **amount** of milk.*

A B C D E F G H I J K L M N Oo P Q R S T U V W X Y Z

Oo

obey *VERB*
*You must **obey** the rules.*
to abide by *You must **abide by** the rules.*
to not break *You must **not break** the rules.*
OPPOSITE **disobey**

object *NOUN*
*We found some interesting **objects** in the cupboard.*
a thing
an article
an item

obvious *ADJECTIVE*
*It was **obvious** that he was lying.*
clear
plain
apparent
evident

obviously *ADVERB*
1 *Mine was **obviously** the best.*
clearly
evidently
undeniably
unmistakeably

2 ***Obviously**, you need to know the password.*
of course
clearly
naturally

occasionally *ADVERB*
*We **occasionally** go swimming.*
sometimes
from time to time
now and then

odd *ADJECTIVE*
*It seemed **odd** that there were no lights on in the house.*
strange
funny
peculiar
curious
weird
OPPOSITE **normal**

offend *VERB*
*It might **offend** her if you don't say thank you.*
to upset
to insult
to annoy
to displease
to affront

offer *VERB*
1 *She **offered** me a piece of cake with my tea.*
to give
to hand
to pass

2 *Tom **offered** to wash up all the dishes after dinner.*
to volunteer

often *ADVERB*
*We **often** go swimming on Saturdays.*
frequently
regularly

Use **repeatedly**, **again and again** or **time after time** for something that happens a number of times: *I tried **again and again**, but I couldn't open the door.*

ogre *NOUN*
*They said that an **ogre** lived in the forest.*
a monster
a beast
a troll

old ADJECTIVE

OVERUSED WORD

Try to use a more interesting word when you want to say **old**. Here are some other words you can use instead:

1 *My grandmother is quite **old**.*
elderly
aged
OPPOSITE **young**

2 *Can we get a new TV? This one is too **old**!*

Use **ancient** for something that is very old: *I found some **ancient** maps in the attic.*

Use **old-fashioned** or **out-of-date** for something that isn't very modern: *There was an **old-fashioned** radio in the kitchen.*
OPPOSITE **new**

3 *My dad collects **old** coins.*
ancient

Use **antique** for something that is old and valuable: *My aunt told me off for putting a cup on her **antique** table.*
OPPOSITE **modern**

4 *He was wearing some **old** jeans.*
tatty
tattered
shabby
scruffy
worn-out
OPPOSITE **new**

open ADJECTIVE

*Someone had left the door **open** and the dog got out into the garden.*
ajar
wide open
unlocked
unfastened
OPPOSITE **closed**

open VERB

1 *He **opened** the door.*
to unlock
to push open

Use **fling open** or **throw open** when you open something suddenly or roughly: *Jack **flung open** the door to the attic and cried, 'Go and see for yourselves!'*

Use **break down** when you open a door by breaking it: *The police had to **break down** the door to get into the house.*

2 *The door **opened**.*
to swing open

Use **burst open** or **fly open** when something opens suddenly or quickly: *Suddenly, the door **burst open** and the teacher marched in, looking very angry.*
OPPOSITE **close**

opening NOUN

*We crawled through a small **opening** in the fence.*
a gap
a hole
a space
a crack
a chink

opinion NOUN

*What's your **opinion** about what happened?*
a view
a belief
a point of view
an impression

opposite *ADJECTIVE*

❶ *They live on the* ***opposite*** *side of the road.*

facing

❷ *North is the* ***opposite*** *direction to south.*

different

opposing

order *NOUN*

You must obey my ***orders*** *or things could go wrong.*

a command

an instruction

order *VERB*

❶ *He* ***ordered*** *us to stand still.*

to tell

to command

to instruct

to demand *He* ***demanded*** *that we stand still.*

❷ *We* ***ordered*** *some sandwiches and drinks.*

to ask for

to request

to send for

ordinary *ADJECTIVE*

❶ *It was just an* ***ordinary*** *day but we had a great time.*

normal

usual

typical

everyday

routine

unexciting

❷ *It's just an* ***ordinary*** *house.*

normal

standard

average

regular

OPPOSITE **special**

organise *(also* **organize***) VERB*

Our teacher ***organised*** *a trip to the zoo.*

to arrange

to plan

to set up

original *ADJECTIVE*

❶ *Try to think of some* ***original*** *ideas for your stories.*

new

fresh

imaginative

innovative

❷ *The* ***original*** *version has been lost.*

first

earliest

initial

outfit *NOUN*

I wore a special ***outfit*** *for my dance show.*

clothes

a costume

outing *NOUN*

We went on an ***outing*** *to the country park.*

a trip

an excursion

an expedition

own *VERB*

Do you ***own*** *a bike?*

to have

to possess

➤ **own up**

He ***owned up*** *to stealing the money.*

to admit *He* ***admitted*** *stealing the money.*

to confess *He* ***confessed*** *to stealing the money.*

owner *NOUN*

The ***owner*** *of the shop asked us what we wanted.*

manager

proprietor

boss

Pp

pack *VERB*
*We **packed** everything into the car.*
to put
to load
to stow
to cram

package *NOUN*
1 *The postman delivered a **package** for my birthday.*
a parcel

2 *Read the cooking instructions on the **package**.*
a packet
a box
a pack
a carton

page *NOUN*
*There's a lovely picture on the next **page**.*
a sheet
a side

paid *VERB* (past tense and past participle of pay)

pain *NOUN*
1 *I've got a **pain** in my stomach and I feel sick.*

Use **ache** for a pain that continues for a long time: *I could still feel an **ache** in my leg where the horse had kicked me.*

Use **twinge** or **pang** for a sudden sharp pain: *I felt a sudden **twinge** in my leg as I was running.*

Use **soreness** or **irritation** for a pain on the surface of your skin: *I felt **soreness** where the strap had rubbed my heel.*

Use **discomfort** for slight pain: *You'll feel a little **discomfort** from the injection.*

2 *She was in terrible **pain** before she had her operation.*
agony
suffering

painful *ADJECTIVE*
*Is your knee still **painful** from when you injured it playing football?*
sore
hurting
aching
tender
throbbing

pair *NOUN*
*The teacher told us to work in **pairs**.*
twos
partners *The teacher told us to work as **partners**.*

A couple is two people who are married or who are each other's girlfriend or boyfriend: *They danced in **couples**.*

pale *ADJECTIVE*
1 *She looked very tired and **pale**.*
white
white-faced
pallid
pasty
wan

2 *He was wearing a **pale** blue shirt.*
light
faded
pastel
OPPOSITE **bright**

pant *VERB*
*He was **panting** by the time he reached the top of the hill.*
to gasp
to gasp for breath
to puff
to huff and puff
to wheeze

paper *NOUN*

WORD WEB

Some types of **paper**:

card
cardboard
newspaper
notepaper
tissue paper
tracing paper
wrapping paper
writing paper

part *NOUN*

1 *He kept a small **part** of the cake for himself.*
a bit
a piece
a portion
a section

A fraction is a very small part: *We only ate a **fraction** of all the food that was there.*

2 *We have completed the first **part** of our journey.*
a stage
a phase

3 *This is a beautiful **part** of the country.*
an area
a region

4 *Which **part** of the city do you live in?*
an area
a district
a neighbourhood

particular *ADJECTIVE*

1 *There was one **particular** dress that she really liked.*
specific
special

2 *She has her own **particular** way of writing.*
individual
personal
special
unique

partner *NOUN*

*Choose a **partner** to work with on the project.*
a friend
a companion
a colleague
a helper

party *NOUN*

*Are you having a **party**?*
a birthday party
a celebration
a gathering
a disco
a dance

pass *VERB*

1 *I **pass** this shop every day on my way to school.*
to go past
to go by

2 *We **passed** an old van which was driving slowly along the road.*
to overtake

3 *Could you **pass** me the salt, please?*
to hand
to give

passage *NOUN*

1 *We walked down a narrow **passage** to the kitchen.*
a corridor
a passageway
a walkway

2 *They say there's a secret **passage** under the castle.*
a tunnel

pat *VERB*
*He **patted** the dog on the head.*
to touch
to stroke
to tap

path *NOUN*
*We walked along the **path**.*
a footpath
a track
A bridleway is a path for horses.

patience *NOUN*
*Our teacher has lots of **patience** and never gets angry.*
tolerance
composure
OPPOSITE **impatience**

patient *ADJECTIVE*
*Lunch isn't quite ready yet, so please be **patient**.*
calm
tolerant
OPPOSITE **impatient**

pattern *NOUN*
*She was wearing a blue dress with a white **pattern**.*
a design
a decoration

pause *VERB*
*He **paused** before opening the door.*
to stop
to wait
to hesitate
to delay

pause *NOUN*
*Let's have a **pause** for lunch.*
a break
an interval
a rest
a halt

pay *NOUN*
*You will get your **pay** at the end of the week.*
wages
salary

pay *VERB* **pays, paying, paid**
1 *He **paid** a lot of money for that bike.*
to give
to spend
to fork out (informal) *He **forked out** a lot of money on that bike.*

2 *If you let me have the game now, I'll **pay** you tomorrow.*
to repay
to reimburse

peace *NOUN*
1 *After the war ended there was **peace** between the two countries.*
friendliness
harmony
an agreement
a truce

2 *We sat on the bench and enjoyed the **peace**.*
quiet
silence
calm
tranquillity
peacefulness
stillness

peaceful *ADJECTIVE*

*It seemed very **peaceful** when the baby had gone to sleep.*

quiet
silent
still
calm
tranquil
OPPOSITE **noisy**

peculiar *ADJECTIVE*

*This cheese has a **peculiar** taste.*

strange
funny
odd
curious
bizarre
extraordinary
OPPOSITE **normal**

people *NOUN*

1 *The streets were full of **people** strolling around in the sun.*

folk
men and women

2 *The president was elected by the **people** of his country.*

the public
the population
the citizens

perfect *ADJECTIVE*

1 *The sun is shining and it's a **perfect** day for a picnic.*

ideal
excellent
idyllic

2 *This is a **perfect** piece of work—I can't find anything wrong with it.*

excellent
flawless
faultless
OPPOSITE **imperfect**

perform *VERB*

1 *The children were excited to see an opera **performed** for the first time.*

to put on
to present

2 *I don't like **performing** in public.*

to act
to dance
to sing
to be on stage

perhaps *ADVERB*

***Perhaps** we'll see you at the park tomorrow.*

maybe
possibly

person *NOUN*

1 *I saw a **person** walking towards me.*

a man
a woman
an adult
a grown-up
a child
a teenager
a boy
a girl
a baby
a toddler

2 *He's a very unpleasant **person**.*

an individual
a character
a human being

personality *NOUN*
*She's got a lovely **personality** and has got a lot of friends.*
a character
a nature
a temperament
a disposition

persuade *VERB*
1 *She **persuaded** her mum to take her swimming.*
to encourage
to urge
to convince
to talk someone into *She **talked** her mum **into** taking her swimming.*

2 *The kitten was hiding under a chair and I tried to **persuade** it to come out.*
to tempt
to coax *I tried to **coax** it out.*
to entice *I tried to **entice** it out.*

pester *VERB*
*My little brother kept **pestering** me when I was trying to read.*
to annoy
to bother
to harass
to hassle
to plague
to bug *(informal)*

Use **nag** or **badger** when you keep reminding someone to do something: *My mum keeps **nagging** me to do my homework.*

phone *VERB*
*I **phoned** my grandma to ask how she was after her fall.*
to call
to ring
to ring up
to telephone
to give someone a ring *I **gave** my grandma **a ring**.*

phone *NOUN*
*There are maths games you can play on your **phone**.*
telephone
mobile
mobile phone
mobile device
smartphone

photograph *NOUN*
*I took a **photograph** of my sister.*
a photo
a picture
a shot
a snapshot
a snap

phrase *NOUN*
*What does the **phrase** 'out of order' mean?*
an expression
a saying
an idiom

pick *VERB*
1 *I didn't know which cake to **pick**.*
to choose
to select
to decide on
to single out
to settle on
to opt for

2 *We **picked** some blackberries for tea.*
to gather
to collect
to harvest

3 *She **picked** some flowers to put in a vase on the table.*
to pluck
to cut

➤ **pick up**
*She **picked up** the book off the floor.*
to lift
to raise

picture *NOUN*

WORD WEB

Some types of **picture**:

A caricature is a funny picture of a real person.
a cartoon
a drawing
An illustration is a picture in a book.
An image is a picture in a film or on the computer.
a painting
a photograph
A portrait is a picture of a person.
A sketch is a rough drawing.

a painting

a portrait

a photograph

a landscape

a caricature

a sketch

piece *NOUN*

1 *She gave me a huge* ***piece*** *of cake.*
a bit
a slice
A **sliver** is a thin piece: *She cut herself a tiny* ***sliver*** *of cake.*
A **wedge** is a thick piece: *He was eating a huge* ***wedge*** *of chocolate cake.*
A **square** is a small square piece: *Would you like a* ***square*** *of chocolate?*
A **lump**, **chunk**, **block** or **slab** is a big thick piece: *There was a big* ***slab*** *of concrete in the road.*

2 *We need another* ***piece*** *of wood.*
a bit
a block
a plank

3 *She handed me a* ***piece*** *of paper.*
a bit
a sheet
A **scrap** is a small piece of paper.

4 *We need a new* ***piece*** *of glass for that window.*
a sheet
a pane

5 *I found* ***pieces*** *of broken plate.*
a bit
a chip
A **fragment** is a very small piece: *There were some tiny* ***fragments*** *of glass on the floor.*

6 *My dress was torn to* ***pieces****.*
shreds *My dress was torn to* ***shreds****.*

pile *NOUN*

There was a ***pile*** *of dirty clothes on the floor.*
a heap
a mound
a stack
a mountain

pillar *NOUN*

The roof was held up by large stone ***pillars****.*
a column
a post
a support

pipe *NOUN*

There was water coming out of the ***pipe****.*
a hose
a tube
A pipeline is a pipe carrying oil or water over a long distance.

pirate *NOUN*

The ship was attacked by ***pirates****.*
a buccaneer

pity *NOUN*

1 *She felt great* ***pity*** *for the hungry children.*
sympathy
understanding
concern

2 *The soldiers showed no* ***pity*** *to their enemies.*
mercy
kindness
compassion

3 *It's a* ***pity*** *you can't come to the party.*
a shame

place *NOUN*

1 *A cross marks the* ***place*** *where the treasure is buried.*
a spot
a position
a point
a location
a site

2 *Our school is in a very nice* ***place****.*
an area
a district
a neighbourhood
a town
a city
a village

3 *Save me a **place** next to you.*
a chair
a seat

plain ADJECTIVE
*His house was quite small and **plain**.*
ordinary
simple
basic
modest
OPPOSITE **fancy**

plan NOUN
1 *He has a **plan** for the weekend.*
an idea
a scheme
a plot
a schedule

2 *We drew a **plan** of the town to show where we all live.*
a map
a diagram
a drawing
a chart
a sketch

3 *I made a **plan** for my story.*
a framework
a structure
a design

plan VERB
1 *When do you **plan** to leave?*
to intend
to aim

2 *He thinks they are **planning** to go to the park without him*
to plot
to scheme

3 *We need to **plan** this trip very carefully.*
to organise
to arrange
to prepare for

plane NOUN (see aircraft)

plant NOUN

WORD WEB

Some types of **plant**:

a bulb
a bush
a cactus
a fern
a flower
a herb
a shrub
a tree
a vegetable
a weed

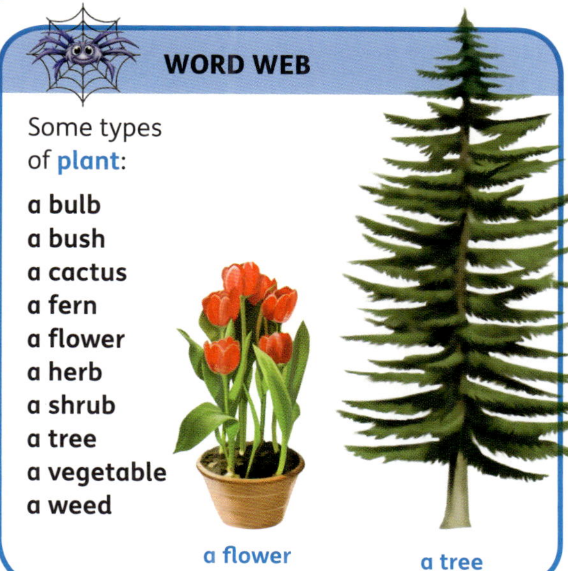

a flower
a tree

plate NOUN
*She brought out a **plate** of fruit.*
a dish
a platter
A **bowl** is a deep dish.

play NOUN
*The children are putting on a **play**.*
a show
a performance
a drama
A **comedy** is a funny play.
A **tragedy** is a sad play.

play VERB
1 *The children were **playing** on the beach.*
to have fun
to enjoy yourself
to amuse yourself

2 *Manchester United **play** Liverpool next week.*
to take on
to compete against
to oppose
to challenge

3 *She **played** a tune on the piano.*
to perform

A B C D E F G H I J K L M N O Pp Q R S T U V W X Y Z

player *NOUN*
*The **players** were getting ready for the game.*
a competitor
a contestant
a participant

playful *ADJECTIVE*
*Kittens can be **playful** and great fun.*
lively
mischievous
frisky
fun-loving
OPPOSITE **serious**

plead *VERB*
*I **pleaded** with my parents to let me go.*
to beg *I **begged** my parents to let me go.*
to implore *I **implored** my parents to let me go.*

pleasant *ADJECTIVE*
1 *We had a very **pleasant** time in the park.*
lovely
enjoyable
agreeable

Use **wonderful**, **fantastic** or **delightful** for something very pleasant: *We had a **wonderful** holiday in Spain.*

2 *He seems a very **pleasant** boy.*
friendly
kind
likeable

Use **thoughtful** if someone thinks about others: *It was **thoughtful** of you to buy me that.*

Use **charming** or **polite** for someone who behaves well and isn't rude to people: *He was always **polite** to his neighbours.*

3 *The weather was very **pleasant** and warm.*
lovely
fine
beautiful
sunny
glorious
wonderful
OPPOSITE **unpleasant**

pleased *ADJECTIVE*
*I was **pleased** that so many people came to my party.*
happy
glad
joyful

Use **delighted** or **thrilled** when you are very pleased about something: *I was **thrilled** when I won the first prize!*

Use **grateful** or **thankful** when you are pleased because someone has been kind to you: *I'm very **grateful** for all your help.*
OPPOSITE **annoyed**

pleasure *NOUN*
*She smiled with **pleasure** when she won first prize in the spelling bee.*
happiness
enjoyment
contentment
amusement

Use **delight** or **joy** for a feeling of great pleasure: *His face lit up with **delight** when he saw his family waiting for him.*

plot *VERB*
*I knew they were **plotting** to steal the jewels from the palace.*
to plan
to scheme

plot *NOUN*
*They had a secret **plot** to steal the money.*
a plan
a scheme
a conspiracy

plump *ADJECTIVE*
*The shopkeeper was a small, **plump** man.*
fat

Use **tubby**, **chubby** or **podgy** for someone who is slightly fat in a nice way: *There was a **chubby** smiling baby in the buggy.*

Use **stout** or **portly** for an older person who is quite fat: *Uncle Toby was a **portly** man.*

Use **overweight** or **obese** for someone who is so fat that they are unhealthy: *It's important to exercise so you don't become **overweight**.*
OPPOSITE **thin**

poem *NOUN*

WORD WEB

Some types of poem:

an acrostic
a calligram
a cinquain
a haiku
a limerick
a nursery rhyme
a rap
a sonnet

poetry *NOUN*

*She loves to write **poetry** and she read me some of her poems.*
verse
poems
rhymes

point *NOUN*

1 *Be careful, those scissors have a very sharp **point**.*
an end
a tip

2 *We soon reached the **point** where the two roads met.*
a place
a spot
a site
a location

3 *At that **point** I hadn't met her.*
a time
a moment
a stage

4 *What is the **point** of this game?*
the purpose
the aim
the object
the use

point *VERB*

1 *He **pointed** towards the castle.*
to indicate *He **indicated** the castle.*
to gesture towards

2 *I **pointed** the hose at the paddling pool.*
to aim
to direct

poisonous *ADJECTIVE*

1 *Some mushrooms are **poisonous**, so please don't eat ones that you pick.*
harmful
toxic

Use **deadly** or **lethal** when something is so poisonous that it can kill you: *Arsenic is a **deadly** poison.*

2 *She was bitten by a **poisonous** snake.*
venomous

poke *VERB*

1 *He **poked** the seaweed with a stick.*
to prod
to push
to jab

2 *She **poked** me in the back to get my attention.*
to nudge
to dig
to prod
to elbow

police officer *NOUN*

*The **police officer** warned us not to play near the road.*
a policeman
a policewoman
an officer
a constable
A detective is a police officer who investigates crimes: A ***detective*** was looking for clues at the scene.

polish *VERB*
*Dad **polished** my shoes for me.*
to shine
to buff

polite *ADJECTIVE*
*He's a very **polite** boy and always says thank you.*
well-mannered
respectful
courteous
civil
OPPOSITE **rude**

pollution *NOUN*
*There's a lot of **pollution** in the river.*
contamination
impurity
waste

poor *ADJECTIVE*
1 *His mother and father were very **poor**.*

Use **hard up** *(informal)* for someone who doesn't have much money to spend: *My dad's a bit **hard up** at the moment, so there's no point asking him for a new bike.*

Use **penniless** or **broke** *(informal)* for someone who does not have any money to spend: *I can't go to the fair because I'm absolutely **broke**!*

Use **needy** or **poverty-stricken** for someone who is very poor and doesn't have enough money for food: *We collect money to help **needy** children.*
OPPOSITE **rich**

2 *This is very **poor** work.*
bad
careless
sloppy
OPPOSITE **good**

popular *ADJECTIVE*
*He is a **popular** TV presenter and we watch him every week.*
famous
well-known
well-liked
OPPOSITE **unpopular**

portion *NOUN*
1 *She gave me a huge **portion** of chips.*
a helping
a serving

2 *I only got a small **portion** of pie.*
a piece
a slice

positive *ADJECTIVE*
*I am **positive** I saw him there.*
certain
sure
convinced

possessions *NOUN*
*We lost all our **possessions** in the fire.*
belongings
property
things

possible *ADJECTIVE*
*It is **possible** that it will rain later.*
likely
conceivable
feasible
OPPOSITE **impossible**

possibly *ADVERB*
1 ***Possibly** they missed the bus.*
perhaps
maybe

2 *This plan could not **possibly** work.*
conceivably
feasibly

post *NOUN*
1 *The fence is supported by wooden **posts**.*
a pole
a stake
a rod

2 *Did you get any **post** this morning?*
mail
letters
parcels

poster *NOUN*
*We put up a **poster** to tell people about our concert.*
a notice
a sign
an announcement
an advertisement
a flyer

postpone *VERB*
*We had to **postpone** the match because of the bad weather.*
to put off
to cancel
to delay

pot *NOUN*
1 *A **pot** of stew was cooking on the stove.*
a pan
a saucepan
a casserole
A cauldron is a very large metal pot.

2 *I grew some flowers in a **pot**.*
a container
a tub

3 *Mum put a **pot** of honey on the table.*
a jar

pour *VERB*
1 *I **poured** some orange juice into a glass.*
to tip

2 *Water was **pouring** over the edge of the bath.*
to run
to spill

Use **splash** when water is pouring noisily: *Water from the roof was **splashing** down into the puddles below.*

Use **stream**, **gush** or **rush** when a lot of water is pouring: *A huge jet of water was **gushing** out of the burst pipe.*

3 *It was **pouring** with rain.*
to teem
to pelt down
to bucket down

power *NOUN*
1 *The police have the **power** to arrest thieves.*
the right
the authority

2 *In stories, magicians have special **powers**.*
an ability
a skill
a talent

3 *The **power** of the waves destroyed buildings.*
force
strength
might
energy

powerful *ADJECTIVE*
1 *He was a rich and **powerful** king.*
mighty
all-powerful

2 *The lion had **powerful** jaws.*
strong
mighty
great
OPPOSITE **weak**

practise *VERB*
1 *I need to **practise** my speech.*
to go through
to run through
to work on
to rehearse

2 *The team meets once a week to **practise**.*
to train

praise VERB
*Our teacher **praised** us for working so hard.*
to congratulate
to commend
to compliment
OPPOSITE **criticise**

precious ADJECTIVE
1 *The necklace that my granny gave me is very **precious**.*
valuable
expensive
priceless

2 *I have a special box for all my **precious** possessions.*
prized
treasured
cherished
much-loved

precise ADJECTIVE
*Please measure out the **precise** amount.*
exact
correct
right
accurate

prepare VERB
1 *We are all busy **preparing** for the party.*
to get ready
to make preparations
to make arrangements
to plan

2 *I helped my mum **prepare** lunch.*
to make
to cook

present NOUN
*I got some lovely **presents** for my birthday.*
a gift

present VERB
1 *She **presented** the prize to the winner.*
to give
to hand
to award

2 *Who will **present** the show tonight?*
to introduce
to host

press VERB
*Don't **press** any of the buttons.*
to push
to touch
to activate

pretend VERB
1 *I thought she was hurt, but she was only **pretending**.*
to put it on
to fake
to play-act

2 *Let's **pretend** we're pirates.*
to imagine
to make believe
to play

pretty ADJECTIVE
1 *You look **pretty** today.*
lovely
beautiful
attractive

Use **stunning** or **gorgeous** for someone who is very pretty: *My sister looked **stunning** in her wedding dress.*

2 *What a **pretty** little cottage!*
quaint
charming
delightful
OPPOSITE **ugly**

prevent VERB
1 *He tried to **prevent** us from leaving.*
to stop
to block

2 *We must act quickly to **prevent** an accident.*
to avoid
to avert

price *NOUN*
1 *I like those trainers, but the **price** is too high.*
the cost

2 *The **price** for going swimming has gone up.*
a charge
a fee
a rate
A **fare** is the price of a journey on a bus or train.

prick *VERB*
*I **pricked** my finger on a needle.*
to jab
to stab
to pierce

prison *NOUN*
*The thief was sent to **prison** for ten years.*
jail
a cell
a dungeon

prisoner *NOUN*
*The **prisoners** were only given bread and water.*
a convict
an inmate
a captive
A **hostage** is a person taken prisoner by a kidnapper.

private *ADJECTIVE*
1 *They have their own **private** beach.*
personal
OPPOSITE **public**

2 *You mustn't read her **private** letters.*
confidential
personal
secret
intimate

3 *We found a nice **private** spot for a picnic.*
hidden
secluded
quiet
isolated
OPPOSITE **busy**

prize *NOUN*
*I hope I win a **prize** at the school raffle.*
an award
a trophy
a cup
a medal

problem *NOUN*
1 *The lack of food was going to be a **problem**.*
a difficulty
a worry
a complication
trouble

2 *We had some difficult maths **problems** to solve.*
a question
a brainteaser
a puzzle

3 *We solved the **problem** of the missing shoe.*
a mystery
a riddle
a puzzle
an enigma

prod *VERB*
1 *She **prodded** the hole with a stick.*
to poke
to push
to jab

2 *Someone **prodded** me in the back.*
to nudge
to dig
to poke

produce *VERB*
1 *This factory **produces** furniture for offices.*
to make
to manufacture
to assemble

2 *Farmers **produce** food for us.*
to grow

3 *She **produced** a photo from her bag.*
to bring out
to take out

promise *VERB*
*Do you **promise** that you will be home by 5 o'clock?*
to give your word
to swear
to vow
to guarantee
to assure *They **assured** us the problem would be fixed soon.*

proper *ADJECTIVE*
1 *Please put the book back in its **proper** place.*
correct
right
precise
suitable

2 *Can we have a ride in a **proper** boat?*
real
genuine
actual

protect *VERB*
1 *The bird always **protects** its chicks.*
to defend
to guard
to look after
to shield

2 *The hedge **protected** us from the wind.*
to shelter
to shield

protection *NOUN*
*Your skin needs some **protection** against the sun.*
defence
a shield
a guard

protest *VERB*
*The children **protested** when the teacher said they had to stay indoors.*
to complain
to object

proud *ADJECTIVE*
*Her parents felt very **proud** when she went up to collect her prize.*
pleased
happy
delighted
honoured
OPPOSITE **ashamed**

prove *VERB*
*Can you **prove** that you live here?*
to show
to establish
to demonstrate

prowl *VERB*
*The tiger **prowled** round the tree.*
to creep
to slink

public *ADJECTIVE*
*This is a **public** beach, so everyone can use it.*
open
communal
shared
OPPOSITE **private**

publish *VERB*
*The school **publishes** a magazine for us to read once a term.*
to bring out
to produce
to issue
to print

puff *VERB*
*I was **puffing** a bit by the time I got to the top of the hill.*
to pant
to huff and puff
to gasp
to gasp for breath

pull *VERB*
1 *We **pulled** the heavy box across the floor.*
to drag
to haul
to lug

❷ *I got hold of the handle and **pulled** hard.*
to tug
to yank
to heave

❸ *The magician **pulled** a bunch of flowers out of a hat.*
to take
to lift
to draw
to produce

❹ *I managed to **pull** the book out of her hands.*
to tear
to wrench
to drag
to rip

❺ *The car was **pulling** a caravan.*
to tow
to draw

punch VERB
*That boy **punched** me!*
to hit
to thump
to wallop
to strike

punish VERB
*The teachers will **punish** you if you misbehave.*
to discipline
to make an example of

pupil NOUN
*This school has about five hundred **pupils**.*
a student
a schoolchild
a schoolboy
a schoolgirl

pure ADJECTIVE
❶ *He was wearing a crown made of **pure** gold.*
real
solid

❷ *We bought a carton of **pure** orange juice.*
natural

❸ *The water here is lovely and **pure**.*
clean
clear
fresh
unpolluted

purse NOUN
*Always keep your money in a **purse**.*
a wallet
a bag

push VERB
❶ *The door will open if you **push** harder.*
to press
to shove
to apply pressure

❷ *I managed to **push** all the clothes into the bag.*
to force
to stuff
to stick
to ram
to squeeze
to jam
to cram

❸ *We **pushed** the table into the corner of the room.*
to move
to shove
to drag

❹ *We **pushed** the trolley towards the checkout.*
to wheel
to trundle
to roll

❺ *Someone **pushed** me in the back.*
to shove
to nudge
to prod
to poke
to elbow

❻ *The angry customer **pushed** past me.*
to shove
to barge
to squeeze
to elbow your way
to thrust

put *VERB* puts, putting, put

OVERUSED WORD

Try to use a more interesting word when you want to say **put**. Here are some other words you can use instead:

1 ***Put*** *all the pencils on my desk.*
to place
to leave

Use **position** when you put something carefully in a particular place: *He **positioned** the clock so that he could see it from his bed.*

Use **arrange** when you put something in a place carefully so that it looks nice: *He **arranged** the flowers in the vase.*

Use **pop** when you put something in a place quickly: *Why don't you quickly **pop** your bike in the shed?*

Use **pile** or **stack** when you put things in a pile: *I **stacked** the papers on my desk.*

Use **drop**, **dump**, **deposit** or **plonk** when you put something in a place carelessly: *She ran in and **dumped** her school bag on the floor.*

2 *I **put** a coin into the slot.*
to slide
to insert

3 *He **put** all the dirty clothes back into his bag.*
to shove
to push
to stick
to bung
to stuff

4 *He **put** some sugar on his cereal.*
to sprinkle
to scatter

5 *Can you **put** some water on these plants?*
to spray
to sprinkle
to pour

6 *I **put** some butter on my bread.*
to spread

7 *We **put** all the pictures on the table so that we could see them.*
to lay
to lay out
to set out
to spread out
to arrange

8 *She **put** her bike against the wall.*
to lean
to rest
to stand
to prop

9 *They have **put** some new lights on the outside of the school.*
to fix
to attach
to install
to fit

10 *You can **put** your car in the car park.*
to park
to leave

➤ **put up with**
*How can you **put up with** this noise?*
to tolerate
to accept
to endure
to bear
to live with

puzzle *NOUN*

1 *I like doing the **puzzles** in my comic.*
a brainteaser
a problem

2 *The disappearance of the keys was a **puzzle**.*
a mystery
a riddle
an enigma

quake *VERB*
*The rabbits were **quaking** in the cold so we took them into the house.*
to shake
to tremble
to quiver
to shiver
to shudder

quality *NOUN*
*The children have produced some work of very high **quality**.*
a standard
a class

quarrel *VERB*
*What are you two **quarrelling** about?*
to argue
to disagree
to squabble

Use **fight** when people argue in a very angry or serious way: *The two brothers **fought** all the time and didn't get on at all.*

Use **fall out** when people quarrel and stop being friends: *I've **fallen out** with my best friend.*

Use **bicker** when people quarrel about little things: *The children were **bickering** over who had the most stickers.*

quarrel *NOUN*
*She had a **quarrel** with her brother.*
an argument
a disagreement
a squabble

A **row** is a loud quarrel: *I had a big **row** with my parents.*

A **fight** is an angry, serious quarrel: *We had a really big **fight** about who should have the main part in the play.*

quest *NOUN*
*They went on a **quest** to find the magic berries.*
a mission
an expedition
a voyage

question *NOUN*
*There was no one who could answer my **question**.*
a query
an enquiry

question *VERB*
*The detective **questioned** everyone who was in the house.*
to ask
to interrogate
to quiz
To grill someone is to ask them a lot of questions in a severe way: *Dad **grilled** us about exactly how the window got broken.*

queue *NOUN*
1 *There was a long **queue** of people waiting for tickets.*
a line

2 *There was a long **queue** of traffic on the road.*

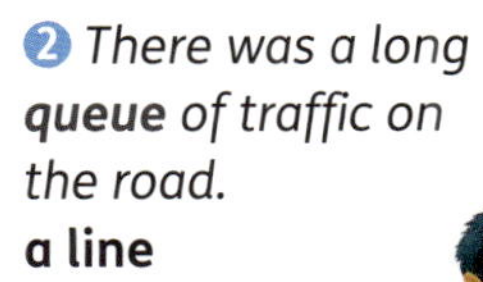

a line
a tailback
a traffic jam

quick *ADJECTIVE*

1 *The journey was **quick** and we arrived early.*
fast
speedy
swift
rapid

2 *He made a **quick** recovery from his illness.*
rapid
speedy

Use **instant** or **immediate** for something that happens very quickly: *The programme was an **instant** success.*

3 *He was walking at a **quick** pace as he was late for school.*
brisk
fast
swift

4 *We had a **quick** lunch and then left.*
hasty
hurried
brief

5 *They only came for a **quick** visit.*
short
brief
fleeting

quiet *ADJECTIVE*

1 *Our teacher told us to be **quiet**.*
silent
hushed
OPPOSITE **noisy**

2 *We found a **quiet** place for our picnic.*
peaceful
calm
isolated
tranquil
OPPOSITE **crowded**

3 *She's a very **quiet** girl.*
reserved
placid
shy
timid
OPPOSITE **noisy**

4 *I listened to some **quiet** music.*
low
soft
OPPOSITE **loud**

quite *ADVERB*

1 *The water's **quite** warm so we can go swimming.*
fairly
pretty
reasonably
rather

2 *I'm not **quite** sure that I will be able to come to the party.*
completely
totally
absolutely
fully

quiz *NOUN*

*We're going to have a maths **quiz** and the team that wins will get a prize.*
a test
a questionnaire
a contest

ragged *ADJECTIVE*
*They wore **ragged** clothes and had no shoes.*
tattered
torn
ripped
frayed
threadbare

rain *NOUN*
*There could be some **rain** later.*
a shower
Drizzle is very light rain: *The rain had slowed down to just a light **drizzle**.*
A **downpour** is a heavy shower of rain: *We got soaked when we got caught in a **downpour**.*
A **storm** or **rainstorm** is heavy rain with thunder: *That night there was a terrible **storm**.*

WRITING TIPS

Here are some useful words for writing about the rain:

- *A **fine**, **light** rain was falling outside.*
- *There was **steady** rain all day.*
- *There were strong winds and **heavy** rain during the night.*
- ***Torrential** rain can cause flooding.*
- *The rain **poured down** all day.*
- *I heard rain **pattering** on the roof.*

rain *VERB*
*It's still **raining**.*

Use **drizzle** or **spit** when it is not raining very hard: *It was only **spitting** so we decided to carry on with our walk.*

Use **pour** when it is raining a lot: *We can't go outside! It's **pouring**!*

rainy *ADJECTIVE*
*We play indoors on **rainy** days.*
wet
showery

Use **drizzly** or **damp** if it is slightly rainy: *It was a **drizzly** day but we still went out to play.*
OPPOSITE **dry**

ran *VERB (past tense and past participle of run)*

random *ADJECTIVE*
*We just asked a few people's opinions in a **random** way.*
chance
unplanned
haphazard

rang *VERB (past tense of ring)*

rare *ADJECTIVE*
*Pandas are very **rare** animals.*
uncommon
unusual
scarce
OPPOSITE **common**

ray *NOUN*
*A **ray** of light shone through the crack in the door.*
a beam
a shaft

reach *VERB*
1 *I **reached** out my hand to pick up the basket.*
to stretch out
to hold out

2 *Can you **reach** the book?*
to touch
to grasp
to get hold of

3 *It was dark when we **reached** London.*
to arrive at/in *It was dark when we **arrived in** London.*

react *VERB*
*I hope she doesn't **react** angrily.*
to respond
to reply

reaction *NOUN*
*She told her parents and waited for their **reaction**.*
a response
a reply

read *VERB* **reads, reading, read**
*I **read** a magazine while I was waiting.*

Use **look at**, **flick through** and **browse through** when you read something quickly: *I **flicked through** the address book until I found her address.*

Use **read through** when you read all of something: *Make sure you **read through** the instructions.*

Use **study** or **pore over** when you read something very carefully: *He spent hours **poring over** the documents.*

ready *ADJECTIVE*
1 *Are you **ready** to leave?*
prepared
all set
waiting
organised

2 *Your goods are **ready** for you now.*
available
prepared

3 *Is lunch **ready**?*
prepared
cooked
made

real *ADJECTIVE*
1 *Is that a **real** diamond?*
genuine
authentic
OPPOSITE **artificial**

2 *Is Tiny your **real** name?*
actual
proper
OPPOSITE **false**

3 *She had never felt **real** sadness before.*
true
sincere
genuine

realistic *ADJECTIVE*
*We used fake blood, but it looked quite **realistic**.*
lifelike
natural
authentic
OPPOSITE **unrealistic**

reality *NOUN*
*Is this a dream or is it **reality**?*
the real world
the facts
the truth
actuality

realise (*also* **realize**) *VERB*
*I suddenly **realised** that I had lost my phone.*
to know
to understand
to become aware
to notice
to see

really *ADVERB*
1 *The water's **really** cold!*
very
extremely

2 *Tom apologised, but I don't think he's **really** sorry.*
truly
honestly
genuinely

3 *Is your dad **really** a spy?*
actually
in reality

reason NOUN

1 *There must be a **reason** why this plant has died.*
a cause
an explanation

2 *What was your **reason** for telling us these lies?*
a motive
an excuse
a justification

reasonable ADJECTIVE

1 *It is **reasonable** to expect you to help.*
fair
right
acceptable
OPPOSITE **unreasonable**

2 *Let's try and discuss this in a **reasonable** way.*
sensible
rational
mature
OPPOSITE **irrational**

3 *You can earn a **reasonable** amount of money.*
fair
quite good
respectable

reassure VERB

*The teacher **reassured** us the test was not hard.*
to console
to comfort
to encourage

rebel VERB

*The other team **rebelled** against the referee's decision.*
to revolt
to rise up
to mutiny
to disobey orders

receive VERB

1 *I **received** some lovely presents.*
to get
to be given *I was **given** some lovely presents.*

2 *She **received** £10 for babysitting.*
to get
to earn
OPPOSITE **give**

recent ADJECTIVE

*Her **recent** film is not as good as the others.*
new
latest
current
up-to-date

recently ADVERB

*Have you done anything fun **recently**?*
lately
in recent days/weeks

reckon VERB

*I **reckon** our side will win.*
to think
to believe
to feel sure

recognise (also recognize) VERB

*I didn't **recognise** my grandad in the picture because he looked so young.*
to remember
to know
to identify

recommend VERB

1 *A lot of people have **recommended** this book to me.*
to suggest
to praise
to speak highly of *A lot of people have **spoken highly of** this book.*

2 *I **recommend** that you see a doctor.*
to suggest
to advise *I **advise** you to see a doctor.*

record NOUN

*We kept a **record** of the birds we saw on holiday.*

an account
a diary
a list
a journal

recover VERB

*Have you **recovered** from your illness?*

to get better
to get well
to recuperate
to get over

red ADJECTIVE

1 *She was wearing a **red** dress.*

crimson
scarlet
maroon

2 *Her cheeks were **red** when she came in from the cold.*

rosy
glowing
flushed

reduce VERB

1 *She **reduced** her speed when she saw the police car.*

to decrease
to lower

2 *We want to **reduce** the amount of litter in the playground.*

to lessen
to cut down

3 *The school shop has **reduced** some of its prices.*

to lower
to cut

Use **slash** when a price is reduced a lot: *That shop is closing down, so all the prices have been **slashed**.*

Use **halve** when something is reduced by half: *The price was **halved** from £10 to £5.*

OPPOSITE **increase**

refreshed ADJECTIVE

*I felt **refreshed** after my rest.*

invigorated
restored
revived
enlivened

refreshing ADJECTIVE

1 *I had a lovely **refreshing** shower.*

invigorating
energising

2 *I need a **refreshing** drink.*

cooling
thirst-quenching

refuse VERB

*I offered to take him to the party, but he **refused**.*

to say no *He **said no**.*
to decline *He **declined**.*
to be unwilling *He **was unwilling**.*

OPPOSITE **accept**

region NOUN

*These animals only live in hot **regions**.*

an area
a place
a zone

regular ADJECTIVE

1 *You should take **regular** exercise.*

frequent
daily
weekly

❷ *The postman was on his **regular** delivery round.*
normal
usual
customary

❸ *The drummer kept a **regular** rhythm.*
even
steady
OPPOSITE **irregular**

rehearse *VERB*

❶ *We **rehearsed** for the concert all afternoon.*
to practise
to prepare

❷ *I think you should **rehearse** your speech.*
to practise
to go through
to run through

relax *VERB*

❶ *I like to **relax** after school by riding my bike around the garden..*
to rest
to unwind
to take it easy
to chill *(informal)*

❷ ***Relax**! There's nothing to worry about.*
calm down!
don't panic!
chill out! *(informal)*

relaxed *ADJECTIVE*

❶ *I felt very **relaxed** lying in the sun.*
calm
carefree
peaceful
chilled *(informal)*
OPPOSITE **stressed**

❷ *Our dad is very **relaxed** and rarely gets cross.*
calm
easy-going
laid back *(informal)*

release *VERB*

*They **released** the animals from the cage.*
to free
to liberate
to set free *They **set** the animals **free**.*
to turn loose *They **turned** the animals **loose**.*

reliable *ADJECTIVE*

*I'm surprised that Joshua is late, he's usually so **reliable**.*
dependable
trustworthy
steady
OPPOSITE **unreliable**

relieved *ADJECTIVE*

*I was very **relieved** when I heard that no one was hurt after the accident.*
happy
glad
thankful

religion *NOUN*

*Different people follow different **religions**.*
a belief
a faith
a creed

WORD WEB

Some different **religions**:

Buddhism	**Islam**
Christianity	**Judaism**
Hinduism	**Sikhism**

reluctant *ADJECTIVE*

*I was **reluctant** to go out in the rain.*
unwilling
unhappy
not keen
hesitant
OPPOSITE **keen**

rely *VERB*

➤ **rely on**

1 *The young chicks* ***rely on*** *their mother for food.*
to depend on
to need

2 *We know we can always* ***rely on*** *you to help us.*
to trust
to count on

remain *VERB*

Please ***remain*** *in your seats.*
to stay
to wait
to continue

remains *NOUN*

1 *We visited the* ***remains*** *of a Roman castle.*
ruins
remnants

2 *We gave the* ***remains*** *of the food to the dog.*
the leftovers
the rest

remark *VERB*

I ***remarked*** *that it was a nice day.*
to comment
to mention
to observe
to point out

remarkable *ADJECTIVE*

This was a ***remarkable*** *achievement.*
extraordinary
amazing
astonishing
incredible
OPPOSITE **ordinary**

remember *VERB*

1 *I can't* ***remember*** *his name.*
to recall
to recollect

2 *I'm going to give you my phone number and you must* ***remember*** *it.*
to learn
to memorise
to make a mental note of
OPPOSITE **forget**

remind *VERB*

Seeing her with her swimming kit ***reminded*** *me that I needed mine.*
to jog someone's memory *Seeing her with her swimming kit* ***jogged my memory****.*

remove *VERB*

1 *Please* ***remove*** *this rubbish from your desk.*
to move
to take away
to get rid of

2 *He opened the drawer and* ***removed*** *some of the papers.*
to take out
to lift out
to extract

3 *She carefully* ***removed*** *the stamp from the envelope.*
to take off
to tear off
to cut off
to detach

4 *Someone had* ***removed*** *the door handle.*
to take off
to break off
to snap off

5 *He walked into the house and* ***removed*** *his shoes.*
to take off
to kick off
to slip off

6 *We scrubbed the walls to* ***remove*** *the dirt.*
to wipe off
to scrape off
to rub off

7 *I* ***removed*** *her name from the list.*
to cross out
to rub out
to erase
to delete

8 *I **removed** some files from my computer.*
to delete
to wipe

9 *The police **removed** him from the building.*
to evict
to throw out

repeat *VERB*
*Could you **repeat** that, please?*
to say again *Could you **say** that **again**, please?*
to reiterate *Mum **reiterated** that we must be home by seven o'clock.*

reply *NOUN*
*I called her name, but there was no **reply**.*
an answer
a response

reply *VERB*
*I asked him another question, but he didn't **reply**.*
to answer
to respond

report *NOUN*
1 *We had to write a **report** of what had happened.*
an account
a description

2 *There was a **report** about our school in the local newspaper.*
an article
a story

reptile *NOUN*

WORD WEB

Some **reptiles**:

an alligator
a crocodile
a dinosaur
a lizard
a snake
a tortoise
a turtle

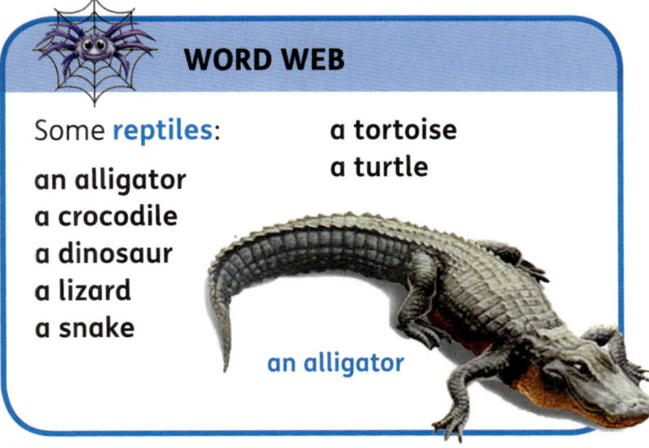

an alligator

rescue *VERB*
1 *They **rescued** the prisoners from the dungeon.*
to free
to release
to liberate
to set free *He **set** the prisoners **free**.*

2 *A lifeboat was sent out to **rescue** the men on the sinking boat.*
to save

responsible *ADJECTIVE*
1 *You are **responsible** for feeding the fish.*
in charge of *You are **in charge of** feeding the fish.*

2 *Who is **responsible** for breaking this window?*
to blame for *Who is **to blame for** breaking this window?*
guilty of *Who is **guilty of** breaking this window?*

3 *We need a **responsible** person to look after the money.*
sensible
reliable
trustworthy
OPPOSITE **irresponsible**

rest *NOUN*
1 *I need a **rest**!*
a break
a pause
a lie-down

A **breather** is a short rest to get your breath back: *We stopped for a **breather** before continuing up the mountain.*

2 *The doctor says that I need plenty of **rest**.*
sleep
relaxation

3 *If you have finished, the dog will eat the **rest**.*
the remainder
the leftovers

rest *VERB*
*We'll **rest** for half an hour before we continue.*
to relax
to take it easy
to have a nap

result *NOUN*

1 *I tried hard and as a **result** I did well.*
a consequence
an outcome

2 *I didn't see the match, but I know the **result**.*
a score

retreat *VERB*

*The soldiers **retreated** towards the fort.*
to go back
to move back
to withdraw
to flee

reveal *VERB*

1 *She drew back the curtain and **revealed** a statue of a man.*
to uncover
to unveil
to unmask

2 *Don't ever **reveal** our secret!*
to tell
to disclose

revenge *NOUN*

*He wanted **revenge** for what they had done.*
vengeance
retribution

review *NOUN*

*I wrote a **review** of the book.*
an evaluation
a judgement
an assessment
a report *I wrote a **report** on the book.*

revolting *ADJECTIVE*

1 *The food was **revolting**.*
horrible
disgusting
inedible

2 *What a **revolting** hat!*
horrible
vile
hideous

rich *ADJECTIVE*

*She dreamed of being **rich** and famous.*
wealthy
well-off
prosperous
OPPOSITE **poor**

ridiculous *ADJECTIVE*

*That's a **ridiculous** thing to say!*
absurd
foolish
stupid
ludicrous
preposterous
OPPOSITE **sensible**

right *ADJECTIVE*

1 *I was very happy because all my answers were **right**.*
correct
accurate

Use **spot on** when something is exactly right:
*I guessed he weighed 24 kilos and I was **spot on**.*

2 *Is that the **right** time?*
exact
precise
correct

3 *I haven't got the **right** books.*
appropriate
suitable
proper
ideal

4 *It's **right** to own up when something is your fault.*
honest
fair
good
sensible
honourable
OPPOSITE **wrong**

ring *NOUN*

*We all stood in a **ring** with Emily in the middle.*
a circle

ring VERB **rings, ringing, rang, rung**

1 *I could hear bells* ***ringing****.*

to sound

Use **chime** or **peal** to describe the sound of large bells: *The church bells* ***chimed****.*

Use **tinkle** or **jingle** to describe the sound of small bells: *The bells around the horse's neck* ***jingled*** *as it trotted along.*

2 *I'll* ***ring*** *you later.*

to call
to phone
to telephone

rip VERB

I ***ripped*** *my jeans.*

to tear
to split

Use **shred** when someone rips something into a lot of little pieces: *She* ***shredded*** *the letter and threw it in the bin.*

rise VERB **rises, rising, risen**

1 *I watched the balloon* ***rise*** *into the sky.*

to climb
to ascend

Use **soar** when something rises very high: *The eagle* ***soared*** *high into the sky.*

OPPOSITE **descend**

2 *The sun was* ***rising*** *when we got up.*

to come up

OPPOSITE **set**

3 *Bus fares are going to* ***rise*** *next week.*

to increase
to go up

OPPOSITE **fall**

risk NOUN

1 *There is a* ***risk*** *that you might fall.*

a danger
a chance
a possibility

2 *Pollution is a* ***risk*** *to health.*

a danger
a hazard

river NOUN

We walked along next to the ***river****.*

A **stream** or **brook** is a small river: *There was a little* ***stream*** *at the bottom of the garden.*

A **canal** is a man-made river: *In the past, goods were transported along* ***canals****.*

WRITING TIPS

Here are some useful words for writing about **rivers**:

- *They sailed along the* ***wide, meandering*** *river.*
- *The river here is* ***broad*** *and* ***slow-moving****.*
- *They came to the edge of a* ***deep, fast-moving*** *river.*
- *The* ***mighty*** *river* ***flows*** *towards the sea.*
- *A river* ***winds*** *through the field.*
- *A* ***shallow*** *river* ***runs*** *through the middle of the forest.*
- *We watched the river* ***rushing*** *past.*

road NOUN

1 *This is the* ***road*** *where I live.*

a street
an avenue

2 *There is a narrow* ***road*** *between the two farms.*

a track
a path
a lane
an alley

3 *We drove along the* ***road*** *from Oxford to London.*

a main road
a motorway

roar *VERB*
*The crowd **roared** as he scored the winning goal.*
to bellow
to shout
to cry

robber *NOUN*
*The **robbers** escaped from the building.*
a burglar
a thief
a pickpocket
a shoplifter

robot *NOUN*
*They invented a **robot** that could play football.*
an automaton
an android
a bot

rock *NOUN*
*He picked up a **rock** and hurled it into the sea.*
a stone

A **boulder** is a very big rock: *We had to climb over some huge **boulders**.*

rock *VERB*
1 *The little boat **rocked** gently in the breeze.*
to sway
to swing

2 *The ship **rocked** violently in the storm.*
to roll
to toss
to pitch

roll *VERB*
*The logs **rolled** down the hill.*
to spin
to tumble
to turn over
to revolve

rope *NOUN*
*The boat was tied up with a strong **rope**.*
a cable
a line
a cord

rose *VERB* *(past tense of* **rise***)*

rotten *ADJECTIVE*
1 *The wood was old and **rotten**.*
decayed
decomposed
OPPOSITE **sound**

2 *The meat was **rotten**.*
bad

Use **mouldy** for cheese: *There was some **mouldy** old cheese in the fridge.*

Use **off** for meat and fish: *We can't eat this meat. It's **off**.*
OPPOSITE **fresh**

3 *That was a **rotten** thing to do!*
nasty
unkind
mean
horrible
OPPOSITE **good**

rough *ADJECTIVE*
1 *We jolted along the **rough** road.*
bumpy
uneven
stony
rocky
OPPOSITE **even**

2 *Sandpaper feels **rough**.*
coarse
scratchy
prickly
OPPOSITE **smooth**

3 *He spoke in a **rough** voice.*
gruff
husky
hoarse
OPPOSITE **soft**

4 *The sea was very **rough**.*
stormy
choppy
OPPOSITE **calm**

5 *Don't be so **rough** with your little brother.*
violent
aggressive
boisterous
rowdy
OPPOSITE **gentle**

6 *At a **rough** guess, I would say there were fifty people there.*
approximate
estimated
vague
OPPOSITE **exact**

round ADJECTIVE
1 *The earth is **round**.*
spherical
rounded

2 *He was wearing a **round** badge.*
circular

row (rhymes with cow) NOUN
1 *I had a **row** with my sister.*
an argument
a quarrel
a squabble
a disagreement

2 *What's that terrible **row**?*
noise
din
racket
rumpus
commotion

row (rhymes with toe) NOUN
*We stood in a straight **row**.*
a line
a queue

rub VERB
1 *He **rubbed** the paint to see if it would come off.*
to scratch
to scrape

2 *He **rubbed** the old coin to make it shine.*
to clean
to polish

➤ **rub out**
*She **rubbed** out what she had just written.*
to erase
to remove
to delete

rubbish NOUN
1 *The **rubbish** is collected once a week.*
refuse
waste
garbage
trash

2 *There was **rubbish** all over the playground.*
litter
waste

3 *The garage is full of old **rubbish**.*
junk

4 *You're talking **rubbish**!*
nonsense
balderdash

rude ADJECTIVE
1 *Don't be **rude** to your teacher.*
cheeky
impertinent
impudent
insolent
disrespectful

2 *It's **rude** to interrupt when someone is talking.*
bad-mannered
impolite
OPPOSITE **polite**

3 *They got told off for telling **rude** jokes.*
indecent
dirty
vulgar

ruin VERB
1 *The storm **ruined** the farmers' crops.*
to spoil
to damage
to destroy
to wreck

2 *The bad weather **ruined** our holiday.*
to spoil
to mess up

rule NOUN
*It is a **rule** that we all wear uniform.*
a regulation
a law

rule VERB
*In the old days, the king used to **rule** the country.*
to govern
to control
to run

ruler NOUN
*Who is the **ruler** of this country?*
a king or queen
a monarch
a sovereign
an emperor or an empress
a president

run VERB **runs, running, ran**

OVERUSED WORD

Try to use a more interesting word when you want to say **run**. Here are some other words you can use instead:

1 *We **ran** across the field.*

Use **jog** if you run quite slowly: *I sometimes go **jogging** with my dad.*

Use **sprint**, **race**, **tear**, **charge** or **fly** if you run as fast as you can: *I **raced** home.*

Use **rush**, **dash** or **hurry** if you are running because you are in a hurry: *I **dashed** back home to pick up my PE kit.*

Use **bolt** or **flee** if you run away fast to escape: *When he saw the policeman he **bolted** for the door.*

Use **career** if you are running fast and out of control: *The two boys came **careering** into the kitchen.*

2 *The dog **ran** towards us.*
to bound

3 *The horses **ran** across the field.*
to trot
to canter
to gallop

4 *The little mouse **ran** into its hole.*
to scurry
to scuttle

5 *Our English teacher **runs** a drama club after school.*
to be in charge of
to manage
to organise
to lead
to head

gallop

➤ **run away**
*I chased them but they **ran away**.*
to escape
to get away
to flee *I chased them but they **fled**.*

rung VERB *(past tense and past participle of* ring*)*

runner NOUN
*Which **runner** won the race?*
an athlete
a competitor

A sprinter is someone who runs fast over short distances.

rush VERB
*I **rushed** to the bus stop.*
to dash
to hurry
to run
to race

Ss

sad ADJECTIVE

OVERUSED WORD

Here are some more interesting words you can use for **sad**:

1 *The little boy looked very **sad**.*
unhappy
upset
miserable
fed up
dejected
despondent
depressed
gloomy
glum
down in the dumps

Use **disappointed** if someone is sad because something has gone wrong: *I was really **disappointed** when we lost.*

Use **tearful** if someone is sad and almost crying: *Amy was **tearful** when she told me about the argument.*

Use **heartbroken** when someone is extremely sad: *I was **heartbroken** when my best friend moved to another town.*

2 *This is very **sad** news.*
upsetting
tragic
depressing
distressing
disappointing
dismal
OPPOSITE **happy**

sadness NOUN

*I was filled with **sadness** and started to cry.*
sorrow
grief
misery
heartache
OPPOSITE **happiness**

safe ADJECTIVE

1 *Once we reached the house I knew that we were **safe**.*
secure
out of danger
out of harm's way
sheltered
protected
OPPOSITE **in danger**

2 *The building was destroyed, but all the people were **safe**.*
safe and sound
unharmed
unhurt
in one piece
OPPOSITE **hurt**

3 *Castles were very **safe** places.*
secure
well-protected
well-defended
impregnable
OPPOSITE **dangerous**

4 *Is this ladder **safe**?*
firm
secure
strong enough
OPPOSITE **dangerous**

5 *Tigers are wild animals and are never completely **safe**.*
harmless
tame
OPPOSITE **dangerous**

safety NOUN

1 *These rules are for your own **safety**.*

security
well-being
protection
OPPOSITE **danger**

2 *I wanted to get to the **safety** of my bed.*

shelter
sanctuary

sail VERB

1 *They **sailed** to far-off lands.*

to set sail
to go by ship
to voyage

2 *We watched the yachts **sailing** on the lake.*

to float
to glide
to drift
to bob

3 *The huge ship **sailed** out of the harbour.*

to steam
to chug

same ADJECTIVE

*The houses look the **same**.*

identical
similar
alike
OPPOSITE **different**

sandwich NOUN

*I had a cheese **sandwich** for lunch.*

a roll
a wrap
a butty *(informal)*

sang VERB *(past tense of* sing*)*

sank VERB *(past tense of* sink*)*

sat VERB *(past tense and past participle of* sit*)*

satisfactory ADJECTIVE

*Your work is **satisfactory**, but I think you could do better.*

all right
OK *(informal)*
acceptable
fair
adequate
passable
OPPOSITE **unsatisfactory**

satisfied ADJECTIVE

*The teacher was **satisfied** with the children's behaviour.*

pleased
happy
content
OPPOSITE **dissatisfied**

save VERB

1 *A firefighter climbed into the burning building to **save** her.*

Use **rescue** when you save someone from danger: *A lifeboat was sent out to **rescue** the men on the boat.*

Use **free**, **release** or **liberate** when you save someone who is a prisoner: *She opened the cage and **liberated** the birds.*

2 *I'm going to **save** this money.*

to keep
to put aside *I'm going to **put** this money **aside**.*
to reserve

saw VERB *(past tense of* see*)*

say *VERB* says, saying, said

OVERUSED WORD

Here are some more interesting words you can use for **say**:

'It's time to leave,' she ***said.***

Use **add** when someone says something more: *'I've got some money,' Joe said. 'About £5,' he* ***added.***

Use **ask** or **enquire** when someone asks a question: *'How old are you?' the teacher* ***asked.***

Use **complain** or **moan** when someone is not happy about something: *'You didn't wait for me,' she* ***moaned.***

Use **confess** or **admit** when someone admits they have done something wrong: *'I'm afraid I've eaten all the biscuits,' George* ***confessed.***

Use **suggest** when someone makes a suggestion: *'Let's play,'* he ***suggested.***

Use **announce** or **declare** when someone says something important: *'We must leave tomorrow,' he* ***announced.***

Use **answer**, **reply** or **respond** when someone is giving an answer: *'No,'* ***answered*** *Lisa.*

Use **shout**, **cry**, **yell**, **scream** or **shriek** when someone says something very loudly: *'You idiot!'* ***yelled*** *Jake.*

Use **mutter**, **mumble**, **murmur** or **whisper** when someone says something very quietly: *'I'm sorry,' she* ***muttered.***

Use **snap**, **growl** or **snarl** when someone says something angrily: *'Be quiet!'* ***snapped*** *Katie.*

Use **stutter**, **stammer** or **splutter** when someone has difficulty saying the words: *'I d-d-don't know,' she* ***stammered.***

Use **laugh** if someone is laughing while they speak: *'That's so funny!' he* ***laughed.***

Use **sneer**, **scoff** or **jeer** if someone is making fun of another person: *'You'll never win the race on that old bike,' Tim* ***scoffed.***

Use **chorus** when people say something together: *'Yes, Miss,' they* ***chorused.***

saying *NOUN*

Do you know the ***saying*** *'too many cooks spoil the broth'?*

a proverb
an expression
a phrase

scare *VERB*

Some of the scenes in the movie really ***scared*** *me.*

to frighten
to give someone a fright
to alarm

Use **terrify** when something scares you a lot: *The thought of starting a new school* ***terrified*** *me.*

Use **startle** or **make someone jump** when something suddenly scares you: *Suddenly the phone rang, which* ***made me jump.***

scared *ADJECTIVE*

Are you ***scared*** *of mice?*

frightened
afraid

Use **terrified** or **petrified** when you are very scared: *I am* ***terrified*** *of snakes.*

scary *ADJECTIVE*

The woods are ***scary*** *at night.*

frightening

Use **eerie** or **spooky** when you think there might be ghosts: *It was really **eerie** being in the old castle at night.*

Use **terrifying** when something is very scary: *In front of us stood a **terrifying** monster.*

scatter VERB

1 *Glass was **scattered** everywhere.*
to spread
to strew *Glass was **strewn** everywhere.*

2 ***Scatter** the seeds on the soil.*
to sprinkle
to sow

school NOUN

WORD WEB

Some types of school:

an infant school
a junior school
a kindergarten
a nursery school
a playgroup
a primary school
a secondary school

scientist NOUN

*I'd like to be a **scientist** because I like discovering why things happen.*
a researcher
an inventor

WORD WEB

Some types of scientist:

an astronomer
a biologist
a botanist
a chemist
a physicist
a psychologist
a zoologist

score NOUN

*What was the **score** at the end of the game?*
points
total

Use **marks** for a score in a test.

scrape VERB

1 *We **scraped** the mud off our shoes.*
to rub
to clean
to scrub

2 *I **scraped** the paint on my new bike.*
to scratch
to scuff
to graze

scratch VERB

1 *Mind you don't **scratch** the paint on the car.*
to damage
to scrape
to mark

2 *His head was itching so he **scratched** it.*
to rub

scream VERB

1 *Everyone **screamed** when they saw the spider.*
to cry out
to shriek
to squeal

2 *'Go away!' she **screamed**.*
to cry
to shout
to call
to yell
to shriek
to screech
to howl

sea NOUN

*They sailed across the **sea**.*
the ocean
the water
the waves
the deep

search VERB

1 *I was **searching** for my watch as I'd lost it.*
to look for
to hunt for
to try to find

❷ *They **searched** the park for the lost dog.*
to comb
to scour

seaside NOUN
*We **spent** the day at the seaside.*
the beach
the coast

seat NOUN
*I sat down on a **seat** by the door.*
a chair

WORD WEB
Some types of **seat**:
an armchair
a bench
A high chair is a child's seat.
a rocking chair
a settee
a sofa
a stool

an armchair

second NOUN
*I'll be there in a **second**.*
an instant
a moment

secret ADJECTIVE
❶ *She wrote everything down in her **secret** diary.*
personal
private

❷ *There is a **secret** garden behind the house.*
hidden
concealed
secluded

see VERB sees, seeing, saw, seen
❶ *I **saw** a horse in the field.*
to notice

Use **observe** or **watch** when you look at something for quite a long time: *You can **observe** birds in your garden.*

Use **spot** or **spy** when you see something that is difficult to see: *We **spotted** a tiny ship on the horizon.*

Use **catch sight of**, **glimpse** or **catch a glimpse of** when you see something for a very short time: *I **caught a glimpse of** a deer as it ran through the forest.*

Use **witness** when you see a crime or accident: *Did anyone **witness** this accident?*

❷ *I'm going to **see** my grandma tomorrow.*
to visit
to pay a visit to
to call on

❸ *I **see** what you mean.*
to understand
to know
to realise
to grasp
to follow

seed NOUN
*I planted some **seeds** in the pot.*
A grain is a seed from a cereal, like wheat.
A pip is a seed from a fruit, like an apple or orange.

seem VERB
*Everyone **seems** very happy today.*
to appear
to look
to sound

seize VERB
❶ *I **seized** the end of the rope.*
to grab
to take hold of
to clutch
to grasp

2 *The thief **seized** my bag and ran off.*
to grab
to snatch

3 *The police **seized** the two men.*
to arrest
to catch
to capture

selfish *ADJECTIVE*
*You shouldn't be so **selfish**.*
mean
self-centred
thoughtless
OPPOSITE **unselfish**

sell *VERB* sells, selling, sold
*This shop **sells** tropical fish.*
to stock
to have for sale
OPPOSITE **buy**

sense *NOUN*
*That dog has got no **sense**.*
common sense
intelligence
brains

sense *VERB*
*I **sensed** someone else was in the room.*
to feel
to be aware
to perceive

sensible *ADJECTIVE*
1 *She is usually a very **sensible** girl.*
careful
thoughtful
level-headed
responsible
reasonable
mature
wise

2 *That would be a **sensible** thing to do.*
logical
prudent
wise
OPPOSITE **stupid**

sensitive *ADJECTIVE*
1 *Tom is feeling very **sensitive** about losing his phone as it was brand new.*
easily hurt
easily upset
easily offended
touchy
OPPOSITE **insensitive**

2 *You shouldn't use this suncream if you have **sensitive** skin.*
delicate
tender

separate *ADJECTIVE*
1 *We need to keep the two sets of stickers **separate**.*
apart
divided

2 *The two boys sleep in **separate** bedrooms.*
different
OPPOSITE **together**

separate *VERB*
1 ***Separate** the stickers into two piles.*
to divide
to split
to remove

2 *Marcus and Aisha wouldn't stop talking, so the teacher **separated** them.*
to move
to split up *The teacher **split** them **up**.*
to break up *The teacher **broke** them **up**.*

serious *ADJECTIVE*
1 *The old man was looking very **serious**.*
sad
solemn

sombre
grave
thoughtful
OPPOSITE cheerful

2 *Are you **serious** about wanting to help?*
sincere
in earnest
OPPOSITE insincere

3 *They were discussing a **serious** issue.*
important
significant
difficult
OPPOSITE unimportant

4 *Littering is a **serious** problem in the city centre.*
bad
terrible
awful
dreadful
OPPOSITE minor

5 *Cancer is a very **serious** illness.*
bad
dangerous
life-threatening
OPPOSITE minor

serve *VERB*
*Mum **served** birthday cake to all the children.*
to dish up
to give
to distribute

set *NOUN*
*I need to get one more card, then I'll have the whole **set**.*
a collection
a series

set *VERB* sets, setting, set
1 *The teacher forgot to **set** us any homework.*
to give

2 *We'll camp for the night when the sun **sets**.*
to go down

3 *Has the glue **set** yet?*
to harden
to solidify

settle *VERB*
➤ settle down
1 *She **settled down** to watch a film.*
to sit down
to sit back
to make yourself comfortable *She **made** herself **comfortable**.*

2 ***Settle down** please, children.*
to calm down
to be quiet

shady *ADJECTIVE*
*We found a **shady** place to eat our lunch.*
cool
shaded
OPPOSITE sunny

shake *VERB* shakes, shaking, shook, shaken
1 *I picked up the money box and **shook** it.*
to rattle

2 *My granny **shook** her finger at me.*
to wave
to waggle
to brandish

3 *The whole house seemed to **shake**.*
to move
to rock
to sway
to wobble
to vibrate
to shudder

4 *The old truck **shook** as it drove along the bumpy lane.*
to judder
to jolt
to rattle

5 *I was **shaking** with cold.*
to tremble
to quake
to quiver
to shiver
to shudder

shape *NOUN*

❶ *I could just see the **shape** of a building.*
the outline
the silhouette

❷ *He's a powerful magician who can take on any **shape** he chooses.*
a form

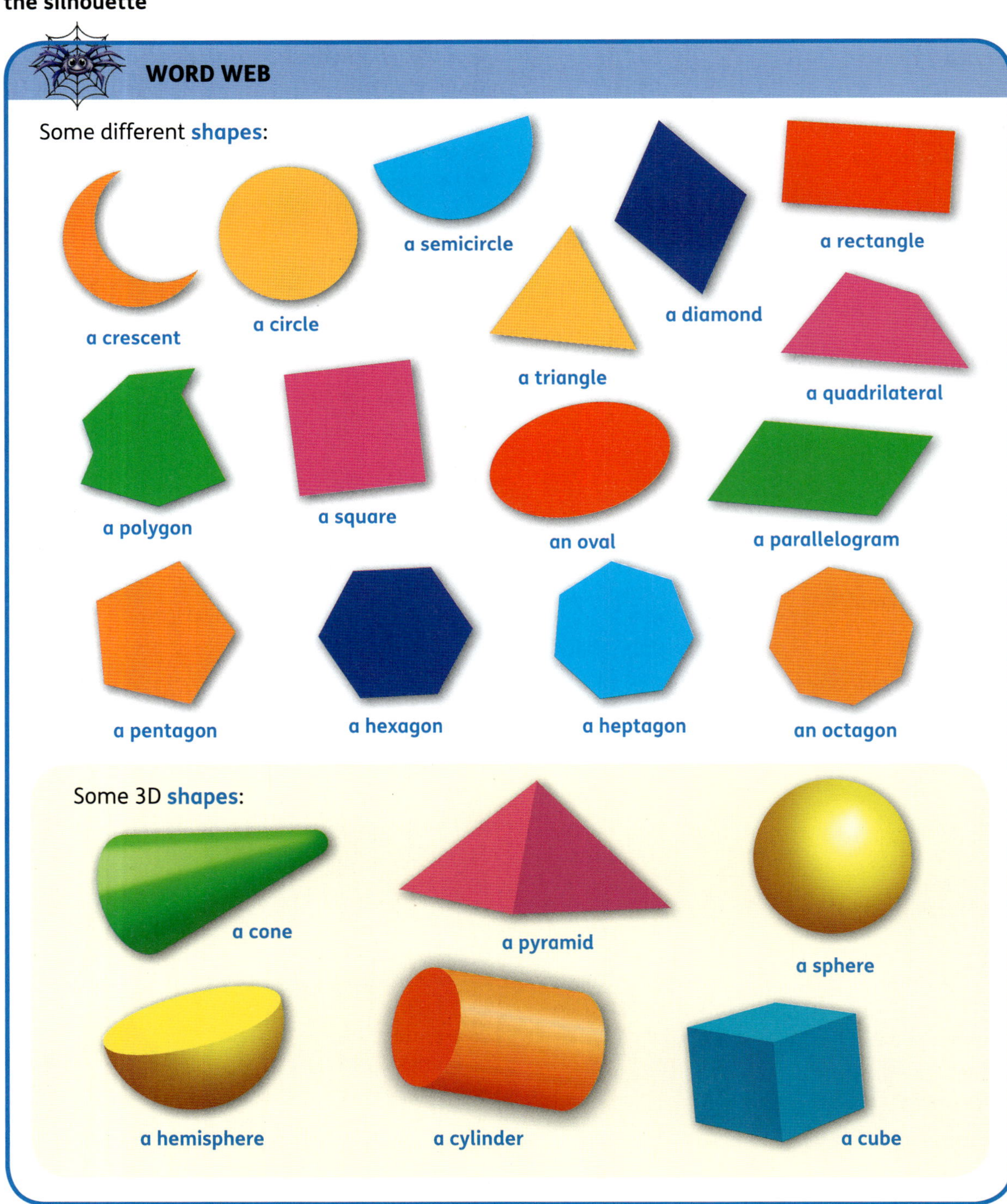

share NOUN
*Don't worry, you will get your **share** of the stickers.*
a part
a portion

share VERB
*We **shared** the food between us.*
to divide
to split

sharp ADJECTIVE
1 *Be careful, that knife is **sharp** and could hurt you.*
razor-sharp
OPPOSITE **blunt**

2 *It hurt our feet walking over the **sharp** rocks.*
pointed
jagged
OPPOSITE **smooth**

3 *A hedgehog's body is covered in **sharp** spines.*
prickly
spiky
OPPOSITE **smooth**

4 *There was a **sharp** bend in the road.*
sudden
tight
OPPOSITE **gradual**

5 *He's a very **sharp** boy.*
clever
intelligent
bright
brainy
quick
smart
brilliant
OPPOSITE **stupid**

shed NOUN
*There's a **shed** at the bottom of the garden.*
a hut
an outhouse
a shack

shed VERB sheds, shedding, shed
1 *Some trees **shed** their leaves in the winter.*
to drop
to lose

2 *Snakes **shed** their old skin each year.*
to cast off

shell NOUN
*The egg is protected by a **shell**.*
a casing
a covering

shelter NOUN
*The trees gave us some **shelter** from the rain.*
protection
refuge
cover

shelter VERB
1 *We **sheltered** from the storm in an old barn.*
to hide
to stay safe
to take cover

2 *The hedge **sheltered** us from the wind.*
to protect
to shield
to screen

shield NOUN
*I used my bag as a **shield** to block the snowballs.*
a screen
a guard
a barrier

shine VERB shines, shining, shone
1 *The sun **shone** all day.*
to blaze down
to beat down
to be out *The sun **was out** all day.*

2 *I saw a light **shining** in the distance.*

Use **glow**, **glimmer**, **gleam** or **shimmer** when something shines gently: *The light from the fire **glowed** softly in the darkness.*

A B C D E F G H I J K L M N O P Q R Ss T U V W X Y Z

Use **flash** when a light shines on and off: *The light from the lighthouse **flashed** in the darkness.*

Use **flicker**, **twinkle** or **sparkle** when a light shines in an unsteady way, like a star: *The Christmas tree lights **flickered** and **sparkled**.*

Use **glint** or **glitter** when something made of metal or glass shines: *His sword **glinted** in the moonlight.*

shiny *ADJECTIVE*

1 *We found a **shiny** new coin.*
bright
gleaming

2 *He was wearing **shiny** shoes.*
polished

3 *We printed our designs on **shiny** paper.*
glossy
OPPOSITE **dull**

shiver *VERB*

1 *I was **shivering** with cold.*
to shake

2 *She was **shivering** with fear.*
to shake
to tremble
to quake
to quiver
to shudder

shock *VERB*

1 *The explosion **shocked** everyone.*
to frighten
to alarm
to shake

2 *News of the terrible accident **shocked** us all.*
to upset
to distress

3 *The swearing in the film **shocked** us.*
to offend
to disgust
to horrify

shocked *ADJECTIVE*

1 *I felt quite **shocked** when I realised I had won.*
surprised
astonished
astounded
staggered

2 *The whole family was **shocked** when their pet rabbit died.*
upset
distressed
traumatised

3 *I was **shocked** when I heard the children swearing.*
disgusted
appalled
horrified

shoe *NOUN*

WORD WEB

Some types of **shoe**:

boots
plimsolls
pumps
sandals
slippers
trainers
wellingtons

shone *VERB (past tense and past participle of* **shine***)*

shook *VERB (past tense of* **shake***)*

shoot *VERB* **shoots, shooting, shot**
We ***shot*** *arrows at the target.*
to fire
to aim
to launch

shop *NOUN*
You can buy comics in the ***shop*** *on the corner.*
a store

WORD WEB

Some big **shops**:

a department store
a hypermarket
a supermarket

Some other types of **shop**:

a baker
a book shop
a boutique
a butcher
a chemist
a clothes shop
a delicatessen
a fishmonger
a florist
a gift shop
a greengrocer
a grocer
a jeweller
a music shop
a newsagent
a post office
a shoe shop
a toy shop

short *ADJECTIVE*
1 *I'm quite* ***short*** *for my age.*
small
little
OPPOSITE **tall**

2 *The animal had a long body and* ***short*** *legs.*
stumpy
stubby
OPPOSITE **long**

3 *It was just a* ***short*** *visit.*
brief
fleeting
quick
OPPOSITE **long**

should *VERB*
You ***should*** *ask your parents before you go anywhere.*
ought to *You* ***ought to*** *ask your parents.*
be supposed to *You* ***are supposed to*** *ask your parents.*
be meant to *You* ***are meant to*** *ask your parents.*

shout *VERB*
'You're here at last!' he ***shouted****.*
to yell
to cry
to call
to bawl
to bellow
to roar

Use **scream** or **shriek** when someone is very frightented or excited: *'Help!' she* ***screamed****.*

Use **cheer** when people are happy about something: *'Hooray!' they* ***cheered****.*

Use **jeer** when people are making fun of someone: *'You're useless!' they* ***jeered****.*
OPPOSITE **whisper**

show *NOUN*
We're putting on a school ***show*** *at the end of term.*
a performance
a production
a play

show *VERB* **shows, showing, showed, shown**
1 *Shall I* ***show*** *you my new bike?*
to let someone see *I'll* ***let you see*** *my new bike.*

2 *He* ***showed*** *me the place where the accident happened.*
to point to
to indicate *He* ***indicated*** *the place where the accident happened.*

3 *We **showed** our work to the visitors.*
to display
to exhibit

4 *She **showed** me how to use the computer.*
to tell
to teach
to demonstrate *She **demonstrated** to me how to use the computer.*
to explain *She **explained** to me how to use the computer.*

shrink VERB shrinks, shrinking, shrank, shrunk

*He drank the potion and it made him **shrink** to the size of a mouse.*
to get smaller
to contract
to shrivel

shrivel VERB

*The plants **shrivelled** in the heat.*
to dry up
to wither

shut VERB shuts, shutting, shut

*She went out of the room and **shut** the door.*
to close
to fasten
to pull shut
to push shut

Use **lock** or **bolt** when you shut something and lock it: *He **bolted** the door securely.*

Use **slam** or **bang** when you shut something noisily: *She ran out and **slammed** the door.*

OPPOSITE **open**

shy ADJECTIVE

1 *He was too **shy** to say that he knew the answer.*
timid
bashful
modest

2 *My cat is a bit **shy** of strangers.*
nervous
cautious
wary

sick ADJECTIVE

1 *I stayed off school because I was **sick**.*
ill
unwell
poorly

2 *After eating all that chocolate I felt **sick**.*
queasy
nauseous

side NOUN

1 *Some people were standing at one **side** of the field.*
an edge
a border

2 *We waited at the **side** of the road.*
the edge
the verge
the margin

3 *A cube has six **sides**.*
a face
a surface

sigh VERB

1 *'It's no use,' she **sighed**.*
to complain
to lament
to moan
to grumble

2 *He **sighed** with relief.*
to exhale
to breathe out

sight NOUN

*She is quite old and doesn't have very good **sight**.*
eyesight
vision

sign NOUN

1 *The **sign** for a dollar is $.*
a symbol
a logo

2 *The **sign** said 'No entry'.*
a notice
a signpost

3 *I'll give you a **sign** when I'm ready for you to start.*
a signal
a gesture

signal NOUN
*Don't move until I give the **signal**.*
a sign
a gesture

silent ADJECTIVE
1 *The hall was empty and **silent**.*
quiet
hushed
peaceful
noiseless
OPPOSITE **noisy**

2 *The teacher told us to be **silent**.*
quiet
OPPOSITE **talkative**

3 *I asked him some questions, but he remained **silent**.*
tight-lipped
wordless

silly ADJECTIVE
1 *It's **silly** to go out in the rain.*
daft
foolish
stupid
idiotic
unwise

2 *Please stop this **silly** behaviour.*
childish
immature

3 *Why are you wearing such **silly** clothes?*
ridiculous
peculiar
odd
unsuitable

similar ADJECTIVE
*The two girls look quite **similar**.*
alike
identical
the same
OPPOSITE **different**

simple ADJECTIVE
1 *That's a **simple** question.*
easy
straightforward
clear
obvious
OPPOSITE **difficult**

2 *We used quite a **simple** design for our poster.*
plain
straightforward
not fancy
OPPOSITE **elaborate**

sing VERB sings, singing, sang, sung
1 *He was **singing** quietly to himself.*
to hum
to croon

2 *The birds were **singing** in the trees.*
to chirp
to cheep
to twitter
to warble

sink VERB sinks, sinking, sank, sunk
*The ship **sank** in a storm.*
to go down
to founder
to be submerged *The ship **was submerged**.*

sit VERB sits, sitting, sat
1 *You can **sit** next to me.*
to have a seat
to take a seat
to settle down

2 *The bird **sat** on a branch.*
to perch
to alight
to settle

A B C D E F G H I J K L M N O P Q R Ss T U V W X Y Z

site NOUN
*This would be a very good **site** for the new school.*
a place
a spot
a position
a location

situation NOUN
1 *This is a complicated **situation**.*
a state of affairs

2 *I wouldn't like to be in your **situation**.*
a position
circumstances *He is in extremely difficult **circumstances**.*

size NOUN
*What is the **size** of this room?*
the measurements
the dimensions
the length
the width
the breadth
the height

skill NOUN
*Everyone admired her **skill** at the game.*
ability
talent
expertise

skin NOUN
1 *Their clothes were made of animal **skins**.*
a hide
a fur
a pelt

2 *You can eat the **skin** of some fruits.*
the rind
the peel

skip VERB
1 *She **skipped** happily down the road.*
to dance
to prance
to trip
to trot

2 *The lambs were **skipping** about in the fields.*
to jump
to leap
to frisk
to prance

slam VERB
*She **slammed** the door angrily.*
to bang

slap VERB
*She **slapped** my hand when I tried to take a cookie.*
to smack
to hit
to strike

sledge NOUN
*The children were playing on **sledges**.*
a toboggan

A sleigh is a big sledge that is pulled by animals.

sleep VERB **sleeps, sleeping, slept**
1 *He was **sleeping** in front of the fire.*
to be asleep
to fall asleep
to doze
to snooze
to slumber
to snore
to have a nap
to nod off

2 *Some animals **sleep** all winter.*
to hibernate

sleepy ADJECTIVE
*I was **sleepy** so I went to bed.*
tired
drowsy
weary
OPPOSITE
wide awake

slide VERB **slides, sliding, slid**
1 *The sledge **slid** across the ice.*
to glide
to skim
to slither

2 *The car **slid** on the icy road.*
to skid
to slip

slight ADJECTIVE
*We've got a **slight** problem.*
small
little
minor
unimportant

slightly ADVERB
*I was **slightly** disappointed with the party.*
a little
somewhat
rather
OPPOSITE **very**

slim ADJECTIVE
*She was tall and **slim**.*
thin
slender

slimy ADJECTIVE
*The bottom of the lake was horrible and **slimy**.*
slippery
slippy
slithery
sticky
gooey

slip VERB
1 *Sam **slipped** and fell over.*
to trip
to stumble
to lose your balance *He **lost his balance**.*

2 *The wheels kept **slipping** on the wet road.*
to slide
to skid

slippery ADJECTIVE
*Take care: the floor is **slippery**.*
slippy
greasy
oily
slimy
icy
slithery

slope NOUN
*We climbed up the steep **slope** to the castle.*
a hill
a bank
a rise

slope VERB
1 *The beach **slopes** down to the sea.*
to drop
to dip
to fall

2 *The field **slopes** gently upwards.*
to rise

3 *The floor **slopes** to one side.*
to tilt
to slant
to lean

sloppy ADJECTIVE
1 *The cake mixture was too **sloppy**.*
wet
runny
watery

2 *This is a very **sloppy** piece of work—you will have to do it again!*
careless
messy
untidy
shoddy

slow ADJECTIVE
1 *They were walking at a **slow** pace.*
steady
leisurely
unhurried
dawdling
sluggish

❷ *We got stuck behind a **slow** lorry on the main road.*
slow-moving

❸ *He made a **slow** recovery from his illness.*
steady
gradual
OPPOSITE **quick**

sly *ADJECTIVE*
*They say the fox is a **sly** animal.*
clever
crafty
cunning
wily
devious

smack *VERB*
*Don't **smack** your little brother!*
to slap
to hit
to spank

small *ADJECTIVE*

OVERUSED WORD

Try to use a more interesting word when you want to say **small**. Here are some other words you can use instead:

❶ *He handed me a **small** box.*
little

Use **tiny**, **titchy** *(informal)* or **minute** for something that is very small: *She was riding a strange-looking bike with **tiny** wheels.*

❷ *They live in a **small** flat.*
little
tiny

Use **cramped** or **poky** for a room or building that is too small: *Our classroom would feel very **cramped** with 50 children in it.*

❸ *I'm quite **small** for my age.*
short
slight
petite

❹ *She gave us **small** helpings.*
mean
measly
stingy

❺ *These trousers are too **small** for me.*
tight
short

❻ *It's only a **small** problem.*
little
slight
minor
OPPOSITE **big**

smart *ADJECTIVE*
❶ *You look very **smart** in your new clothes.*
neat
elegant
stylish
well-dressed
chic
OPPOSITE **scruffy**

❷ *He's a **smart** boy.*
clever
intelligent
bright
sharp
OPPOSITE **stupid**

smash *VERB*
❶ *A glass fell on the floor and **smashed**.*
to shatter
to break into pieces

Use **splinter** when wood smashes: *The boat hit a rock and **splintered**.*

❷ *The car **smashed** into a tree.*
to crash
to collide with *The car **collided with** a tree.*

smear VERB

*The baby had **smeared** jam all over the walls and made a terrible mess.*
to wipe
to rub
to spread
to daub

smell NOUN

*What's that **smell**?*
A **scent**, **perfume** or **fragrance** is a nice smell, like the smell of perfume or flowers: *These roses have a lovely **scent.***
An **aroma** is a nice smell of food cooking: *A delicious **aroma** of fresh bread was coming from the kitchen.*
An **odour** is a bad smell: *There was a strong **odour** from the bin.*
A **stink**, **stench** or **pong** *(informal)* is a nasty smell: *There was a horrible **stink** of sweaty socks!*

smell VERB smells, smelling, smelled or smelt

*Your feet **smell**!*
to stink
to reek
to pong *(informal)*

smelly ADJECTIVE

*That cheese is really **smelly**!*
stinky
stinking
foul-smelling
pongy *(informal)*
odorous

smile VERB

*She looked up and **smiled** at me.*

Use **grin** or **beam** when someone smiles because they are happy: *The children **beamed** when they saw the presents.*

Use **smirk** when someone smiles in an annoying way: *Henry **smirked** when I got told off.*

smooth ADJECTIVE

❶ *Roll out the dough on a **smooth** surface.*
level
even
flat
OPPOSITE **uneven**

❷ *I stroked the cat's lovely **smooth** fur.*
soft
silky
velvety
sleek
OPPOSITE **rough**

❸ *We rowed across the **smooth** surface of the lake.*
calm
flat
still
OPPOSITE **rough**

snake NOUN

*We were frightened because we saw a poisonous **snake**.*
a serpent

WORD WEB

Some types of **snake**:

an adder
a boa constrictor
a cobra
a grass snake
a python
a rattlesnake
a viper

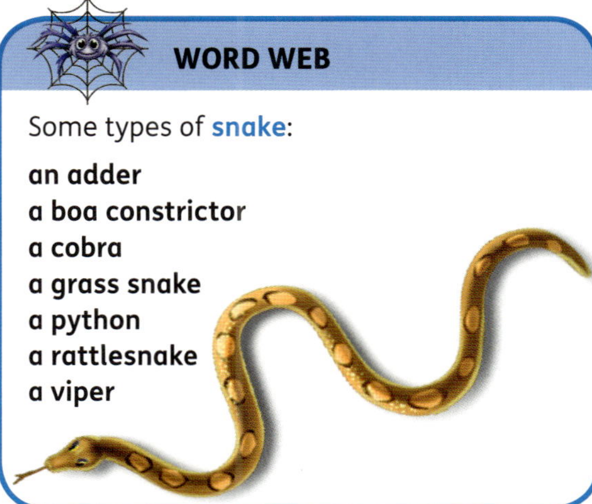

snatch VERB

*He **snatched** the sandwich from my hand.*
to grab
to take
to pull
to seize

A B C D E F G H I J K L M N O P Q R Ss T U V W X Y Z

sneak VERB
*She **sneaked** out of the room.*
to creep
to slip
to steal

soaking ADJECTIVE
*My clothes were **soaking** after I walked home in the rain.*
drenched
dripping wet
wringing wet
sopping
wet through
saturated

soft ADJECTIVE
1 *Work the clay with your hands until it is **soft**.*
doughy
squashy
malleable
OPPOSITE **hard**

2 *The bed was warm and **soft**.*
springy
OPPOSITE **hard**

3 *The kitten's coat was lovely and **soft**.*
smooth
fluffy
furry
silky
velvety
OPPOSITE **rough**

4 *Our feet sank into the **soft** ground.*
boggy
marshy
spongy
squashy
OPPOSITE **hard**

5 *There was **soft** music playing in the background.*
quiet
gentle
low
soothing
OPPOSITE **loud**

soldier NOUN
*They sent **soldiers** to help people after the floods.*
troops *They sent **troops**.*
the army *They sent **the army**.*

solid ADJECTIVE
1 *The walls are **solid**.*
dense
rigid
strong
OPPOSITE **hollow**

2 *Water becomes **solid** when it freezes.*
hard
firm
OPPOSITE **soft**

solve VERB
*Have you **solved** the mystery yet?*
to work out
to figure out
to clear up
to crack
to unravel
to get to the bottom of

song NOUN
*As he walked along he sang a little **song**.*
a tune
a ditty

WORD WEB

Some types of **song**:

an anthem
a ballad
A carol is a Christmas song.
a folk song
A hymn is a religious song.
A lullaby is a song to send a baby to sleep.
a melody
a nursery rhyme
a pop song
a rap

soon *ADVERB*
*Lunch will be ready **soon**.*
shortly
before long
in a short while
in no time

sore *ADJECTIVE*
*My knee is **sore**.*
hurting
painful

Use **aching** if something is sore for a long time: *I sat down to rest my **aching** feet.*

Use **throbbing** if something is sore with a banging pain: *My knee was still **throbbing**.*

Use **bruised** if something has a bruise on it: *Mum gently bathed my **bruised** knee.*

Use **tender** if something is sore when you touch it: *I can walk around now, but my leg is still a bit **tender**.*

sorry *ADJECTIVE*
1 *He was **sorry** when he saw the damage he had done.*
apologetic
ashamed
upset
remorseful
regretful
OPPOSITE **unrepentant**

2 *I feel **sorry** for the little girl.*
sympathetic *I feel **sympathetic** towards the little girl.*
full of pity
sad
OPPOSITE **unsympathetic**

sort *NOUN*
1 *What **sort** of sandwich do you want?*
a type
a kind
a variety

2 *A terrier is a **sort** of dog.*
a breed

3 *A ladybird is a **sort** of beetle.*
a species

4 *What **sort** of trainers do you want to buy?*
a brand
a make

sort *VERB*
*We **sorted** the books into three different piles.*
to arrange
to group
to organise
to classify

sound *NOUN*
*I heard a strange **sound** coming from the kitchen.*
a noise

WORD WEB

Some loud **sounds**:

bang
boom
buzz
clang
clank
clatter
crash
pop
rattle
ring
roar
rumble
thud
thump
whistle

Some gentle **sounds**:

bleep
click
drip
fizz
hum
plop
splash
tick
whirr

sour *ADJECTIVE*
*Lemon has a **sour** taste.*
bitter
sharp
acid
tart
OPPOSITE **sweet**

space *NOUN*
1 *Is there enough **space** for me there?*
room
capacity
2 *We squeezed through a **space** between the two rocks.*
a gap
a hole
an opening
3 *The astronauts will spend ten days in **space**.*
outer space

WORD WEB
Some types of spacecraft:
a spaceship
a rocket
a space shuttle

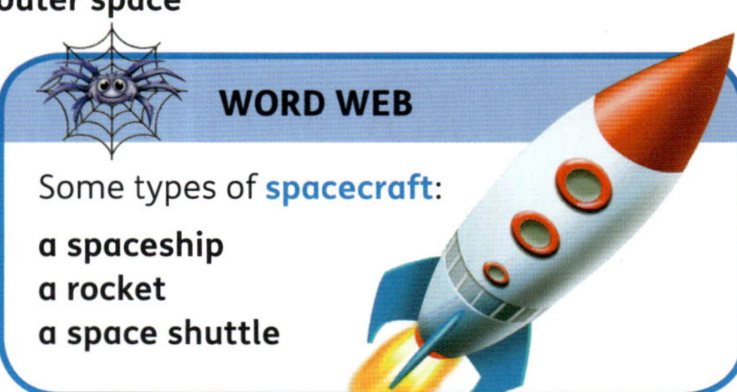

spare *ADJECTIVE*
*Remember to take a **spare** pair of shoes.*
extra
additional

spark *NOUN*
*I saw a **spark** come from the fire.*
a flash
a glint

sparkle *VERB*
*The sea **sparkled** in the sunlight.*
to shine
to glisten
to shimmer
to glint
to glitter
to twinkle

speak *VERB* **speaks, speaking, spoke, spoken**
*Everyone started to **speak** at once.*
to talk
to say something
to chatter
to start a conversation

special *ADJECTIVE*
1 *Your birthday is a very **special** day.*
important
significant
unusual
extraordinary
2 *I've got my own **special** mug.*
personal
individual
particular
specific
OPPOSITE **ordinary**

spectacular *ADJECTIVE*
*We watched a **spectacular** fireworks display.*
exciting
impressive
magnificent
wonderful
thrilling
sensational

speed NOUN
❶ *We were walking at a fairly average **speed**.*
a pace

❷ *The pilot told us the **speed** of the aeroplane.*
velocity

❸ *They worked with amazing **speed**.*
quickness
swiftness
haste

speed VERB **speeds, speeding, sped**
*A sports car **sped** past us.*
to shoot
to zoom
to whizz
to flash

spell NOUN
*She was under a magic **spell**.*
an enchantment
a charm
a bewitchment

spend VERB **spends, spending, spent**
*I've already **spent** all my pocket money.*
to use
to pay out *I **paid out** a lot of money for that jacket.*

spiky ADJECTIVE
*The plant has **spiky** leaves.*
sharp
prickly
pointed
barbed

spill VERB **spills, spilling, spilled** or **spilt**
❶ *Mind you don't **spill** your drink.*
to drop
to knock over
to upset

❷ *She **spilt** milk all over the kitchen floor.*
to pour
to tip
to slop
to splash

Use **scatter** or **strew** when you spill something dry with lots of small pieces: *The packet broke and rice was **scattered** all over the floor.*

❸ *Some water had **spilt** on to the floor.*
to drip
to leak
to splash

❹ *Water was **spilling** over the edge of the bath.*
to pour
to run
to stream
to gush
to splash

spin VERB **spins, spinning, spun**
❶ *I **spun** round when I heard his voice.*
to turn
to whirl
to swivel

❷ *We watched the dancers **spinning** across the floor.*
to twirl
to whirl
to pirouette

❸ *The back wheel of my bike was still **spinning**.*
to turn
to revolve
to rotate

spirit NOUN
*The house is supposed to be haunted by evil **spirits**.*
a ghost
a phantom
a spectre

spiteful ADJECTIVE
*It wan't nice to say those **spiteful** things about your friend.*
nasty
unkind
horrible
mean
malicious
OPPOSITE **kind**

splash VERB
❶ *They **splashed** us with water.*
to shower
to spray
to squirt

❷ *They **splashed** water all over the floor.*
to spill
to slop
to slosh

split VERB **splits, splitting, split**
❶ *He **split** the log with an axe.*
to cut
to chop

❷ *The bag **split** open and the oranges fell out.*
to break
to tear
to rip

❸ *We **split** the sandwich between us.*
to share
to divide

spoil VERB
❶ *The water had **spoilt** some of the books.*
to damage
to ruin
to destroy

❷ *The bad weather **spoilt** our holiday.*
to ruin
to wreck
to mess up

spoke VERB (*past tense of* **speak**)

spoken VERB (*past tense and past participle of* **speak**)

spooky ADJECTIVE
*I don't like that **spooky** old house.*
creepy
ghostly
eerie
scary

sport NOUN
*Do you enjoy **sport**?*
exercise
games

WORD WEB

Some team **sports**:

baseball
basketball
cricket
football
hockey
ice hockey
netball
rounders
rugby
volleyball

Some individual **sports**:

athletics
badminton
canoeing
cycling
fishing
golf
gymnastics
ice skating
jogging
judo
ju-jitsu
karate
kick-boxing
skiing
snooker
snowboarding
swimming
table tennis
tae kwondo
tennis
trampolining

cycling
kick-boxing
gymnastics
running
football
canoeing

A B C D E F G H I J K L M N O P Q R Ss T U V W X Y Z

spot *NOUN*

1 *Leopards have dark **spots** on their bodies.*
a mark
a dot
a blotch
a patch

2 *Oh, no! I've got a **spot** on my nose!*
a pimple

Acne is a lot of spots on your face:
*Some teenagers get very bad **acne**.*

A rash is a lot of spots you get when you are ill:
*Chickenpox gives you a **rash**.*

3 *There were a few **spots** of paint on the door.*
a mark
a dot
a drop
a blob
a smear
a smudge
a speck

4 *We found a lovely **spot** for a picnic.*
a place
a site
a location

spot *VERB*

1 *I **spotted** my friend at the bus stop.*
to catch sight of
to notice
to see
to spy

2 *Can you **spot** the difference?*
to detect
to notice

spray *VERB*

1 *He **sprayed** some water on to the plants.*
to splash
to sprinkle
to squirt

2 *She **sprayed** us with water.*
to splash
to shower
to squirt

spread *VERB* spreads, spreading, spread

1 *The bird **spread** its wings and flew away.*
to open
to stretch out

2 *We **spread** a cloth on the ground.*
to lay out
to unfold
to open out
to arrange

3 *I **spread** some jam on to the bread.*
to put
to smear

spun *VERB* *(past tense and past participle of* spin*)*

squabble *VERB*

*My brothers are always **squabbling**.*
to argue
to quarrel
to disagree
to fall out
to fight
to bicker

squash *VERB*

1 *Mind you don't **squash** those flowers.*
to crush
to flatten
to damage
to break

2 *We all **squashed** into the back of the car.*
to squeeze
to crowd

3 *I **squashed** everything into the suitcase.*
to push
to shove
to cram
to squeeze
to jam

squeeze *VERB*

1 *We all **squeezed** into the tiny room.*
to squash
to crowd
to pack

❷ *I **squeezed** everything into the bag.*
to push
to shove
to squash
to pack
to cram
to jam

squirt VERB

❶ *Water **squirted** out of the hole.*
to spurt
to gush
to spray
to shoot
to spout
to squeeze

❷ *She **squirted** water at me.*
to spray
to splash
to shoot
to fire

stage NOUN

*We have finished the first **stage** of our journey.*
a part
a phase

stain NOUN

*Her shirt was covered in **stains** from cooking.*
a mark
a spot
a smudge
a smear

stale ADJECTIVE

*All we had to eat was water and **stale** bread.*
old
dry
mouldy
OPPOSITE **fresh**

stammer VERB

*'B-b-but why?' he **stammered**.*
to stutter
to splutter

stamp VERB

*He **stamped** on my toe.*
to stomp
to tread
to trample

stand VERB stands, standing, stood

❶ *We all **stood** when the visitors arrived.*
to get up
to get to your feet *We all **got to our feet**.*
to rise *We all **rose**.*

❷ *I can't **stand** this noise!*
to bear
to put up with
to tolerate

standard NOUN

*The **standard** of your work has improved.*
level
quality

stare VERB

*Why is everyone **staring** at me?*
to look
to gaze

Use **gape** if you stare in a surprised way: *My friends all **gaped** at me as I climbed onto the horse.*

Use **glare** if you stare in an angry way: *My aunt **glared** at me, so I knew I had to behave.*

start VERB

❶ *What time does the programme **start**?*
to begin
to commence
OPPOSITE **finish**

❷ *We're going to **start** a running club.*
to set up
to create
to establish
to launch

❸ *She **started** the engine.*
to switch on
to turn on

A B C D E F G H I J K L M N O P Q R Ss T U V W X Y Z

start *NOUN*
*When is the **start** of the hockey season?*
the beginning
the opening
OPPOSITE **end**

starving *ADJECTIVE*
*Is lunch ready? I'm **starving**!*
famished
ravenous
starved

state *VERB*
*'It's time to go,' she **stated**.*
to say
to declare
to announce
to assert

state *NOUN*
*The classroom was in a very messy **state**.*
a condition

statue *NOUN*
*In the main hall is a **statue** of a woman.*
a carving
a sculpture
A **bust** is a statue of someone's head and shoulders.

stay *VERB*
1 ***Stay** here until I come back.*
to remain
to wait
to hang around
to linger

2 ***Stay** on this path until you reach the river.*
to continue
to carry on

3 *I'm going to **stay** with my grandma.*
to visit

4 *He **stayed** asleep all morning.*
to remain
to continue *He **continued** sleeping all morning.*

steady *ADJECTIVE*
1 *Make sure the ladder is **steady**.*
firm
stable
secure
balanced
OPPOSITE **wobbly**

2 *The music had a **steady** rhythm.*
even
regular
constant
OPPOSITE **irregular**

steal *VERB* **steals, stealing, stole, stolen**
*Someone's **stolen** my purse.*
to take
to pinch
to nick *(informal)*

steep *ADJECTIVE*
*There was a **steep** drop down to the river.*
sharp
vertical
sheer
OPPOSITE **gradual**

step *NOUN*
1 *He took a **step** forwards.*
a pace
a stride

2 *I climbed up the **steps**.*
stairs

stick *NOUN*
1 *We collected some **sticks** to make a fire.*
a twig
a branch

2 *He was holding a long **stick**.*
a pole
a rod
a cane
A **baton** is a stick you use to conduct an orchestra or in a relay race.
A **truncheon** is a stick that a policeman carries.
A **club** is a stick you use as a weapon or in golf.

A **bat** is a stick you use in cricket, rounders or baseball.
A **walking stick** or **crutch** is a stick to help you walk.

stick *VERB* **sticks, sticking, stuck**
1 *I **stuck** the pictures in my book.*
to glue
to fix
to paste

2 *Sometimes the door **sticks** a bit.*
to jam
to get stuck

3 *She **stuck** a pin into my arm.*
to jab
to stab
to pierce

sticky *ADJECTIVE*
*She picked up some of the **sticky** mixture.*
gooey
tacky
gluey
gummy

stiff *ADJECTIVE*
1 *Use **stiff** cardboard for the base.*
hard
rigid
OPPOSITE **soft**

2 *The ingredients make a **stiff** paste.*
thick
firm
OPPOSITE **soft**

3 *The door handle was a bit **stiff**.*
stuck
jammed

4 *I woke up with a **stiff** neck.*
sore
painful

still *ADJECTIVE*
1 *It was a very **still** evening.*
quiet
calm

2 *We all stood perfectly **still**.*
motionless

stir *VERB*
*She **stirred** the mixture with a spoon.*
to mix
to beat
to whisk

stole *VERB (past tense of* **steal***)*

stolen *VERB (past participle of* **steal***)*

stone *NOUN*
*He threw a **stone** into the water.*
A **pebble** is a small round stone: *We found some pretty **pebbles** on the beach.*
A **rock** is a big stone: *We climbed over the **rocks** and down to the sea.*
A **boulder** is a very big heavy stone: *Huge **boulders** came tumbling down the mountainside.*

stood *VERB (past tense and past participle of* **stand***)*

stop *VERB*
1 *The policeman **stopped** the traffic.*
to halt
to hold up

2 *The bus **stopped** outside the school.*
to pull up
to draw up
to park
to come to a halt
to grind to a halt
to come to a standstill

3 *He **stopped** for a moment.*
to hesitate
to pause
to wait

4 *Shall we **stop** for lunch?*
to break off
to knock off

A B C D E F G H I J K L M N O P Q R Ss T U V W X Y Z

5 *I wish you would **stop** teasing your brother!*
to finish
to quit
to give up

6 *This silly behaviour has got to **stop**.*
to end
to finish
to come to an end
to cease

7 *It is time to **stop** this nonsense.*
to end
to put an end to
to put a stop to
to conclude

8 *We must **stop** him from getting away.*
to prevent
to block

storm *NOUN*

*That night there was a terrible **storm** and we were glad to be inside the house.*

A **thunderstorm** is a storm with thunder.
A **blizzard** is a storm with snow: *The **blizzard** had left huge snowdrifts the next morning.*

A **gale**, **hurricane** or **tornado** is a storm with a very strong wind: *A lot of buildings were damaged by the **hurricane**.*

story *NOUN*

*He told us a **story** about a fox.*
a tale
a yarn

WORD WEB

Some types of **story**:

an adventure story
a fable
a fairy tale
a fantasy story
a folk tale
a legend
a myth
a parable
a science fiction story
a traditional tale

straight *ADJECTIVE*

*That picture isn't **straight**.*
level
upright
OPPOSITE **crooked**

strain *VERB*

1 *I had to **strain** to reach the handle.*
to struggle
to try hard
to make an effort

2 *I **strained** a muscle when I was running.*
to hurt
to injure
to damage
to pull

strange *ADJECTIVE*

1 *What a **strange** animal the sloth is!*
funny
peculiar
odd
curious
unusual
extraordinary
remarkable
weird
OPPOSITE **normal**

2 *When I woke up I was in a **strange** place.*
different
new
unfamiliar
unknown
foreign
OPPOSITE **familiar**

stranger *NOUN*

*He was a **stranger** in the town.*
an unknown
an outsider
a newcomer
A **foreigner** is someone who comes from a different country.

stray *VERB*
*Some of the children had **strayed** off the path.*
to wander
to straggle
to go astray
to roam

strength *NOUN*
*I had to use all my **strength** to open the door.*
force
might
power
energy
force

stress *NOUN*
*I was feeling a lot of **stress** about my homework.*
strain
pressure
anxiety
worry

stretch *VERB*
*You can **stretch** elastic.*
to pull out
to lengthen
to extend
to tighten
to tauten

strict *ADJECTIVE*
*Our teacher is quite **strict**.*
harsh
severe
stern
firm
rigid

string *NOUN*
*We tied the parcel up with **string**.*
cord
rope
twine
ribbon

stripe *NOUN*
*She was wearing a blue dress with white **stripes**.*
a line
a band
a strip

strong *ADJECTIVE*

OVERUSED WORD

Here are some more interesting words you can use instead of **strong**:

1 *You have to **strong** to be a weightlifter.*
tough
powerful

Use **muscular**, **brawny** or **strapping** for someone who has big muscles: *The lifeguard was tall and **muscular**.*

2 *She has been very ill and is not **strong** enough to go outside yet.*
well
fit
healthy

3 *The rope wasn't **strong** enough to hold my weight.*
tough
thick

4 *Concrete is a **strong** material.*
tough
solid
hard-wearing
heavy-duty
durable
unbreakable
indestructible

5 *The shelter was quite **strong**.*
well-made
well-built
sturdy

6 *This orange squash is too **strong**.*
concentrated

OPPOSITE **weak**

struggle *VERB*

1 *The thief **struggled** to get away.*
to fight
to wrestle

2 *We were **struggling** to carry all the boxes.*
to try hard
to strain
to make a big effort
to exert yourself

stubborn *ADJECTIVE*

*He was **stubborn** and refused to come with us.*
obstinate
defiant
wilful
pig-headed
determined
dogged

study *VERB*

1 *We're **studying** the Romans at school.*
to learn about
to read about
to research
to investigate

2 *He **studied** the map carefully.*
to look at
to examine

stuff *NOUN*

1 *There was some sticky **stuff** on the floor.*
a substance *There was a sticky **substance** on the floor.*

2 *We cleared all the old **stuff** out of the cupboards.*
things
odds and ends
bits and pieces

3 *Don't forget to take all your **stuff** with you.*
things
belongings
possessions
kit

stuffy *ADJECTIVE*

*The room was **stuffy**.*
warm
airless
stifling
OPPOSITE **airy**

stumble *VERB*

*I **stumbled** over a big stone.*
to trip
to slip
to lose your balance

stupid *ADJECTIVE*

1 *That was a **stupid** thing to do!*
silly
daft *(informal)*
foolish
unwise
idiotic

2 *You must be **stupid** if you believe that!*
daft
dim
dense
brainless
thick *(informal)*
OPPOSITE **intelligent**

subtract *VERB*

*Can you **subtract** 6 from 9?*
to take away
to deduct
to find the difference between *Can you **find the difference between** 6 and 9?*

succeed *VERB*

1 *I know she will **succeed** in becoming a pilot.*
to manage
to be successful

2 *All children should try to **succeed** at school.*
to do well

③ *Did your plan* ***succeed****?*
to work
to be successful ***Was*** *your plan* ***successful****?*
OPPOSITE **fail**

success NOUN
The concert was a great ***success****.*
a triumph
a hit
OPPOSITE **failure**

successful ADJECTIVE
Our team was ***successful*** *in the competition.*
victorious
triumphant

sudden ADJECTIVE
① *There was a* ***sudden*** *change in the weather.*
unexpected
abrupt

② *He made a* ***sudden*** *dash for the door.*
quick
swift
hasty
hurried

suggest VERB
I ***suggested*** *that we should go back home.*
to propose
to advise
to recommend

suggestion NOUN
What do you think we should do?
What's your ***suggestion****?*
an idea
a proposal
a plan

suit VERB
That dress ***suits*** *you.*
to look nice on *That dress* ***looks nice on*** *you.*
to look right on *That dress* ***looks right on*** *you.*

sulky ADJECTIVE
He's been ***sulky*** *all afternoon.*
moody
sullen
bad-tempered
grumpy

sung VERB *(past participle of sing)*

sunk VERB *(past participle of sink)*

sunny ADJECTIVE
It was a lovely ***sunny*** *day.*
bright
fine
clear
cloudless
summery
OPPOSITE **cloudy**

supply NOUN
There's a ***supply*** *of paper in the cupboard.*
a store
a stock
a reserve
a hoard

support VERB
① *Those pillars* ***support*** *the roof.*
to hold up
to prop up
to reinforce
to bear

② *You should* ***support*** *your friends when they are in trouble.*
to help
to defend
to stand up for
to stick up for
to back
to side with

A B C D E F G H I J K L M N O P Q R Ss T U V W X Y Z

3 *We went to **support** our team.*
to encourage
to cheer on
to express support for

suppose VERB

1 *I **suppose** we ought to go home now.*
to think
to guess
to reckon

2 *I **suppose** she must be the new teacher.*
to assume
to presume

sure ADJECTIVE

1 *I'm **sure** she lives somewhere round here.*
certain
positive
convinced
confident

2 *He's **sure** to remember.*
bound
certain
OPPOSITE **unsure**

surprise NOUN

1 *Winning was a big **surprise**.*
a shock
a bombshell
a bolt from the blue
a revelation

2 *He looked at me in **surprise**.*
amazement
astonishment
wonder

surprise VERB

*It **surprised** everyone when our team won the game.*
to amaze
to astonish
to astound
to shock
to startle
to stagger
to stun

surprised ADJECTIVE

*I was really **surprised** to see him.*
amazed
astonished
astounded
staggered
flabbergasted
shocked

surrender VERB

*After a long game, the team **surrendered**.*
to give in
to capitulate
to yield

surround VERB

*The house was **surrounded** by a wall.*
to encircle
to ring
to enclose

surroundings NOUN

*She found herself in very strange **surroundings**.*
a setting
a location
an environment *She found herself in a strange **environment**.*

survive VERB

*The plane crashed, but everyone **survived**.*
to live
to stay alive

suspect VERB

*I **suspect** he is lying.*
to think
to believe
to guess
to have a feeling *I **have a feeling** she is lying.*
to have a hunch *I **have a hunch** she is lying.*

suspicious ADJECTIVE

1 *She felt something **suspicious** was happening.*
dubious
suspect
fishy

❷ *I was a bit **suspicious** of him because I thought he was lying.*
distrustful
mistrustful
unsure
wary
OPPOSITE **trusting**

swam VERB *(past tense of* swim*)*

swear VERB **swears, swearing, swore, sworn**
❶ *He **swore** he would not be late.*
to promise
to vow
to give your word *He **gave his word** that he would never do it again.*

❷ *The teacher told him off because he **swore**.*
to use bad language
to curse

sweet ADJECTIVE
❶ *This orange juice is too **sweet**.*
sugary
OPPOSITE **bitter**

❷ *That little dog is really **sweet**!*
lovely
lovable
cute
adorable
OPPOSITE **ugly**

swim VERB **swims, swimming, swam, swum**
*We **swam** in the river.*
to bathe
to go swimming

swing VERB **swings, swinging, swung**
❶ *The loose rope was **swinging** backwards and forwards.*
to sway
to wave

❷ *The monkey **swung** from a branch.*
to hang
to dangle

switch NOUN
*Don't touch any of those **switches**.*
a button
a knob
a control

switch VERB
*I **switched** the light on.*
to turn
to flip
to put *I **put** the light on.*

swoop VERB
*The owl **swooped** down on its prey.*
to dive
to drop
to descend *The owl **descended** on its prey.*

sympathy NOUN
*Everyone gave me a lot of **sympathy** when I was ill.*
compassion
understanding
pity

A B C D E F G H I J K L M N O P Q R S Tt U V W X Y Z

Tt

tag NOUN
*Look at the price on the **tag**.*
a label
a ticket
a sticker

take VERB **takes, taking, took, taken**
1 *I offered him a sandwich and he **took** one.*
to pick up
to take hold of

Use **grab**, **snatch** or **grasp** if someone takes something roughly: *Sara rudely **snatched** the book out of my hands.*

2 *Please **take** this cup of tea to Mum.*
to carry
to bring

3 *The nurse **took** us to the ward.*
to lead
to accompany
to guide

4 *Dad **took** us to the station in his car.*
to drive
to transport
to give someone a lift *Dad **gave us a lift** in his car.*

5 *The burglar **took** the jewels.*
to steal
to pinch
to seize
to run off with

➤ **take out**
*The dentist **took out** one of my teeth.*
to remove
to pull out
to extract

talent NOUN
*He's a tennis player with a lot of **talent**.*
ability
skill
flair
aptitude
a gift *She has a great **gift** for music.*

talented ADJECTIVE
*He is a very **talented** musician.*
clever
gifted
skilful
able

talk NOUN
1 *I had a **talk** with my teacher.*
a chat
a conversation
a discussion

2 *Mr Rose gave us a **talk** on owls.*
a speech
a lecture

talk VERB
1 *We **talked** about our hobbies.*
to speak
to chat
to converse
to have a conversation
to have a discussion

2 *The teacher told us to stop **talking**.*
to chat
to chatter
to natter
to gossip

talkative ADJECTIVE
*My best friend is very **talkative** and always has a lot to say.*
chatty
communicative
garrulous

tall *ADJECTIVE*
1 *She is quite **tall** for her age.*
big
lanky
OPPOSITE **short**

2 *There are some **tall** buildings in the city.*
big
high
lofty
towering
soaring
OPPOSITE **low**

tame *ADJECTIVE*
*The animals in the farm are all very **tame**.*
gentle
docile
domesticated
obedient
OPPOSITE **wild**

tangle *NOUN*
*The wires have all got into a **tangle**.*
a muddle
a jumble
a knot
a twist

tangled *ADJECTIVE*
*The string was all **tangled**.*
knotted
twisted
snarled
entangled

tap *VERB*
*She **tapped** quietly on the door.*
to knock
to rap

taste *NOUN*
1 *The chilli had a strong **taste**.*
a flavour
a tang

2 *Can I have a **taste** of your chocolate?*
a bit
a bite
a piece
a mouthful
a nibble
a morsel

3 *He let me have a **taste** of his orange juice.*
a sip
a drop
a mouthful
a spoonful

taste *VERB*
*Would you like to **taste** my drink?*
to try
to sample

tasty *ADJECTIVE*
*Can I have some more of that **tasty** chicken?*
delicious
flavoursome
appetizing
mouth-watering

Use **savoury** for something that is tasty and not sweet: *There was a plate of lovely **savoury** snacks.*

teach *VERB* **teaches, teaching, taught**
1 *A teacher's job is to **teach** children.*
to educate

2 *My brother **taught** me how to use the computer.*
to show
to tell
to train *He **trained** us to use the computer.*

teacher *NOUN*
*We have a new maths **teacher**.*
A professor is a teacher at a university.
A tutor is a teacher for one person or a small group.
An instructor is someone who teaches you a skill: *My sister had a lesson with her driving **instructor**.*

team NOUN
*I'm in the school football **team**.*
a side
a club

tear VERB **tears, tearing, tore, torn**
*Be careful you don't **tear** your dress.*
to rip
to split

Use **shred** when something is torn into many small pieces: *He **shredded** the paper into tiny pieces.*

tease VERB
*Sometimes my friends **tease** me about my hair.*
to make fun of
to laugh at
to torment
to taunt
to mock

telephone VERB
*I'll **telephone** you later.*
to phone
to call
to ring
to give someone a ring

tell VERB **tells, telling, told**
1 *He **told** me he'd be home for tea.*
to say *He **said** he'd be home for tea.*
to mention *He **mentioned** he'd be home for tea.*
to promise *He **promised** he'd be home for tea.*

2 *My dad **told** me how to use a calculator.*
to show
to teach
to explain *He **explained** how to use a calculator.*

3 *You should **tell** the police.*
to inform
to notify

4 *She finally **told** me the secret.*
to reveal *She **revealed** the secret to me.*
to divulge *She **divulged** the secret to me.*

5 *My dad **told** us a story.*
to relate *He **related** a story.*
to narrate *He **narrated** a story to us.*

6 *Can you **tell** us what happened?*
to describe *Can you **describe** what happened?*
to recount *Can you **recount** what happened?*

7 *Mum **told** us to stop shouting.*
to order
to instruct
to command

➤ **tell off**
*The teacher **told** us **off** for talking during class.*
to scold
to reprimand
to rebuke

temper NOUN
1 *The man was in a terrible **temper**!*
a rage
a fury

2 *You seem to be in a very good **temper** today.*
mood
humour

terrible ADJECTIVE
1 *The weather was **terrible**!*
awful
dreadful
appalling
horrible

2 *This is **terrible** news!*
sad
awful
shocking
upsetting
alarming

3 *I'm a **terrible** tennis player.*
hopeless
useless

terrified ADJECTIVE
*I was absolutely **terrified**!*
petrified
horrified
scared stiff

terrify VERB
*Snakes **terrify** me.*
to frighten
to scare
to petrify

terror NOUN
*People ran away from the fire in **terror**.*
fear
fright
panic
alarm

test NOUN
1 *We've got a spelling **test** tomorrow.*
an exam
a quiz

2 *This is a **test** to see if the printer works.*
a trial
a check

test VERB
*Now we must **test** the machine to see if it works.*
to try
to try out
to check

thank VERB
*I **thanked** them for their present.*
to say thank you
to express your gratitude
to show your appreciation *Let's **show our appreciation**.*

thanks NOUN
*We gave her flowers to show our **thanks**.*
gratitude
appreciation

➤ **thanks to**
*We're safe now, **thanks to** you!*
because of
due to

thaw VERB
1 *The snow has started to **thaw**.*
to melt

2 *I took the meat out of the freezer to **thaw**.*
to defrost
to warm up

thick ADJECTIVE
1 *He drew a **thick** line.*
wide
broad

Use **bold** for printed letters that are thick: *I used **bold** letters for the title.*

2 *The castle had **thick** stone walls.*
solid
strong

3 *She cut herself a **thick** slice of cake.*
big
large
fat

4 *We had to walk through **thick** mud.*
deep
dense

5 *He was wearing a **thick** coat.*
heavy
warm
OPPOSITE **thin**

thief NOUN
*The money was stolen by a **thief**.*
a robber

A **burglar** goes into a person's house to steal: *A **burglar** got in through the window.*

A **pickpocket** steals things from a person's pocket: *There are **pickpockets** on the buses.*

A **mugger** attacks someone in the street to steal from them: *A **mugger** took his phone.*

A **shoplifter** steals things from shops: *There are security cameras to catch **shoplifters**.*

thin ADJECTIVE
1 *She drew a **thin** line across the page.*
fine
narrow
faint
OPPOSITE **thick**

2 *The dog was very **thin** and seemed hungry.*
slim
slender

Use **skinny**, **scrawny** or **bony** for someone who is too thin: *The evil witch had horrible **bony** hands.*

OPPOSITE **fat**

3 *This paint is too **thin**.*
watery
weak
runny
diluted
OPPOSITE **thick**

4 *She was only wearing a **thin** cotton dress.*
light
flimsy
OPPOSITE **thick**

thing *NOUN*

1 *We found some very interesting **things** in the attic.*
an object
an article
an item

2 *Don't forget to take all your **things** with you when you leave.*
belongings
possessions
stuff

3 *A corkscrew is a **thing** for opening bottles.*
a tool
a device
a gadget
a machine

4 *A very strange **thing** happened today.*
an event
an incident
an occurrence

5 *We had to do some very difficult **things**.*
an action
an act
a job
a task

think *VERB* thinks, thinking, thought

1 ***Think** before you act.*
to concentrate
to use your mind
to reflect

2 *He was sitting in a chair just **thinking**.*
to meditate
to muse
to daydream

3 *I **thought** about what had happened.*
to reflect on *I **reflected on** what had happened.*
to mull over *I **mulled over** what had happened.*
to ponder *I **pondered** what had happened.*
to consider *I **considered** what had happened.*

4 *My parents are **thinking** about moving.*
to consider *They are **considering** moving house.*
to plan *They are **planning** to move.*
to contemplate *They are **contemplating** moving.*

5 *I **think** that you are right.*
to believe
to reckon
to suppose

thought *NOUN*

*I've just had an interesting **thought**.*
an idea
a brainwave
a notion

thoughtful *ADJECTIVE*

1 *He was sitting on his own, looking **thoughtful**.*
serious
pensive
reflective

2 *You should try to be more **thoughtful**.*
considerate
kind
caring
helpful
unselfish
OPPOSITE **thoughtless**

threaten VERB
*An ogre was **threatening** the villagers.*
to menace
to intimidate
to bully
to terrorise

throw VERB **throws, throwing, threw, thrown**
1 *She **threw** a stone and broke the glass.*

Use **fling** or **hurl** when you throw something with a lot of force: *Someone had **hurled** a brick through the greenhouse window.*

Use **sling**, **toss** or **chuck** *(informal)* when you throw something carelessly: *She **tossed** the letter into the bin.*

Use **lob** when you throw something high into the air: *I **lobbed** the ball over the fence.*

2 *He **threw** the ball towards the batsman.*
to bowl

➤ **throw away**
*I **threw** my old shoes **away**.*
to throw out
to get rid of
to dispose of
to discard
to dump

tidy ADJECTIVE
1 *My aunt's house is always very **tidy**.*
neat
shipshape
orderly
uncluttered
trim
spick and span

2 *The children all looked **tidy**.*
neat
smart
well-groomed

3 *Are you a **tidy** person?*
neat
organised
house-proud
OPPOSITE **untidy**

tie VERB **ties, tying, tied**
1 *I can't **tie** my shoelaces.*
to do up
to fasten

2 *Why don't you **tie** the two bits together?*
to fasten
to join
to fix
to knot

3 *They **tied** the boat to a post.*
to fasten
to secure
to moor
to lash

4 *He **tied** the animal to the fence.*
to tether

tight ADJECTIVE
1 *My trousers are a bit **tight**.*
small
tight-fitting
close-fitting

2 *Make sure the jar has a **tight** lid.*
firm
secure

3 *Pull the rope until it is **tight**.*
stretched
taut
OPPOSITE **loose**

time NOUN
1 *He sat in silence for a long **time**.*
a while
a period

2 *Things were different in that **time**.*
a period
an era
an age

3 *This is a good **time** to go.*
a moment
an opportunity

tiny *ADJECTIVE*
*Some insects are **tiny.***
minute
minuscule
microscopic

Use **miniature** for a tiny version of something larger: *The fairy rode on a **miniature** horse.*
OPPOSITE **big**

tip *NOUN*
1 *She stood up on the **tips** of her toes.*
the end
the point

2 *We could only see the **tip** of the iceberg.*
the top

tip *VERB*
1 *I could feel the bench beginning to **tip** back.*
to lean
to tilt

2 *She **tipped** water all over the floor.*
to pour
to spill

➤ **tip over**
*The boat **tipped over** in the rough sea.*
to capsize
to overturn

tired *ADJECTIVE*
1 *We were **tired** after our walk.*
weary

Use **exhausted** or **worn out** when you are very tired: *I was **exhausted** after our long day.*

Use **sleepy** or **drowsy** when you want to sleep: *This warm fire is making me **sleepy**.*

2 *I'm **tired** of this game.*
fed up *I'm **fed up** with this game.*
bored *I'm **bored** with this game.*

told *VERB (past tense and past participle of* **tell***)*

tomb *NOUN*
*The explorers found the entrance to a **tomb**.*
a burial chamber
a crypt

took *VERB (past tense of* **take***)*

tool *NOUN*
*You can use a special **tool** to get the lid off.*
a device
a gadget
an implement
a utensil

WORD WEB

Some **tools** for woodwork:

a drill
a hammer
a plane
pliers
a screwdriver
a spanner

Some **tools** you use in the garden:

a fork
a hoe
a rake
shears
a spade
a trowel
a watering can

top *NOUN*
1 *We climbed to the **top** of the mountain.*
the summit

2 *We saw mountain **tops** far away.*
a peak
a tip

3 *We drove over the **top** of the hill.*
the crest

4 *Put the **top** back on the jar.*
a lid
a cover
a cap
OPPOSITE **bottom**

tore *(past tense of* **tear***)*

torn *(past participle of* **tear***)*

total *ADJECTIVE*
1 *What will the **total** cost be?*
full
whole

2 *The party was a **total** disaster.*
complete
absolute
utter

totally *ADVERB*
*That's **totally** ridiculous!*
absolutely
completely
utterly
downright

touch *VERB*
1 *He **touched** my arm lightly.*
to pat
to tap
to brush

2 *You mustn't **touch** the things on display.*
to handle
to hold
to feel

3 *Please don't **touch** the controls.*
to fiddle with
to mess about with
to play with

4 *If the wires **touch** there is a spark.*
to meet
to make contact
to come into contact

tough *ADJECTIVE*
1 *The rope is made of very **tough** nylon.*
strong
hard-wearing

2 *He thinks he's a really **tough** guy.*
strong
hard
rough
OPPOSITE **weak**

tower *NOUN*
1 *We built a **tower** of blocks.*
a stack
a pile
a mound

2 *The castle has a tall **tower**.*
a turret
a chimney
A steeple is the tower on a church.
A minaret is the tower on a mosque.

track *NOUN*
1 *They walked up the steep **track**.*
a path
a footpath
a trail

2 *The animal had left **tracks** in the snow.*
traces
footprints
a trail

track *VERB*
*They **tracked** the deer through the woods.*
to trail
to tail
to trace
to follow

tragedy *NOUN*
*The plane crash was a terrible **tragedy**.*
a disaster
a catastrophe
a calamity

train *VERB*
1 *Mr Green **trains** our swimming team.*
to coach
to instruct
to teach

2 *Our team **trains** every Thursday.*
to practise

trainer *NOUN*
1 *My brother is a **trainer** at the gym.*
a coach
an instructor

2 *Bring your **trainers** tomorrow for PE.*
running shoes
sports shoes

training *NOUN*
*It's football **training** after school today.*
practice
coaching

transform *VERB*
*The caterpillar **transforms** into a butterfly.*
to change
to turn
to develop
to become *The caterpillar **becomes** a butterfly.*

trap *VERB*
*We **trapped** the smugglers in the cave.*
to catch
to corner

travel *VERB*
*We **travelled** all around the world.*
to go
to journey
to tour

WORD WEB

Some ways to **travel**:

to cycle
to drive
to hitch-hike
to fly
to ride
to sail
To voyage is to travel by sea.
to walk

traveller *NOUN*
*The **travellers** saw many amazing things on their journey.*
an explorer
a voyager
A tourist is someone who travels for a holiday.
A nomad is someone who travels around instead of living in one place.
A pilgrim is someone who travels to a religious place.

tread *VERB* **treads, treading, trod, trodden**
*Mind you don't **tread** on the flowers.*
to step
to walk
to stand
to trample
to stamp

treasure *NOUN*
*We found a box of buried **treasure**.*
gold
silver
jewels
riches

treat *NOUN*
1. *We were allowed to stay up late as a **treat**.*
a reward
a favour
2. *The cake shop sells lots of tasty **treats**.*
delicacies
snacks

tree *NOUN*

WORD WEB

Some types of deciduous **tree**:

ash
beech
birch
elm
hawthorn
hazel
horse chestnut
larch
maple
oak
poplar
sycamore
willow

Some types of evergreen **tree**:

fir
holly
palm
pine
yew

a palm tree

Some types of **trees** around the world:

baobab
buffalo thorn
jacaranda
mango
marula
mopane
palm

tremble *VERB*
*I was **trembling** with fear.*
to shake
to quake
to quiver
to shiver
to shudder

trick *NOUN*
1 *We played a **trick** on our friends.*
a joke
a prank
a hoax
a con

2 *The dolphins did some amazing **tricks**.*
a stunt

trick *VERB*
*He **tricked** us into giving him our money.*
to cheat
to fool
to deceive
to swindle

trickle *VERB*
*Water **trickled** slowly out of the tap.*
to drip
to dribble
to leak
to seep

trip *NOUN*
*We went on a **trip** to the seaside.*
an outing
an excursion
a journey
a visit

trip *VERB*
*I **tripped** on the step and fell.*
to stumble
to slip
to lose your balance *I **lost my balance**.*

trod *VERB (past tense of* **tread***)*

trodden *VERB (past participle of* **tread***)*

trouble *NOUN*
1 *We have had a lot of **troubles** recently.*
difficulties
problems
cares
worries

2 *There was some **trouble** in the playground.*
bother
fighting
hassle

true *ADJECTIVE*
1 *The book is based on a **true** story.*
real
genuine
actual

2 *What he said isn't **true**.*
correct
accurate
right
factual
OPPOSITE **made-up**

trust *VERB*
*Can I **trust** you to behave while I am away?*
to rely on
to depend on
to count on

try *VERB* **tries, trying, tried**
1 *I **tried** to climb over the wall.*
to attempt
to make an effort

2 *Can I **try** the cake?*
to taste
to sample

3 *Would you like to **try** my new bike?*
to try out
to test
to have a go *Would you like to **have a go** on my new bike?*

try NOUN
*Would you like to have a **try** at tossing the pancake?*
a go
an attempt
a turn

tunnel NOUN
*There is a secret **tunnel** leading to the castle.*
a passage
An underpass is a tunnel under a road.

turn VERB
1 *I **turned** round to see who was behind me.*
to spin
to whirl
to twirl
to swivel

2 *I **turned** the key in the lock.*
to rotate

3 *The wheel began to **turn**.*
to revolve
to rotate
to spin

4 *In the autumn some leaves **turn** red.*
to become
to go
to change to

5 *Tadpoles **turn** into frogs.*
to become
to change into
to transform into
to develop into

6 *I **turned** the light on.*
to switch
to put

7 *We **turned** the attic into a playroom.*
to change
to convert
to transform

turn NOUN
*Be patient—it will be your **turn** in a minute.*
a go
a try
a chance
an opportunity

twinkle VERB
*The lights **twinkled** in the distance.*
to shine
to sparkle
to glitter

twist VERB
1 *I **twisted** the wire around the pole.*
to wind
to loop
to coil
to curl
to bend

2 *She **twisted** the ribbons together.*
to plait
to wind
to weave *She **wove** the ribbons together.*

type NOUN
1 *What **type** of music do you like?*
a kind
a sort

2 *A collie is a **type** of dog.*
a breed

3 *A ladybird is a **type** of beetle.*
a species

4 *I don't like that **type** of trainers.*
a brand
a make

typical ADJECTIVE
*It was a **typical** winter's day.*
normal
ordinary
average
standard
usual
OPPOSITE **unusual**

Uu

ugly ADJECTIVE
1 *We screamed when we saw the **ugly** monster.*
horrible
hideous
frightful
repulsive
grotesque

2 *Cinderella had two **ugly** sisters.*
plain
unattractive
OPPOSITE **beautiful**

uncomfortable ADJECTIVE
1 *These shoes are so **uncomfortable**!*
tight
stiff
cramped

2 *The bed was very **uncomfortable**.*
hard
lumpy
OPPOSITE **comfortable**

understand VERB understands, understanding, understood
*Do you **understand** what I'm saying?*
to follow
to grasp
to see
to get
to comprehend

unexpected ADJECTIVE
*He did something very **unexpected**—he ran away!*
surprising
startling
unpredictable

unfair ADJECTIVE
1 *It's **unfair** if she gets more pudding than me.*
wrong
unjust
unreasonable

2 *I thought the referee was **unfair**.*
biased
unjust
OPPOSITE **fair**

unfriendly ADJECTIVE
*The other children were very **unfriendly**.*
unkind
nasty
hostile
rude
mean
unwelcoming
OPPOSITE **friendly**

unhappy ADJECTIVE
*I was **unhappy** at my last school.*
sad
miserable
depressed
glum
dejected
down in the dumps *(informal)*

A B C D E F G H I J K L M N O P Q R S T Uu V W X Y Z

Use **gloomy** or **despondent** if you think something bad is going to happen: *Don't be **despondent**—we can fix your bike.*

Use **upset** or **heartbroken** if something sad has happened: *I was really **upset** when I fell out with my friends.*

Use **fed up** if you are unhappy and bored: *I was **fed up** because it rained all day.*

OPPOSITE **happy**

unkind ADJECTIVE

*Jo hates to see people being **unkind** to animals.*

horrible
nasty
mean
cruel
spiteful

OPPOSITE **kind**

unknown ADJECTIVE

*When I answered the phone I heard an **unknown** voice.*

unfamiliar
strange
unrecognised
unidentified

OPPOSITE **known**

unlucky ADJECTIVE

*We were **unlucky** to miss the bus.*

unfortunate
out of luck

OPPOSITE **lucky**

unpleasant ADJECTIVE

1 *He said some **unpleasant** things to me and I was upset.*

horrible
nasty
mean
unkind
rude
unfriendly
upsetting

2 *The meat had an **unpleasant** taste.*

horrible
nasty
disgusting
revolting
terrible

OPPOSITE **pleasant**

untidy ADJECTIVE

1 *My bedroom is always **untidy**.*

messy
chaotic

Use **jumbled** or **muddled** if a lot of things are mixed together in an untidy way: *There was a huge **jumbled** pile of clothes on the floor.*

Use **scruffy** to describe someone's clothes or appearance: *Tom never looks smart—he always looks **scruffy**!*

2 *This work is very **untidy**!*

messy
careless
sloppy

OPPOSITE **tidy**

unusual ADJECTIVE

*It's **unusual** to have snow in May.*

extraordinary
odd
peculiar
strange
surprising
uncommon

OPPOSITE **ordinary**

upset ADJECTIVE

*Sita was crying and looked very **upset**.*

sad
unhappy
distressed
troubled

Use **hurt** if you are upset by something unkind that someone has done: *I felt **hurt** that I wasn't invited to the party.*

upset VERB upsets, upsetting, upset

1 *The pictures of the war on TV **upset** me.*
to distress
to sadden
to frighten
to scare
to worry
to trouble

2 *Some of the nasty things he said really **upset** me.*
to hurt
to bother
to hurt someone's feelings *Some of the things he said **hurt my feelings**.*

upside down ADJECTIVE

*The picture on the screen was **upside down**.*
the wrong way up
topsy-turvy
inverted
OPPOSITE **the right way up**

urgent ADJECTIVE

1 *She got an **urgent** message from her friend and she had to go.*
very important
pressing
top-priority

2 *We have to do something. It's **urgent**.*
essential
vital
crucial
imperative
OPPOSITE **unimportant**

use VERB

1 *They **used** machines to dig the tunnel.*
to employ
to make use of

2 *Do you know how to **use** this tool?*
to handle
to manipulate

3 *He taught me how to **use** the machine.*
to work
to operate

4 *Have we **used** all the paint?*
to finish

useful ADJECTIVE

1 *Mobile phones are very **useful**.*
handy
practical
convenient

2 *She gave us some very **useful** advice.*
helpful
valuable
OPPOSITE **useless**

useless ADJECTIVE

1 *This old bicycle is **useless**!*
unusable
worthless
OPPOSITE **useful**

2 *I was a **useless** goalkeeper.*
hopeless
terrible
incompetent
OPPOSITE **good**

3 *Complaining is **useless**—you have to do something.*
pointless
fruitless
futile
OPPOSITE **useful**

usual ADJECTIVE

1 *I went to bed at my **usual** time of eight o'clock.*
normal
ordinary
regular

2 *The **usual** answer is no.*
normal
typical
general

Vv

vague *ADJECTIVE*
*He only gave a **vague** description of the dog.*
general
unclear
confused
hazy
OPPOSITE **exact**

vain *ADJECTIVE*
*He's so **vain** that he's always looking in the mirror.*
conceited
arrogant
big-headed
proud
boastful
OPPOSITE **modest**

valuable *ADJECTIVE*
*The coins in my collection are quite **valuable**.*
expensive
costly

Use **precious** if something is valuable and important to you: *The jewellery my grandmother gave me is very **precious** to me.*

Use **priceless** if something is so valuable you can't say how much it is worth: *These old paintings are **priceless**.*

OPPOSITE **worthless**

variety *NOUN*
1 *There is a **variety** of colours to choose from.*
an assortment
a choice
a mixture
a range

vegetable *NOUN*

WORD WEB

Some types of **vegetable**:

A B C D E F G H I J K L M N O P Q R S T U Vv W X Y Z

a courgette
a lettuce
broccoli
a potato
a leek
a cucumber
a yam
beetroot
a squash
an avocado
spinach
celery
sweetcorn
an onion
a cabbage
a cauliflower
a pumpkin

vibrate *VERB*

*The whole house **vibrates** when a lorry goes past.*
to shake
to wobble
to rattle
to shudder

victory *NOUN*

*We celebrated our team's **victory**.*
a win
a success
a triumph
OPPOSITE **defeat**

villain *NOUN*

*The police caught the **villain** in the end.*
a criminal
a crook
a baddy

violent *ADJECTIVE*

1 *We're not allowed to play **violent** games.*
aggressive
rough

Use **ferocious** or **savage** if someone is very violent: *He defeated the dragon in a **ferocious** battle.*

2 *That night there was a **violent** storm.*
severe
fierce
raging

virtually *ADVERB*

*It's **virtually** impossible to answer that question!*
almost
nearly
practically
as good as

visit *VERB*

*I'm going to **visit** my grandma next week.*
to see
to call on
to stay with

visitor *NOUN*

*Are you expecting a **visitor** this afternoon?*
a guest
a caller
company *Are you expecting **company**?*

Ww

wail *VERB*
*'I want to go home!' she **wailed**.*
to howl
to bawl
to cry

wait *VERB*
1 ***Wait** here until I get back.*
to stay
to remain

Use **hang on** or **hold on** when you wait only a short time: ***Hang on** a minute. I won't be long.*

2 *She **waited** for a while before she opened the door.*
to pause
to hesitate

wake *VERB*
➤ **wake up**
*I **wake up** at seven o'clock every morning when I have to go to school.*
to awaken
to get up
to rise

walk *VERB*
*We **walked** home from school.*

OVERUSED WORD

Try to use a more interesting word when you want to say **walk**. Here are some other words you can use instead:

Use **stride** or **march** when someone walks with big steps: *The professor came **striding** up to the building.*

Use **hurry** or **rush** when someone walks quickly: *She **hurried** down the road to the shop.*

Use **wander**, **stroll**, **amble** or **saunter** if someone walks slowly in a relaxed way: *Manjit slowly **wandered** over to the door.*

Use **stomp** or **clump** if someone walks noisily: *Tara **stomped** angrily out of the room.*

Use **creep**, **sneak** or **tiptoe** if someone walks very quietly: *I **crept** quietly downstairs, trying not to wake anyone.*

Use **limp**, **hobble**, **shuffle**, **stagger** or **stumble** if someone can't walk very well: *The old man **hobbled** along the street.*

Use **trudge** or **plod** if someone walks in a tired way: *Wearily, we **trudged** home.*

Use **strut** or **swagger** if someone walks in a very proud way: *I couldn't bear seeing him **strutting** about on the stage, so proud of himself!*

Use **hike** or **trek** if someone walks a long way over rough ground: *We spent two weeks **hiking** in the mountains.*

wander VERB

*We **wandered** around town all afternoon.*

to roam
to rove
to drift
to ramble

want VERB

1 *Do you **want** an ice cream?*

to fancy
to feel like
to need
to desire *(formal)*

Use **be dying for** or **be desperate for** if you want something very badly: *It's so hot! I'm **desperate for** a drink!*

Use **wish for**, **long for** or **yearn for** if you want something badly but do not think you will be able to have it: *She had always **longed for** a pony of her own.*

2 *I **want** to be a professional dancer.*

to dream of *I **dream of** being a professional dancer.*
to set your heart on *I have **set my heart on** being a professional dancer.*

warm ADJECTIVE

1 *The water was **warm**.*

lukewarm
tepid

2 *It was a nice **warm** day.*

hot
mild
sunny
summery

3 *I was lovely and **warm** in my thick coat.*

cosy
snug

4 *We sat down in front of the **warm** fire.*

hot
blazing
roaring

OPPOSITE **cold**

warn VERB

1 *He **warned** us to stay away from the old quarry.*

to advise
to remind
to tell

2 *Someone had **warned** the police about the robbery.*

to alert
to tip someone off

3 *This time I will just **warn** you. If you do it again, you will be in big trouble.*

to caution
to give someone a warning *This time I will just **give you a warning**.*

warning NOUN

1 *They ignored her **warning** and went outside.*

caution
advice

Use **threat** for something bad someone says they will do to you: *He ignored their **threats** because he wasn't afraid of them.*

2 *He stopped the car without any **warning**.*

notice
signal
indication

wash VERB

1 *Go and **wash** your hands.*

to clean
to rinse

2 *You should **wash** more often.*

to have a bath
to bath
to have a shower
to shower

3 *I **washed** my hair with shampoo.*
to shampoo

4 *We need to **wash** this floor because it's really dirty.*
to clean
to mop
to scrub
to wipe

waste NOUN

*We sort out all our **waste** so that the paper, glass and metal can be recycled.*
rubbish
litter
junk
refuse
trash
garbage

wasteful ADJECTIVE

*It's **wasteful** to take more food than you can possibly eat.*
extravagant
lavish
uneconomical

watch VERB

1 *I had the feeling that someone was **watching** me.*
to look at
to observe

Use **stare at** if you watch someone for a long time: *Ali was **staring at** the ship, trying to see who was on board.*

Use **gaze at** if you are watching something beautiful or interesting: *We **gazed at** the dancers, amazed by their leaps and jumps.*

2 *Will you **watch** my things while I go for a swim?*
to keep an eye on
to look after
to take care of
to guard
to mind

water NOUN

1 *Would you like a glass of **water**?*
mineral water
spring water
tap water

2 *We sat by the side of the **water**.*
a lake
a pond
a reservoir
a river
a stream
the sea
the ocean
a brook

WRITING TIPS

Here are some useful words for writing about **water**:

- *The water in the river **flowed** along smoothly.*
- *Water was **pouring** into the boat.*
- *Cold water **gushed** and **splashed** over the rocks.*
- *The water **trickled** and **gurgled** over the pebbles.*
- *A few drops of water were still **dripping** from the tap.*
- *The water of the lake **lapped** against the shore.*

She'd forgotten to turn off the tap when she fetched the bucket of water and all I can say is that there was ten times as much water on the kitchen floor as there was in the play-house when Lotta was scrubbing.—LOTTA SAYS NO, Astrid Lindgren

wave VERB

1 *She **waved** to me from across the street.*
to signal
to gesture

2 *The flags were **waving** in the wind.*
to stir
to sway
to flap
to flutter

3 *He **waved** the stick over his head.*
to swing
to brandish

wave NOUN
*We played in the **waves**.*
the surf
A **breaker** is a very big wave: *Huge **breakers** crashed onto the shore.*

way NOUN
1 *Is this the **way** to London?*
a road
a route
a direction
a course
a track

2 *This is the best **way** to build a den.*
a method *This is the best **method** of building a den.*
a technique *This is the best **technique** for building a den.*
a system *This is the best **system** for building a den.*

3 *The teacher spoke in a very nice **way**.*
a manner
a fashion
a tone

4 *She ties her hair up in a very pretty **way**.*
a style

weak ADJECTIVE
1 *She still feels quite **weak** after her illness.*
ill
poorly
feeble
frail
shaky
delicate
sickly

2 *You're too **weak** to fight against me!*
weedy
puny

3 *I think these wooden posts are too **weak**.*
thin
flimsy
fragile
rickety

4 *This orange squash is too **weak**.*
watery
tasteless
diluted
thin
OPPOSITE **strong**

weakness NOUN
*The monster's one **weakness** is that it can't hear.*
a fault
a flaw
a defect
OPPOSITE **strength**

wealthy ADJECTIVE
*Her parents are **wealthy**.*
rich
well-off
prosperous
OPPOSITE **poor**

wear VERB wears, wearing, wore, worn
1 *He was **wearing** a smart blue jacket.*
to have on
to be dressed in
to be sporting

2 *What shall I **wear** today?*
to put on
to dress in

weird ADJECTIVE
1 *They wear some **weird** clothes!*
strange
funny
peculiar
odd
OPPOSITE **ordinary**

2 *We heard a **weird** noise in the night.*
eerie
spooky
uncanny

well ADJECTIVE
*I hope you are **well**.*
fit
healthy
OPPOSITE **ill**

well ADVERB
1 *You have done this work very **well**.*
carefully
competently
properly
successfully
thoroughly

Use **brilliantly** or **excellently** if you do something very well: *Everyone in our team played **brilliantly**!*

Use **cleverly** or **skilfully** if you do something in a clever way: *He painted **skilfully**.*
OPPOSITE **badly**

2 *They don't treat their pets very **well**.*
kindly
lovingly
caringly
OPPOSITE **badly**

well-known ADJECTIVE
*He's a very **well-known** pop star.*
famous
celebrated
OPPOSITE **unknown**

went VERB *(past participle of* go*)*

wet ADJECTIVE
1 *My shoes are **wet**.*

Use **damp** if something is slightly wet: *I wiped the table with a **damp** cloth.*

Use **soaked**, **soaking wet**, **dripping wet** or **drenched** if something is very wet: *My clothes were **soaked** after I fell in the pool!*

2 *The field is too **wet** to play on.*
muddy
soggy
waterlogged

3 *It was a **wet** day.*
rainy
drizzly
showery
damp
OPPOSITE **dry**

while NOUN
*After a **while** I started to get the idea of the game.*
a time
a period of time
an interval

whisper VERB
*'Which way shall we go?' he **whispered**.*

Use **murmur** if you speak very gently: *'I must be dreaming,' she **murmured** .*

Use **mutter** or **mumble** if you speak quietly and not clearly: *The witch was **muttering** a spell to herself.*

Use **hiss** if you speak in a loud or angry whisper: *'Get out of here!' he **hissed**.*

white ADJECTIVE
*She was wearing a **white** dress.*
cream
ivory
snow-white

whole ADJECTIVE
*We ate the **whole** cake.*
complete
entire

wicked ADJECTIVE
1 *The land was ruled by a cruel and **wicked** king.*
bad
evil
vicious

2 *That was a **wicked** thing to do.*
wrong
bad
immoral
sinful
OPPOSITE **good**

wide *ADJECTIVE*
*We had to cross a **wide** river.*
broad
big
large
OPPOSITE **narrow**

wild *ADJECTIVE*
1 *They are **wild** animals and can be dangerous.*
untamed
ferocious
undomesticated
OPPOSITE **tame**

2 *Their behaviour can be a bit **wild** sometimes.*
noisy
rough
boisterous
unruly
rowdy
OPPOSITE **calm**

will *VERB*
1 *I **will** tell my teacher tomorrow.*
to intend to *I **intend to** tell my teacher tomorrow.*
to plan to *I **plan to** tell my teacher tomorrow.*
to be going to *I'm **going to** tell my teacher tomorrow.*

2 *I **will** help you with your homework.*
to be willing to *I **am willing to** help you.*
to be happy to *I **am happy to** help you.*

willing *ADJECTIVE*
*Are you **willing** to help us tidy up after the birthday party?*
happy
ready
prepared
eager
keen
inclined
OPPOSITE **unwilling**

win *VERB* **wins, winning, won**
1 *I was delighted when my team **won**.*
to be victorious
to triumph
to succeed
to come first
to finish first
OPPOSITE **lose**

2 *She **won** a medal in the cross-country race.*
to get
to earn
to receive
to gain
to secure

wind (*rhymes with **find***) *VERB* **winds, winding, wound**
1 *She **wound** her scarf round her neck.*
to wrap
to loop
to coil
to twist

2 *The path **winds** through the woods.*
to twist and turn
to curve
to meander
to snake

wind (*rhymes with **tinned***) *NOUN*
*Outside, the **wind** was blowing.*
A **breeze** is a gentle wind: *It was a hot day, but there was a lovely cool **breeze**.*

A **gale** is a strong wind: *We couldn't play outside because there was a **gale** blowing.*
A **hurricane** is a very strong wind: *A lot of houses were damaged by the **hurricane**.*

WRITING TIPS

Here are some useful words for writing about **wind**:

- *A **gentle** wind was **blowing** across the field.*
- *The **strong** wind **howled** and **roared** and **whistled** through the trees.*
- *The **icy** wind **buffeted** the small boats on the lake.*

windy ADJECTIVE
*It was a cold, **windy** night.*
breezy
blustery
stormy
OPPOSITE **calm**

winner NOUN
*James is the **winner**!*
the champion
the victor
OPPOSITE **loser**

wipe VERB
1 *I'll **wipe** the table before we eat.*
to clean
to mop

2 *She used a duster to **wipe** the furniture.*
to dust
to polish

3 *Please could you **wipe** the mud off your shoes?*
to rub
to scrape

wire NOUN
*There were electrical **wires** all over the floor.*
a cable
a lead
a flex

wise ADJECTIVE
1 *My grandfather is a very **wise** man.*
clever
intelligent
sensible

2 *You have made a **wise** decision.*
good
sensible
OPPOSITE **foolish**

wish VERB
➤ **wish for**
*I had always **wished for** a puppy.*
to want
to long for
to yearn for

wish NOUN
*Her greatest **wish** was to see her family again.*
a desire
a longing
a yearning
an ambition

witch NOUN
a sorceress
an enchantress

wizard NOUN
a sorcerer
an enchanter
a magician

wobble *VERB*

1 *The ladder* ***wobbled*** *as I climbed up it.*

to shake
to sway
to be unsteady
to teeter
to totter

2 *The jelly* ***wobbles*** *when you move the plate.*

to shake
to quake
to quiver
to vibrate

woman *NOUN*

What was the ***woman's*** *name?*

a lady
a girl

A **wife** is a married woman.
A **mother** is a woman who has children.
A **widow** is a woman whose husband has died.

won *VERB (past tense and past participle of* **win***)*

wonder *NOUN*

We stared at the lights in ***wonder****.*

amazement
admiration
awe

wonder *VERB*

I was ***wondering*** *what to do next.*

to think about
to consider
to ponder
to ask yourself *I was* ***asked*** *what to do next.*

wonderful *ADJECTIVE*

We had a ***wonderful*** *time at the park.*

great
amazing
brilliant
fantastic
marvellous

OPPOSITE **terrible**

wood *NOUN*

1 *Our garden shed is made of* ***wood****.*

timber
planks

2 *We need more* ***wood*** *for the fire.*

logs

3 *We walked through the* ***wood****.*

woods
woodland

A **forest** is a large wood: *They were scared to go into the huge, dark* ***forest****.*
A **copse** is a very small wood: *There's a* ***copse*** *at the top of the hill.*

woolly *ADJECTIVE*

I wore a nice warm ***woolly*** *jumper.*

fleecy
furry
thick
cuddly

word *NOUN*

I can't think of the right ***word****.*

a term
a phrase
an expression

wore *VERB (past tense of* **wear***)*

work *NOUN*

1 *Just sit quietly and get on with your* ***work****.*

a job
a task
schoolwork
homework

2 *What* ***work*** *do you want to do when you grow up?*

a job
an occupation
a profession
a career
a trade

3 *The* ***work*** *can be back-breaking.*

labour
toil

work VERB
1 *We **worked** hard all morning.*
to be busy *We **were busy** all morning.*
to toil
to labour

2 *When I grow up I want to **work** in a bank.*
to be employed
to have a job

3 *The lift isn't **working**.*
to go *The lift won't **go**.*
to function *The lift isn't **functioning**.*
to run *The lift isn't **running**.*

4 *I don't think your plan will **work**.*
to succeed
to be successful

world NOUN
*He has travelled all over the **world**.*
the earth
the globe
the planet

worn VERB *(past participle of* **wear***)*

worried ADJECTIVE
1 *I was **worried** because they were so late.*
anxious
concerned
uneasy

2 *Are you **worried** about changing schools?*
nervous
apprehensive
fearful
OPPOSITE **relaxed**

worry VERB
*Don't **worry**, everything will be all right.*
to fret
to be anxious
to be concerned

worry NOUN
*I seem to have so many **worries** at the moment.*
a concern
a fear
an anxiety

wound *(rhymes with* **spooned***)* NOUN
*He had a nasty **wound** on his arm.*
an injury
a cut
a gash

wound *(rhymes with* **spooned***)* VERB
*The explosion **wounded** a lot of people.*
to injure
to hurt

wound *(rhymes with* **found***)* VERB *(past tense and past participle of* **wind***)*

wrap VERB
1 *I **wrapped** the parcel in paper.*
to cover
to pack

2 *I **wrapped** my scarf round my neck.*
to wind
to loop
to twist

wreck VERB
1 *The explosion **wrecked** several buildings.*
to destroy
to demolish
to smash up

2 *He drove into a lamppost and **wrecked** his car.*
to smash up

3 *You've **wrecked** my phone!*
to break
to ruin
to smash

wriggle VERB
*Worms were **wriggling** in the soil.*
to wiggle
to squirm
to writhe

wrinkle NOUN
*He has **wrinkles** on his forehead.*
a line
a crease
a furrow

wrinkled ADJECTIVE
*I saw the kind, **wrinkled** face of my grandma.*
wrinkly
creased
crumpled
furrowed
lined
OPPOSITE **smooth**

write VERB **writes, writing, wrote, written**
1 *He **wrote** the word 'birthday' at the top of the page.*

Use **print** when you write something without the letters joined up: *He **printed** each word carefully in capital letters.*

Use **jot down** or **note down** when you write something quickly: *I quickly **jotted down** her phone number.*

Use **scribble** or **scrawl** when you write something quicky and messily: *I **scribbled** a quick message to the others.*

2 *Please **write** your name here.*
to sign
to put

3 *I **wrote** a list of all the things we would need to make the pancakes..*
to compile
to make
to draw up

4 *I **wrote** a story about a girl who found a pair of magic shoes.*
to make up
to create

To draft is to write a rough plan of something: *We **drafted** our stories in pairs.*

To post is to write something on the internet: *I **posted** a poem on the school website.*

5 *We're going to **write** a piece of music.*
to compose
to create

writer NOUN
*I want to be a **writer** when I grow up.*
an author

WORD WEB

Some types of **writer**:

An author is someone who writes books.
A blogger is someone who writes their own blog on the internet.
A journalist is someone who writes for a newspaper.
A novelist is someone who writes novels.
A playwright is someone who writes plays.
A poet is someone who writes poems.
A screenwriter or **a scriptwriter** is someone who writes stories for films or television.

written VERB *(past participle of **write**)*

wrong ADJECTIVE
1 *The information that he gave us was **wrong**.*
false
inaccurate
untrue
incorrect
faulty

2 *I thought she lived here, but I was **wrong**.*
mistaken
incorrect

3 *It is **wrong** to steal.*
dishonest
immoral
bad
wicked
OPPOSITE **right**

wrote VERB *(past tense of **write**)*

Yy

yell *VERB*
*The man **yelled** at us to go away.*
to shout
to scream
to shriek
to bawl
to bellow

yellow *ADJECTIVE*
*The bridesmaids wore **yellow** dresses.*
lemon
gold
primrose

young *ADJECTIVE*
1 *I was too **young** to understand what was happening.*
little
small

Use **immature**, **childish** or **babyish** when someone behaves in a way that seems too young: *Stop being so **childish**!*
OPPOSITE **old**

2 *My dad is forty, but he still looks **young**.*
youthful
OPPOSITE **old**

Zz

zap *VERB*
You have to zap aliens in this game.
to kill
to shoot
to destroy
to blast
to hit

zero *NOUN*
1 *The temperature went down to **zero**.*
nought
nothing

2 *The other team won by three goals to **zero**.*
nil

zoom *VERB*
The car zoomed along the road.
to speed
to race
to tear
to hurtle

Become a Word Explorer!

Contents

Word building

Have you ever thought about making up a word? If there isn't an exact word to describe something, you could try creating your own by thinking what it **looks**, **smells** or **tastes** like and then adding one of these endings.

-y	*a fish**y** smell, an orange**y** colour, a chocolate**y** taste*
-like	*a snake-**like** creature, a giraffe-**like** neck, a silk-**like** cloth*

You can also make new words to describe what something looks, smells or tastes like using these endings:

-looking	*a strange-**looking** man, a fierce-**looking** dog*
-smelling	*sweet-**smelling** perfume, disgusting-**smelling** socks*
-tasting	*delicious–**tasting** soup, foul-**tasting** medicine*

If you are describing an **ogre**, you could write:

*He had thick **leathery** skin and huge **shark-like** teeth. His eyes were small and **evil-looking**, and from his mouth came **foul-smelling** breath.*

Similes

Similes are comparisons using '**as**' or '**like**'. They can liven up your writing and of course, you can make up your own!

Here are some similes using 'as':

- blind **as** a bat
- clear **as** a bell
- cunning **as** a fox
- dry **as** a bone
- fit **as** a fiddle
- good **as** gold
- hard **as** nails
- light **as** a feather
- quiet **as** a mouse
- strong **as** an ox

Here are some similes using 'like':

- built **like** a tank
- chatter **like** a monkey
- eyes **like** a hawk
- fit **like** a glove
- fight **like** cats and dogs
- memory **like** an elephant
- move **like** a snail
- sing **like** a bird
- swim **like** a fish

Collective nouns

Collective nouns are words that are used to talk about groups of things, usually animals. There is often more than one way to refer to the groups, but some common examples include:

- an **army** of caterpillars, frogs, ants
- a **band** of gorillas
- a **brood** of chickens
- a **colony** of ants, rabbits, beavers
- a **flock** of sheep, birds
- a **gaggle** of geese
- a **herd** of horses, cows, goats, yaks, llamas, hippopotamuses
- a **litter** of puppies, kittens, cubs
- a **murder** of crows
- a **nest** of snakes
- a **pack** of wolves
- a **pod** of walruses, seals, dolphins, whales
- a **pride** of lions
- a **school** of sharks, salmon, whales
- a **shoal** of fish
- a **troop** of monkeys, kangaroos
- a **swarm** of bees, insects
- an **unkindness** of ravens

Writing stories

Top 10 tips

EXPLORER TIPS

Before you write:

1. Plan your story—you can do this using question words such as **who**, **what**, **when**, **where**, **why** and **how**. Try using the page opposite to help you.
2. Tell your story to a friend before you write. Would you want to read this story? Would your friend? Change your plan if necessary.

While you are writing:

3. Keep to your new plan when you write. Now is not a good time to change your mind.
4. Write in sentences and think about punctuation.
5. Don't forget paragraphs. If you need to begin a sentence with an adverbial of time (e.g. *Later that day . . . When it was all over . . .*) or place (e.g. *Outside, in the woods . . .*) you probably need to start a new paragraph.

After you have written the first draft:

6. Use your **Oxford Junior Illustrated Dictionary** to check your spelling.
7. Use this thesaurus to make sure you have chosen the best words.
8. Look at the **OVERUSED WORDS** list on page 9. Try to use other words where they can add meaning to your story.
9. Can you add some details about your characters?
10. Can you add more information about your setting to help your reader to 'see' it in their mind?

Planning

Characters:

Who are you writing about?

What are they like?
Can you use more precise adjectives?

Action:

What does someone do?

How do they do it?
Can you use more precise verbs?

Why do they do it?

Time:

When do the different events happen? Use adverbs and phrases such as *earlier*, *meanwhile* and *during the afternoon*.

Place:

Where do the events take place?

What is the place like?
Can you use more precise adjectives?

Dialogue:

What does someone say?

How do they say it?
Can you use more precise verbs?

Atmosphere:

What is it like?
Can you use more precise adjectives?

Editing your work using the thesaurus

Once you have written a first draft, use this thesaurus to make your writing more effective. Don't forget the **WRITING TIPS**, **OVERUSED WORDS** and **WORD WEB** panels. Here are some examples where the thesaurus has been used to edit sentences from a first draft.

Writing about sports day

The teams ~~went~~ strode on to the pitch.

Sahil ~~ran~~ flew round the track.

The bean bag was ~~caught~~ grabbed by a member of the other team.

Ellie-May's dad ~~threw~~ hurled the welly across the pitch.

The ~~losing~~ defeated teams agreed that it was a well-deserved win.

Jack ~~jumped~~ cleared the first three hurdles without any problems.

The headteacher ~~said~~ declared Team Jupiter were the winners.

The teams were ~~taken~~ led outside by their captains.

Writing about life on a river

The city is beside the ~~big~~ mighty river.

~~Boats~~ Barges can be seen travelling up and down the river.

Nowadays, tourists can enjoy ~~trips~~ excursions on the water.

Sometimes there are people in ~~boats~~ canoes.

In the past, a lot of coal was ~~taken~~ transported by ship.

Writing a fairy story

The goblin ~~ran~~ careered into the clearing.

The goblin was soon found and ~~caught~~ arrested.

Fairy Foxglove was ~~going~~ strolling through the forest.

For the next few days, any sudden movement made the goblin ~~jump~~ start.

Fairy Foxglove ~~threw~~ tossed the goblin's stick into the stream.

'Call yourself a goblin?' ~~said~~ sneered Fairy Foxglove.

She had ~~lost~~ mislaid her wand.

The goblin tried to ~~take~~ seize her bag.

Writing about what aliens saw when they landed on Earth

They were filled with ~~amazement~~ wonder.

Suddenly, ~~a bird~~ an albatross landed on top of the spacecraft.

The bird was now ~~flying~~ gliding above the ocean

'We must leave now,' the leader ~~said~~ announced.

They could hear the water ~~hitting~~ lapping against their spaceship.

The Martians ~~looked~~ peeped out of their spacecraft.

What a ~~beautiful~~ glorious sight!

The sea was ~~blue~~ azure.

They looked again, but this time they ~~looked~~ gazed in delight.

When they received the order to leave, they were ~~very sad~~ heartbroken.

Different types of writing

Whether you are writing fiction or non-fiction, it is important to think about **who** you are writing it for (your **audience**) and **why** you are writing it (your **purpose**). Here are some examples.

Story

You might be writing a story for a younger child, with magical characters.

Once upon a time, Fairy Foxglove was strolling through the secret forest when an obnoxious little goblin had the nerve to try and pinch her magic fairy dust.

Article

You might be writing an article for a school newsletter, in which you describe in an entertaining way a recent trip to a theme park.

Year 3 enjoyed a delightful excursion to the safari park last week. They were fortunate to see some magnificent animals and to have an exhilarating ride on a roller coaster.

Advertisement

You might be writing an advertisement in which you try to persuade other pupils to join a new after-school activities club.

Roll up! Roll up! Join our superb circus society! Become a juggler, acrobat or clown!

Learn sensational new skills and make new friends.

Membership is available to children in every year group and costs £1 per week.

EXPLORER TIP

Write a draft of your text first, then go through it and underline the common adjectives and verbs that you have used. Look these up in the thesaurus to see if you can find some more interesting, accurate or persuasive ones!

EXPLORER TIP

Look at the texts on this page and on p240. They were all edited in the way shown on pages 236 and 237. Can you guess which words were added after using the thesaurus?

Writing a thank-you letter

21, Bank Street,
Melden,
Oxfordshire
OX36 9LH

Dear Aunty Jen,

How are you?

Thank you for the pens you sent me for my birthday. I took them into school and everyone said you must be the best to spend me a pressy like that! They're BRILLIANT!

School's fine. We've got a concert next week and I'm trying to learn the words of the songs. Wish me luck!

Hope to see you soon.

Lots of love,

Sarah

LOOK OUT FOR

- the salutation (*Dear Aunty Jen*) and sign-off (*lots of love*)
- the informal tone (informal words such as *pressy* and *the best*, the contractions *we've* and *I'm*, block capitals and exclamation marks)
- Sarah asking Aunty Jen how she is and sending some other news

Mrs J Edwards,
15, Hill Street,
Stoneyhill,
West Yorkshire
BD56 9TT

Writing a letter of complaint

3, Park Road,
Crowne,
Oxfordshire
OX64 9EH

Mrs Davies,
Ye Old Sweet Shoppe,
1, High Street,
Sweetly,
Oxfordshire
OX81 9PS

5th May, 2018

Dear Mrs Davies,

On 23rd November, whilst passing your shop, I was enticed to enter by the aroma of the fudge that you were cooking.

I then purchased and devoured an entire bag of fudge, and as a result gained a kilogram in weight.

As you are clearly responsible for this unfortunate incident, I would like to be assured that in future you will not leave the door open when preparing your mouth-watering fudge.

Yours sincerely,

Ethel Smith

Mrs Ethel Smith

LOOK OUT FOR

- the salutation (*Dear Mrs Davies*) and matching sign-off (*Yours sincerely*)
- the formal tone (formal words such as *enticed* and *incident*, and no block capitals or exclamation marks)
- Mrs Smith stating clearly what the problem is, why Mrs Davies is to blame, and what should happen next

Mrs Davies,
Ye Old Sweet Shoppe,
1, High Street
Sweetly,
Oxfordshire
OX81 9PS